ALL UNDER HEAVEN

D0873334

SUNY Series in Chinese Philosophy and Culture
David L. Hall and Roger T. Ames, editors

ALL UNDER HEAVEN

*Transforming Paradigms
in Confucian-Christian Dialogue*

John H. Berthrong

STATE UNIVERSITY OF NEW YORK PRESS

Parts of the Appendix appeared in an earlier version in *Confucian-Christian Encounter in Historical and Contemporary Perspective* (1991): 226–254 © 1991 Edwin Mellen Press and is reprinted with permission.

Published by
State University of New York Press, Albany

© 1994 State University of New York

All rights reserved

Printed in the United States of America

No part of this book may be used or reproduced
in any manner whatsoever without written permission
except in the case of brief quotations embodied in
critical articles and reviews.

For information, address State University of New York Press,
State University Plaza, Albany, N.Y., 12246

Production by Cathleen Collins
Marketing by Dana Yanulavich

Library of Congress Cataloging in Publication Data

Berthrong, John H., 1946–
    All under heaven : transforming paradigms in Confucian-Christian
dialogue / John H. Berthrong.
        p.   cm. — (SUNY series in Chinese philosophy and culture)
    Includes bibliographical references and index.
    ISBN 0-7914-1857-X (alk. paper). — ISBN 0-7914-1858-8 (pbk. :
alk. paper)
    1. Christianity and other religions—Confucianism.
2. Confucianism—Relations—Chrisitanity.   3. Christianity—
Philosophy.   4. Philosophy, Confucian.   5. Neo-Confucianism.
I. Title.   II. Series.
BR128.C43B46   1994
261.2′9512—dc20   93-17291
                                                                                            CIP

10 9 8 7 6 5 4 3 2 1

Contents

Acknowledgments

The making of this inquiry into comparative religion has required that I draw upon the contributions of many in diverse fields. First, there are my teachers at the Chicago Theological Seminary and the University of Chicago who introduced me to the pleasures of process thought and Sung Neo-Confucianism. I owe them a set of windows on the world. This group includes W. Widick Schroeder, David Roy, Anthony Yu, Edward Ch'ien and Joseph Kitagawa. Not only did they teach me much about Western philosophy and Chinese culture, they also instilled a love for scholarly precision and historical accuracy I retain, however imperfectly, from their seminars.

Second, I also have an obligation to various Confucians and scholars of the tradition who have assisted me in trying to understand the Confucian Way over the last three decades. What comprehension I have of Confucianism I owe to Tu Wei-ming, Julia Ching, Cheng Chung-ying, Thomas Metzger, Liu Shu-hsien, Wing-tsit Chan and Wm. Theodore de Bary—and to one who has taught us all, Mou Tsung-san. The Confucians within this group have shown that the tradition lives and grows with integrity and wit in their teachings. They have reassured me that I am not just talking to myself. One of the real pleasures of this work has been its concrete dialogical nature.

Third, I must acknowledge a remarkable group of irenic Canadian and international church women and men who pioneered interfaith dialogue over the last three decades. These include Kay Hockin, Garth Legge, Fred Baylis, David Lochhead, Hal Llewellyn, David Chappell (also of the University of Hawaii) and Thomas Edmonds of the Division of World Outreach of the United Church of Canada. Will Oxtoby of the University of Toronto is also a member of this group of devoted servants of the church. Whatever I know of the true spirit and real mission of the Christian gospel is due to these colleagues. I also need to thank friends in the former Sub-Unit on Dialogue of the World Council of Churches for encouraging the international context for Confucian-Christian dialogue. Without the leadership of people like Stanley Samartha, Peter Lee, Franklin Woo and Wesley Ariarajah the modern dialogue movement would never have opened itself to conversation with the Confucian Way.

Fourth, I include a group of colleagues at Boston University, the larger Boston intellectual community and all the other scholars working on the question of the relationship of Confucianism and Christianity. There is no better place in North America to pursue this study than in Boston. My colleagues here at Boston University, Robert Cummings Neville, David Eckel, Paula Fredriksen, Peter Berger, Chung Chai-sik and Joseph Fewsmith all graciously provided support and insight when I sought it, and sometimes even when I did not. I also need to thank such colleagues as Diana Eck, Mary Evelyn Tucker, Rodney Taylor, David Dilworth and Judith Berling for their ability to walk along the same road as mentors and friends.

No imagination or conscience grasped by the Christian and Confucian traditions of filial piety could ever fail to overlook the importance of family as the primordial matrix of scholarship. My final thanks is to Evelyn and Sean for all the time they have given up over the last three years reading my work and listening to endless recensions of my reflections on the meaning and value of Confucian-Christian dialogue.

Introduction

THE DIFFERENCE OF THE OTHER

Theology and philosophy as well as high and low culture have a way of mirroring each other in the religious life of humankind. There are periods in religious and intellectual history when the relationship of the academic and cultural disciplines is a happy one, or at least productively challenging. Some times simply are in tune with themselves; T'ang and Sung China along with the High Middle Ages in Europe are recorded in the historical memories of Buddhists, Confucians and Christians as such eras. Then there are other times; the late Chou dynasty and the Wei-Chin period (220–420 C.E.) in China, the Renaissance and the postmodern North Atlantic world represent periods of dislocation and transformation. We inhabit such a transitional time of otherness, of estrangement from inherited wisdom and practice.

The Wei-Chin period in China is instructive; the Wei-Chin intellectuals worried about the survival of their culture and were intrigued by the arrival of a foreign religion, Buddhism. In many respects, late Greco-Roman antiquity resembled this transitional era except for the fact that Christianity represented an internal religious movement rather than a missionary faith from a completely different cultural world. In transitory times nothing holds together as it was before and the key themes of discourse are alarity, isolation, hopelessness, difference, pluralism, conflict; all this forms a bleak picture of cultural dissonance. A great age had come to an end and no one was sure what the dawn would bring.

THE DIFFERENCE OF THE AUDIENCE

This essay in comparative theology has two focal points. One is the pressing theological question of a Christian response to religious pluralism in the modern world. While not seeking to survey the whole field of interreligious relations

1

and scholarship, I will examine the present state of Christian thinking on this topic as it pertains to the renewed Confucian-Christian dialogue. The second focus is the Confucian tradition, a fact that may prove to be a point of bemusement because even in the field of interfaith dialogue Confucianism is not ordinarily considered as a conversation partner for Christians. Very little is known in Christian theological circles about the development of the spiritual or religious dimensions of the Confucian tradition compared to the modern Christian understanding of Judaism, Islam and Buddhism. Hence it is necessary to present selected historical material about the Confucian tradition in order to display the importance of this new bilateral interfaith dialogue.

The two religious traditions compared in this essay have usually been studied by different audiences. The first audience is the growing body of Christian theologians and historians of religions interested in comparative theology. I hope this part of the audience will include all persons interested in comparative religion and philosophy whatever their religious affiliations. The second audience comprises the professional students of Chinese intellectual history who are also interested in the Confucian encounter with the modern world, including Confucian-Christian interaction.

Chapters 3 and 4 will be of special interest to the growing international body of ecumenical Confucian scholars concerned with the historical roots of Confucian-Christian dialogue as well as the New Confucian contribution to the conversation between these two communities of faith. It is my hope that this central section of the essay will be of interest to Confucian and non-Confucian scholars alike. I am convinced that modern Confucian intellectuals such as Mou Tsung-san and Tu Wei-ming deserve a wider audience than they had previously, especially among Christian intellectuals. No one can understand East Asia without understanding its Confucian past and its Confucian future.

The duality of vision will sometimes be confusing in terms of which audience I am addressing. Some material, such as the more technical expositions of Chu Hsi's Sung synthesis and Mou Tsung-san and Tu Wei-ming's reformed modern Confucianism, will initially make more sense to the China scholars. The theological reflections on the nature of dual transcendence in Chapter 5 will be better understood by the theological audience. Sometimes, such as the discussion of multiple religious participation in chapter 6, both communities of scholars will be addressed. This confusion of audience and interest reflects the actual state of the Confucian-Christian dialogue. While such a mixture of audience and theme is puzzling, it is not boring. As Whitehead once noted, it is ultimately better for a proposition to be interesting than strictly true. I believe that it is better to preserve some interesting confusion instead of pretending to an orderly discourse where this patently does not yet exist. If the New Confucians and the process theologians and philosophers are correct about the creative and pluralistic nature of our cosmos, boring order will never be a problem for Confucian-Christian dialogue.

Modern North Atlantic discourse, foremost being postmodern deconstructionism, argues that we can never return to the naive onto-theological visions of unity found in so much historic Western and Eastern thinking. What we can think about but never really comprehend is the other, the strange, the different—all those things that defy our ability to bring order, unity and peace to our world.[1] On the postmodernist reading of the situation, we must learn to live with chaos and the strangeness of the other. Or we can embrace this newness as a joyful expansion of our horizons of consciousness. For some intellectuals the emergence of new worldviews, new Gods and bodhisattvas are to be celebrated.

As is so typical of theological discourse, the question of otherness haunting modern Western consciousness comes in a specialized form for the Christian faithful. The presenting issue is religious pluralism. Suddenly, the other is manifested by the irreducible other, the great religions of humankind demanding a Christian theological response. The other religious have revived and are not going to depart the scene or simply provide a pool of converts for successful Christian mission. This question of a theology of religion has become a pressing issue for all Christian communions. Further, the answer given to the question of religious pluralism will impact all the other teaching disciplines of the Christian churches as well as the communal practice of Christians around the globe. Along with the other great question of otherness—gender and the rise of feminism— religious pluralism is upon us with a vengeance, although this is the not first time in the history of the Christian tradition that theologians have noticed the otherness of different communities of faith. Certainly men and women have noticed each other as different throughout the history of humankind. Historically, and usually with some hostility, Christians have been aware of Jews and Muslims. But there is an energy about these questions today that is different. The questions of gender and religious difference have become self-conscious issues defying the traditional answers that the church has given over the centuries.

Of these two great issues of otherness, this study will focus on the question of religious pluralism.[2] Christian theologians are beginning a new cycle in the framing of the question of the persistent religious pluralism of humankind. The dream of a Christian century and world as the complete victory of the faith are fading. What does pluralism mean for the historic Christian narrative of faith when Christians discover that they are not alone in the story of salvation history? Suddenly pluralism does not seem merely proleptic to a future monoreligious human history. Pluralism appears permanent, a pragmatic and theological fact amid other surds of being that must be understood if the gospel is to be preached with integrity. If persons of other communities of faith are to be fellow pilgrims for all time, what does this mean for Christian mission, systematic theology and social ethics?

One intriguing aspect of pluralism is that while many people believe it is an intellectual and social problem, others do not. Some want to ignore it while others see it as a blessing. Others are so used to it that they wonder, if they notice at all, at the angst it engenders among the circle of Christian theologians. For many secular historians of religion the real question is when Christians will grow up to the reality of pluralism. Yet both Christian theologians and the secular historians of religion are nervous about the intellectual twin of pluralism: relativism. Just as no one seems to like being called a syncretist, few embrace the label of relativist, implying as it does an abandonment of any social ethics and public standards of excellence in all the professions and conduct of civil life.[3]

This study of Confucian-Christian dialogue is, therefore, by the very nature of its subject matter, a study in comparative religion and philosophy. Its specialized form of engagement is an analysis of modern ecumenical Confucian-Christian dialogue. Along with an examination of the promise and pitfalls of modern dialogue, there is also a brief Southern Sung interlude focused on Chu Hsi (1130–1200) and Ch'en Ch'un (1159–1223). This excursus into the Southern Sung is necessary to set the stage for the modern dialogue between Confucians and Christians. Without understanding the Sung reformation of the Confucian Way, no one can comprehend modern Confucian discourse. The Confucian synthesis of Chu Hsi and his disciples is still the benchmark for all East Asian internal discourse. Clearly there are many Confucians who disagree vigorously with Chu Hsi. Mou Tsung-san and Tu Wei-ming present one articulate strand of modern Confucianism that most definitely does not agree with Chu Hsi. Yet we cannot understand Mou and Tu without recourse to Chu Hsi and the two centuries of Neo-Confucian genius in the Northern and Southern Sung.

On the Christian and Western side, the essay is informed by the thought of Alfred North Whitehead and his followers in what is now called process thought. Given the interest in the transcendence-immanence question in the emerging Confucian-Christian dialogue, I have made special reference to Charles Hartshorne. As I will explain below, I also offer my own version of process thought as a suitable tool for comparative philosophy and theology. But before

I present the 'triple thread' of my process-based hermeneutic, I need to frame the actual Confucian-Christian dialogue out of which these concerns have arisen.

EPISODES OF DIALOGUE

There is a reason why the organization and themes of *All under Heaven* are not as orderly as would normally be the case in a scholarly study of comparative theology and philosophy. As Aristotle pointed out long ago, the organization of any exposition needs to follow the subject matter under review. A number of chapters were written in response to the first and second international Confucian-Christian dialogues, July 1988 in Hong Kong and July 1991 in Berkeley, California. One of the delights of such meetings is that the conversation takes on a life of its own. Questions are raised; tentative answers are given; new questions are asked; tangential issues suddenly become important. While these essays in comparative theology are not a chronicle of either of the international meetings, they are responsive to some of the main issues raised in both conferences.

Confucianism, declared dead not long ago, has refused to die and is alive in East Asia and the Asian diaspora; Confucians are now prepared to advertise the renewal of the tradition. Too much has happened to the tradition over the last century for the mere repetition of past glories. For instance, the historical centers for the transmission of the tradition have passed from the complete control of Confucians throughout its East Asian homeland. As de Bary (1988, 1991) has noted, the three traditional transmission points for Confucianism were the family, the educational system and the state civil service examination system. With the loss of direct Confucian control over the family, education and the state civil service there is little doubt that many people anticipated the precipitous demise of the tradition. Moreover, many believed the tradition was internally moribund and lacked the ability to replicate itself in new generations in the modern world.

The trials and tribulations of the Confucian tradition engendered by the confrontation with Western modernism mirror the fate of all the great religious traditions of humankind in the last century. What is now clear is that all the historic religions have survived, albeit invariably transformed by the encounter with Western secular and religious modernism. It appears the case that Confucianism, especially because of the Communist revolution in China, has taken longer to begin its response to modernism than some of the other traditions such as Buddhism, Christianity, Hinduism, Judaism or Islam.[4] Hence any Confucian-Christian dialogue will be as tentative as it is complex. The Chinese

Confucians are finding a modern voice in which to explain and commend their tradition. The Japanese Confucians have also been at work answering the challenge of Western modernity ever since the Meiji Restoration. Some traditional elements of Confucianism will be dropped and some historically minor forms of Confucian discourse will come to the fore. These are the components for an untidy dialogue. The dialogue itself mirrors the pluralism of the age, an age waiting to figure out what the new global configurations of religious interaction will produce in the twenty-first century. Anyone who pretends to more organization is missing what is going on in both traditions.

One of the main topics of conversation in both the 1988 Hong Kong and 1991 Berkeley meetings was the different way Confucians and Christians have regarded divine transcendence and immanence. There was a general consensus that both traditions have doctrines of divine transcendence and immanence; there was also a clear recognition that Confucianism and Christianity have developed the notions of transcendence and immanence in distinctive fashions. Along with Taoism and Buddhism, it is hard to think of another major world tradition farther removed historically and conceptually from Christianity in these matters than Confucianism. While the difference between the two traditions was found important, it was also noted that there now are tendencies in both traditions forcing them to reconsider their historical positions. Could it actually be the case that modern Confucians and Christians are moving to a new understanding of divine transcendence and immanence closer in style and substance than before?

In order to answer the question of convergence of the two traditions, some historical background is necessary. Chapter 3 and its exploration of the history of the Confucian Way as well as Chu Hsi's pivotal role in defining the tradition from the Southern Sung to the modern period addresses this point. It is impossible to understand the development of Confucianism from the Southern Sung to the present without a study of Chu Hsi, just as it would be impossible to understand the development of Western Christian thought without study of Augustine, Aquinas, Luther and Calvin. As many contemporary Christian theologians no longer agree with the details of the theologies of Augustine, Aquinas, Luther or Calvin, few New Confucians follow every twist and turn of Chu Hsi's *tao-hsüeh* ("The Study of the Way," Chu Hsi's favorite term for his own project). Yet without some knowledge of Chu Hsi, we cannot understand the role of a New Confucian such as Mou Tsung-san and Tu Wei-ming in contemporary Chinese intellectual history. Hence I have tried to provide enough background information to make the topics of dialogue with

Confucianism comprehensible historically and in terms of the perennial religious issues they evoke for an emerging global ecumenical discourse.

Another topic which comes up repeatedly in modern Confucian-Christian dialogue is the question of multiple religious participation. As we shall see in chapter 6, this is a question of great interest to Confucians and Asian Christians. In East Asia there is nothing new about the discussion of such issues. Some East Asian Confucians have believed that such multiple religious participation was acceptable and some thought it was unlikely to have a happy outcome. Given the much more exclusive claims made by Christian doctrine, such questions are rejected almost entirely in Western Christian circles. Nonetheless, the Confucians press Christian participants about their possible appropriation of the Confucian Way.

Other topics from the two international Confucian-Christian dialogue conferences could have been elaborated. I have selected these two major themes because they were considered important issues at both meetings and because they are recognized as ongoing matters for discussion. These topics illustrate the kinds of conversation that goes on when Confucians and Christians talk. In that respect they are dialogical in nature. Neither question might be the way that either tradition would discuss the issues at hand if there were no dialogue. When faced with the living representatives of the two traditions, these were two issues that demanded comment.

Because the issues are drawn from actual dialogue, the contours of the discussions are not as clear as if the outline had been generated internally from either tradition. One of the things that actual dialogue reveals is that the agenda will never be as orderly as it would be among members of the same tradition. The reason for this is the very reason for dialogue. Together, Confucians and Christians are exploring new ground, topics never before taken in tandem. Along with the systematic issues germane to each tradition individually, new joint questions emerge. The discussion of such questions will be amorphous for a time, with much alternating between historical explanation and contemporary thematization. Just making sure that the partners are talking about the same things takes a great deal of time. And once the discovery of a good topic has been made, each tradition needs to ponder its response in light of the actual dialogue situation.

It is also important to note that no bilateral dialogue concerning the complex tapestry of human religious interaction is ever conducted in splendid isolation. For instance, any discussion of Confucian-Christian dialogue needs to keep an eye on parallel developments in Buddhist-Christian and Taoist-Christian dialogue. In East Asia we must likewise be sensitive to Shinto-Christian dialogue. The religious history of East Asia is the history of its own internal diversity. One cannot ultimately isolate only one element, such as Confucianism, from all the rest. For instance, in order to understand Chu Hsi's intellectual world one must comprehend something of Wei-Chin Taoist thought along with the history of T'ang Buddhism. Important as such considerations are, they have been bracketed for this study.

THE TRIPLE THREAD

Throughout this study, I will defend the position that all intellectual endeavors have a metasystemic orientation. I am acutely aware how much such a statement runs against the grain of contemporary philosophy and even a great number of theological studies. Nonetheless, I believe that every text is controlled by certain assumptions about how the world works.[5] Sometimes this metasystem is not thematized; sometimes it is denied as even existing; sometimes it is admitted that there is a metaphysical outlook—but that the metaphysics is so sublime or mystical that it cannot be put into words. I hold that it is possible to describe the main themes of any metasystem. This description may lose the power of the original in terms of the specifics of its details, but it is a description nonetheless. While I do hold with the Calvinists that *finitum non capax infiniti*, I also believe that we can describe accurately or inaccurately what is going on in any text. Such a systematic description may not do justice to the artistic, mystical, ethical, social or intellectual richness of the text involved. Nonetheless, descriptions can be better or worse and it is our responsibility to try to give the better one if possible.

As was noted above, such a bald appeal to metaphysics, or to metasystem as I prefer to call it (I will defend the neologism in later chapters), is not a popular way to begin such a comparative enterprise in a philosophic mode. It smacks of seeking a logocentric foundation for our discourse, a style of discourse such thinkers as Rorty, Derrida, Foucault, Lenivas, Heidegger, Nietzsche and others have exposed as a useless and even pernicious language game. While I share the contemporary fascination with the notion of the other and awareness of the rupture of the modern onto-theological traditions of the North Atlantic West, I still affirm that a chastened metasystem is both possible and plausible. Games are still games and some rules might be more binding than it appears in cultures in the midst of paradigm shifts.

However, there is yet another way of describing the triple thread in terms of contemporary discourse. The three traits of form, dynamics and unification can be seen as an attempt to frame a new descriptive vocabulary useful for comparative philosophy and theology. I will not claim that these are the foundations of reality, traditionally understood as the essence of all that is. I will claim that they are a way of describing reality that is sensitive to two major philosophic schools, the Western school of Whitehead and the East Asian school of Chu Hsi. Minimally, it will lead to an edifying conversation between process philosophy and Confucian thought.

If we see the following tripartite formulation as the offering of a new vocabulary then we are not committed to any extravagant claims for its ontological or cosmological validity. We are, with Peirce, appealing to a self-critical group of scholars in terms of presenting a new way of describing reality making use of the insights of Whitehead and Chu Hsi. The triple thread is nothing more than a suggestion about how to describe reality in an adequate and coherent fashion. It is claimed to be adequate in that it allows for a comparison of the Western and East Asian partners in conversation. It is coherent in that it allows for the description of everything in the thematized worlds of Chu Hsi and Whitehead. Following Whitehead's reticence in such matters, I do not claim that this particular vocabulary is a metaphysical description of the foundations of reality.

I have chosen to call this systematic endeavor a metasystem in order not to force the dialogical conversation with Confucianism prematurely into the Western channels of cosmology, ontology and metaphysics. Surely, there are Neo-Confucian analogies to these Western philosophic concerns, but the overlap is never perfect. To assume that the East Asian Confucian community is carrying out such time-honored Western debates can obscure what is going on. Hence I have resorted to the term metasystem to point to those areas of self-reflection about the issues of cognition and reality so near and dear to the hearts of the Confucians and process thinkers in the West.

The metasystem informing the comparative philosophic categories in this essay is derived from two sources: the modern process movement inspired by A. N. Whitehead and the Sung dynasty *tao-hsüeh* of Chu Hsi. The governing assumptions of this schema are the three notions of form, dynamics and unification. My claim is that any text, in any way whatsoever, can be described in terms of form, the dynamic interaction of form and the world and the necessary unification of these two traits into the why, how and what of any entity or event among the other things of the world. What is meant by form, dynamics and unification will be spelled out in more detail in various chapters although this is not the central aim of this study. In a future study specifically designed to deal with the process tradition I will deal more directly with the notion of form, dynamics and unification as a comparative metasystem.

There is nothing revolutionary about this combination of Anglo-American and Chinese sources. Ever since Joseph Needham (1956) remarked on the fascinating similarities between Chu Hsi's *tao-hsüeh* and Whitehead's organic philosophy, scholars have used process thought to interpret the Neo-Confucian synthesis of the Southern Sung Neo-Confucian master. Many of the most creative members of the process tradition, very broadly conceived, have taken the lead in the fields of comparative philosophy and theology.[6]

Very briefly stated, my short working definitions of form, dynamics and unification can be summarized as:

Form

Every thing that is or might be has some form of definiteness that separates it from other things. In the history of Western thought the most notable terms for the formal aspects of the world have been Plato's ideas, Aristotle's forms or Whitehead's eternal objects. Justus Buchler's notion of traits is a modern naturalist version of form as I will define the term. On the Chinese side, Chu Hsi is famous for his defense of the role of *li* or principle as the form qua the defining characteristic of any particular things. In the classical Confucian tradition, Hsün Tzu was also interested in the formal side of reality. Chu Hsi often called principle the whatness of a thing or the howness of its creation. Forms include such diverse things as colors, number, ordinal location, shape, taste, color, tone, principles, the norms of conduct and so forth.

Dynamics

There is always a protean power of self-creation or generation as noted by Whitehead and Chu Hsi. Wherever we find dialectic as the generation of interacting forces, we find the dynamic element of the cosmos as growth, newness and creativity. The very matter-energy of the universe is constantly in flux. It is what Whitehead called creativity and what Chu Hsi thematized as *ch'i,* the most difficult of Chinese philosophic concepts to approximate in English. *Ch'i* is the formless power of all creation; it is also the primordial nature of God for Whitehead in its aspect as unceasing eros driven by creativity. It is interesting that even though *ch'i* is a foundational concept in Chu Hsi's thought, neither he nor Ch'en Ch'un devoted much time to a separate discussion of the importance of *ch'i* in their thought.[7]

Unification

The notion of unification describes the ever-present unity of form and dynamics. Form finds a creative power in the dynamics of the universe. There is always the unification of form and energy into some new thing or value, some new configuration of what was with what seeks to become. Unification points to the emergence of discrete things and also that they are what they are and not something else. Unification points to the harmony achieved by the self and every other entity by means of its fusion of form and dynamics. Unification, by its very nature, demands a pluralistic universe. To unify form and dynamics leads to something new. In Whitehead's terms, this is the creative advance into novelty. For Chu Hsi it is often thematized by *t'ien-ming* as the Will of Heaven for the increase of ethical perfection and the spiritual testing of sagely persons.

There are other ways to formulate this triad within the many mansions of process thought and Confucian discourse. However, I believe that the triad of form, dynamics and unification is a good device for the comparative side of process thought in that the three terms can claim both Chu Hsi and Whitehead as sources of inspiration.[8] One of the threads of my argument is that process thought is inherently pluralistic in nature and therefore capable of cross-cultural formulation. Thus one would expect a number of diverse specifications of process thought and modes of thematization of its important issues. The triad of form, dynamics and unification has the benefit of being useful in the encounter of process thought and the Neo-Confucian tradition as defended by Chu Hsi and his East Asian disciples.

The tripartite thread also has another element that needs an introductory definition. Along with form, dynamics and unification, I will often make use of the notion of axiology in defining process theology and Confucian thought. I believe that process thought, Neo-Confucianism and New Confucianism represent religio-philosophic metasystems defined by the values and harmonies generated by the creation of individual entities. In short, they are essential axiologies. As Neville (1992, 106) has noted, "Whitehead saw human experience to be thoroughly valuational, affective, shot through with enjoyments, pains, purposes, and moving episodes." Neville goes on to point out that "in terms of his cosmology this means that the process of concrescence in any occasion is the achievement of some value." Chu Hsi's notion of *li* as principle embodying a pattern of value reflecting a person's appropriation of the Mandate of Heaven as human nature (*hsing*) is one Neo-Confucian formulation of an axiological cosmology, a Chinese analogy to Whitehead's insistence on values at the center of all creative activity. For Neo-Confucians, New Confucians and process thinkers, values are crucial elements in the analysis of being. Hence it is entirely appropriate to call all three formal axiological metasystems.

THE REASONS WHY

Interreligious dialogue is a strange academic beast. It is an activity demanding multiple interpretive skills and *phronesis*. It needs the academic care of a exegete, the tact of a diplomat and the understanding of a historian of religion. Why engage in such activity beyond the stock answer that, like mountains, religions are there for us to describe, understand and commend if we find them worthy of belief? I hold that there are at least three plausible responses to the question. First, in terms of fundamental comparative theology and philosophy, the challenge is to describe and understand pluralism. Second, I agree with Hans Küng who argues that there will be no lasting peace among nations until there is peace among religions. Although not all communal conflict is religiously motivated, much is and this sad fact of interreligious conflict must be addressed. Third, the North Atlantic part of Western civilization is in a period of transition from modernity per se to what has been called postmodernism; a very important element of this transformation has been stimulated by the awareness of other human cultures.

While it is important for Western civilization to continue to ponder its own history, it is perhaps time for it to open its windows to consider different approaches to the question of civilized life. Westerners cannot become Chinese, Koreans, Vietnamese or Japanese, but they can begin to see some perennial religious and philosophic questions from different angles. Just as the infusion of knowledge of the ancient Greek world via Islam stimulated the medieval synthesis, so too might reflection on Confucian theories of society and Taoist artistic sensibilities contribute to the intellectual culture of an increasingly global world. For the first time in centuries Western intellectuals seem to be disposed to take other cultures seriously as possible sources of knowledge and wisdom.

Some might pause now and enjoy an ironic laugh at the extent of this prodigious list of the potential rewards of interreligious dialogue. It is a long list to be sure. It promises almost as much as the second coming of the Messiah. Can it deliver what it promises? As with all such pre-millenarian faiths, probably not. Interreligious dialogue will not bring world peace, spiritual enlightenment or the renewal of Western civilization. But it might contribute to the achievement of at least some of these goals. Here is the list:

First, a main problem of this study is whether religious pluralism is legitimately a question for comparative philosophy and theology. If ever there were a religious question seeking dialogue with the philosophic disciplines, it is pluralism. Do we see the world as monistic, dualistic or pluralistic? All these and every other possible response are questions summoning new ontologies, cosmologies and metaphysics. Whitehead once noted (1927) that dogmas preserve a tradition's integrity, but it is a good idea to let the windows of the ark open from time to time to let in some new ideas to stimulate the received tradition in order to refresh the air for all inhabitants. Who can argue that there is something stale about the endless recycling of ideas in modern academic philosophy and religious studies? Wouldn't it be worth a small price to open the windows of the Western world to encounter with the traditions of East Asia for instance? Who knows, if the Japanese can build such good automobiles, might they also not have something to say about other facets of human life?

Second, as Hans Küng has noted repeatedly, peace among the nations also demands peace among the religions. It is not sufficient for religious leaders to decry hostility between their followers; disavowal is no longer enough. Nor will it do to make the old distinction between the "good" tradition that everywhere and always teaches peace, and the "bad" followers, who in their zeal for the faith, pervert the message of peace into violence against the other, the neighbor. All the religious of the world have a responsibility to review their theologies of religion and teachings about the other traditions in order to find out if they indeed foster peace or war. The purging of the teachings of contempt for other human beings is a paramount duty of all religious authorities.

This reexamination of the teachings and practice of each religion with regard to the other traditions did not seem like a very important matter during the Cold War and its attendant secular concerns. The end of the Cold War has demonstrated that it has now become an even more pressing task. Much interreligious hostility, as we now see in hindsight, was moderated or controlled by the dynamics of the superpower conflict. With the demise of the Soviet Union, it has become clear that interethnic and interreligious tensions did not go away. Although they have not yet become international confrontations using weapons of mass destruction, the renewed conflicts in the Middle East, parts of the old Soviet Union and the Balkans mandate some kind of conversation between religious leaders designed to reduce conflict wherever it has religious roots.

While interreligious dialogue will not solve all the problems of global historic conflict, conversation must take place in order to build understanding and then trust if we are to better frame new visions of civil society. Without dialogue it is very hard to see any improvement in the resolution of tensions short of the reemergence of a new Cold War or the enforced hegemony of the United States acting in concert with the other major industrial countries. Neither of these military solutions promises anything more than merely sweeping the old problems under the rug yet again. Dialogue is surely a better option.

Third, there is the possibility of the renewal of all our historic civilizations through dialogue. We have come to a time when Asian students study Plato, Aristotle, Kant and Hume. Western students are exposed to Lao-tzu, Confucius, Chu Hsi and the classics of the Indian and Asian Buddhist traditions. Nothing is more global than ideas in motion. Notions such as karma, dharma, yin and yang and the tao have become common on the tongues of educated persons in the North Atlantic world. The Japanese are beginning to chart ways to export the best of their culture along with their computers, electrical appliances and automobiles. The Chinese, Koreans and Indians are not far behind.

That ideas are more potent in transforming a culture than trade goods is easy to demonstrate. What would China be without Buddhism? What would the West be without the transmission of Aristotle and Plato via the Islamic philosophic synthesis? However, something else is happening here which has never really happened before. All religions are moving from what can be called regional religions, confined to particular cultural areas, such as Christianity before the sixteenth century, and also from the reality of the world religions of the colonial period of European expansion towards the emergence of global religions. Global religions are those that have come to understand, for better or for worse, that there are many religions in the world and that they are increasingly interconnected by the very nature of modern civilization. Global religions realize that there is no escape from the problem of pluralism.

I am not one of those people who believes that Western civilization is on the brink of collapse. This is a fashionable though nonempirical observation. Western civilization is the dominant force in the world today; its culture moves where it will, its educational patterns are replicated globally and its political, economic and military technologies touch every human being. This does not mean that it is a wise or compassionate culture in its dealings with other civilizations. Nor does it mean that it is not a civilization highly self-critical of its own achievements and acutely aware of its own shortcomings. Self-criticism is one of the key features of Western culture since the European Enlightenment. Nonetheless, for all its strength, Western civilization is now facing the pluralism of the emerging global civilization as is every other great culture.

All our cultures are moving from regional to global, that is, cultures recognizing the interconnectedness of the modern world. One of the features of this shift to an emerging global culture is the mutual recognition of the historic religious traditions as enduring realities. This essay in Confucian-Christian dialogue is a recognition and a manifestation of these changing realities. It is a preliminary exploration of what changes the mutual impact of Confucianism and Christianity might achieve. It is written in the sure conviction that in the twenty-first century the Pacific Rim will become a corridor for Confucian-Christian dialogue. Two great traditions will learn how to come to terms with each other and with the new world of mutual relations and understanding; they may even come to learn from each other.

THE STRUCTURE OF THE ESSAY

Chapters 1 and 2 set the stage for modern Confucian-Christian dialogue. They do so by means of situating this new bilateral interreligious conversation within the matrix of modern ecumenical Christian dialogue, theory and practice. These two chapters frame the historical and theological context, primarily from the Christian side. They are also designed to set the stage for the introduction of the Confucian history, themes and partners explored in chapters 3 and 4. And last, but not least, the first two chapters also suggest some joint dialogical issues that set the agenda for chapters 5 and 6.

Chapters 3 and 4 introduce Chu Hsi, Mou Tsung-san and Tu Wei-ming to the dialogue. Prior to the discussion of Chu Hsi's seminal exposition of the Confucian Way, I present an abbreviated introduction to the development of the Confucian tradition. Without some kind of historical introduction to the Confucian tradition, we cannot understand why modern Confucians have become interested in interreligious dialogue. Compared to the study of Buddhism, the history of the Confucian tradition is not very well known in the West, and its religious dimensions are even less well understood. Chu Hsi, the grand master of the Sung revival, is a good place to start because his synthesis of Neo-Confucianism still dominates the Confucian tradition throughout East Asia. As we shall see in chapters 3 and 4, Chu Hsi's synthesis is undergoing a major reformulation in the hands of contemporary Confucians such as Mou Tsung-san and Tu Wei-ming as they seek to explain, understand and commend the Confucian Way as an element in the emerging ecumenical civilization of the twenty-first century.

Chapters 5 and 6 present a more detailed exposition of process theology's contribution to the Confucian-Christian dialogue. These two chapters also reconnect the discussion with some of the initial theological questions raised in chapters 1 and 2 as well as the Confucian contributions of chapters 3 and 4.

Chapters 5 and 6 sketch some of the possible avenues of future dialogue between Confucians and Christians. These chapters also defend the whole notion of interreligious dialogue as an important element of an authentic Christian theology of pluralism.

The appendix is an examination of the present state of scholarship concerning the religious dimensions of the Confucian tradition. It is designed to guide additional study of this issue for those who seek a better understanding of Confucianism as a living tradition in East Asia. In order to limit the length of discussion, the focus is on English language material representing what can only be called a revolution in Confucian studies over the last four decades.

The basic structure of the essay falls into three parts. The first two chapters set the context for the new Confucian-Christian dialogue. This is done primarily in terms of ecumenical Christian interfaith dialogue theory. The next two chapters introduce, for a Western audience, the Confucian side of the dialogue. The last two chapters are a process theology response to the issues raised in the first four chapters. Like Whitehead's famous description of "the true method of discovery" (1978, 5) as an airplane flight, this essay takes off from the specifics of one airport, flies to another field and returns to its base for its final reflections. Its modest intent is that it will be of interest to people in both airports and to the wider audience of scholars concerned with improving our ability to talk to each other, and even better, to begin to understand and appreciate what we have heard in our dialogues.

There is no better way to end this introduction and begin the essay than with the words of Abraham Joshua Heschel:

> The religions of the world are no more self-sufficient, no more independent, no more isolated than individuals or nations. Energies, experiences and ideas that come to life outside the boundaries of a particular religion or all religions continue to challenge to affect every religion.

All under Heaven

TRANSFORMING PARADIGMS
IN CONFUCIAN-CHRISTIAN DIALOGUE

When one loves humaneness without loving learning, it is
corrupted into foolishness
When one loves sagacity without loving learning, it is corrupted
into deviousness
When one loves trustworthiness without loving learning, it is
corrupted into blind faith
When one loves forthrightness without loving learning, it is
corrupted into rudeness
When one loves courage without loving learning, it is corrupted
into truculence.

(Analects 17:8; de Bary 1991b, 40)

DUAL TRANSFORMATIONS

The title of this essay in comparative theology, *All under Heaven: Transforming Paradigms in Confucian-Christian Dialogue*, carries a double meaning. First, it indicates that I believe modern Confucian-Christian dialogue to be a serious matter with far-ranging theological implications for the Christian community. Although I understand through our conversations that the Confucian partners believe much the same thing, it is for them to define the importance and place of Confucian-Christian dialogue for the Confucian Way.[1] Indicative of this Confucian interest in dialogue are recent essays on the religious dimension of the tradition by scholars such as Tu Wei-ming, Liu Shu-hsien and Cheng Chung-ying. While the Confucian-Christian dialogue is only a small part of the ferment of the larger theological scene, it illustrates many of the problems and rewards of the interfaith dialogue movement. Its small scale and freshness make it a prime candidate to be examined as an important moment in the renewal of the Christian theology by means of self-conscious dialogue with other communities of faith.

Second, the field of interfaith relations and comparative theology is burgeoning in terms of the Christian response to the question of pluralism. Yet there is certainly no agreement about what the major theological or philosophical issues in dialogue are or what practical and theoretical impact these encounters will have on the global church and the wider intellectual communities of the North Atlantic world[2] and East Asia. Nonetheless, there is an emerging consensus that Christians are in the middle of a paradigm shift in terms of the theological evaluation of religious pluralism and the proper role of the churches in ecumenical interreligious dialogue.[3] Nor is the debate solely confined to the intellectual and systematic aspects of the Christian faith; often the motive for dialogue is the pragmatic cooperation of diverse religious communities seeking a religiously harmonious, politically just and ecologically sustainable world.

The question of religious (or secular) pluralism is not the only major theological issue confronting the churches now. I am convinced that churches, along with the challenge of religious pluralism, are facing at least three other transforming encounters as part of the increasingly self-conscious global religious history of humankind. While these four paradigmatic shifts are separate issues in some regards, they are all created by the spreading solvent of secular Western European and North American modernism[4] and the religious upheaval caused by the global peregrinations of the North Atlantic missionary movement. This modern Christian missionary movement was and is both partner and critic of what can be called North Atlantic modernism. The technologies of travel and communication and the ideology of imperial expansion were the highly ambiguous material facilitators of Christian missions—an unsteady mixture for a religion whose founder often pointed out that his kingdom was not of this world. Nonetheless, the question of religious pluralism may, in the end, prove to be the most provocative of the four religious and social issues facing the churches today because it so clearly challenges many of the hallowed theological convictions of even the liberal post-Enlightenment churches of the North Atlantic world.

THE FOUR TRANSFORMING ENCOUNTERS

First, the changing role of women and men in all religious institutions and society at large is presently an intellectual, practical and emotional issue for debate mostly in the North Atlantic section of the Christian world, but I trust that it will soon become a concern for the entire ecumenical church. Feminism and womanist thought will be manifested in Jewish, Islamic, Hindu, Jain, Buddhist, Sikh, Confucian, Taoist, Shintoist and all other religious traditions in response to the missionary impact of the feminist and womanist agenda which is an important part of North Atlantic modernism.[5] Further, I believe that the main Western missionary movement these days is feminism and womanism, even if this seems shocking to many feminists or womanists. Nonetheless, feminism and womanism share the ambiguous history and global reach of the West as an expansive and aggressive culture.

That feminists and womanists argue for different styles and even psychologies for women does not mean they are any less convinced that they have a true and transforming message for all peoples and cultures. Nothing could be a more missionary crusade than the social, moral and intellectual demands of the feminist and womanist movements.

Many feminist and womanist theologians would dispute the claim for theological priority that I have assigned to the question of pluralism. They argue (O'Neill 1990) that all this talk of dialogue is merely discussion among men and will not be nearly as dramatic as male thinkers assume until and unless women are given a place at the debating table. The feminists and womanists argue that all religious traditions face a truly profound task in dealing with their gender-based agenda. O'Neill makes the point that many theologians involved in the dialogue movement are keen to trumpet the benefits or perils of religious pluralism without noticing the most primal and essential element of human pluralism, namely, the fact of two sexes. From O'Neill's perspective, most of the theologians of pluralism have simply missed the most obviously pluralistic part of their actual lives. Until the pluralism of gender is addressed all dialogue theology will be hopelessly biased towards the experience of less than half of humanity.

Second in the list of transforming encounters is the impassioned universal human cry for political, economic and cultural freedom often thematized in terms of distributive social justice. To paraphrase Hegel, if you tell people they are free then they are likely to think and act as if they were free. Once they have discovered the notion of freedom, they will seek to realize it in all the spheres of civilized human life. The debate is complicated by the very germane question of whether or not the whole issue of freedom is framed parochially in terms of Western individualism. A key issue in the debate is whether modernist notions of freedom can be made to fit societies that do not share the Western notion of the sovereign individual as the locus of human rights. The dramatic transformations of Eastern Europe, the former USSR Soviet Union and the ongoing debate in China about human rights bear witness to this phenomenon. Clearly all people seek freedom, but the definition of what constitutes a free person and a free society is not so clear in different cultural situations.

In the Christian churches this debate about personal and collective freedoms or rights has found voice in political and liberation theologies. There is a great deal of debate about whether these theologies have developed out of purely religious concerns or are reflections of intense nonreligious ideological forces in their host cultures. One result of these inquiries is that all easy forms of unjustified privilege will be challenged relentlessly. Notions of deference and deserved authority are rejected; strife rules discourse between the so-called oppressors and the oppressed. Now we are also seeing an increase of interethnic tension with the end of the so-called Cold War. In China the role of conflict as a justified element of political life is being keenly debated even though this is a stark departure from the notions of Confucian propriety embodied in the now rapidly fading memory of the quasi-Confucian ideologies of the imperial past.[6]

The ecumenically-minded churches are facing a real dilemma in the area of social justice with the collapse of the Marxist left. For the last few generations of Christian social ethicists, notions of a reformed Marxist society or some kind of democratic socialism dominated the thinking of North Atlantic and South American theologians concerned with issues of social justice. As Peter Berger (1992) has noted, if you want to find out what is politically correct on the left, all you have to do is consult the political manifestos of the mainline North American church hierarchies. The problem such theories must now face is the fact that all state socialism, in its strict form as a command economy, promises only poverty and underdevelopment for everyone. Politically and economically, the various forms of North Atlantic and Pacific Rim market economies empirically are the only social systems capable of increasing wealth and giving people a chance for economic development. Berger (1986) has also pointed out that the market economy has been woefully deficient in presenting itself as a compassionate alternative to the idealistic dreams of the socialist left. So we are left with a victorious free market that hardly anyone can now love and socialist ideals of social cooperation and community that few can now believe in. The whole field of Christian social ethics lacks any engaging or driving vision of where we need to go as a global community.

Although Christian liberation theologians, engaged Buddhists and concerned Confucians, not to mention Islamic revivalists, all seek some form of workable social ethics, there is a distinct lack of hopeful and realistic vision in their work when faced with the collapse of the left. However, we must not lose sight of the question of social justice merely because we have reached an impasse generated by the loss of faith in the older socialist version of liberation and political theology. The question is still a crucial one for all societies: what makes for a just society and how do we work toward making the ideals of social justice a reality? My argument, in part, is that the question of religious pluralism is also important in answering the question of social justice. In the modern world it is unrealistic to suggest that there is a separate Christian, Islamic, Hindu, Confucian or Buddhist solution to the question of social justice. Just as with ecological concerns, these are questions that need a common solution if there is to be any solution at all.

Third, all humanity faces a monumental and persistent ecological crisis. We are degrading the environment and consuming nonrenewable natural resources at such a horrendous and prodigious rate that the mind boggles. A prudent person ought to be deeply concerned but not hysterical. This is fundamentally a crisis of values and not just a question of technological adjustment, though an ecologically enlightened technology and ecumenical science may help to first undo and then to reverse the effects of unrestrained destructive industrial technologies.[7]

The ecological crisis does not lend itself to a single solution derived from any one religious community or even any grouping of nation states, however collectively powerful. Like the question of social justice, it is not a question that can be addressed only by Christians, Jews, Muslims, Hindus, Jains, Buddhists, Sikhs, Confucians, Taoists, Shintoists, secular humanists, Marxists, or even native elders. In fact, I have reached the conclusion that none of the great historic religious traditions of Jasper's Axial Age have much to say about the praxis of ecological sanctification, much less salvation, until they have learned a great deal more about modern ecumenical science and its potential for ecologically sound technologies. The battle between science and religion is a false one; what is needed is cooperation between science and religion in helping to resolve the ecological crisis in terms of a reformed praxis for both religion and science. And perhaps all the members of the so-called "universal" religious traditions need to heed the long ignored voice of the primal or traditional cosmic traditions that claim to have preserved a better sense of balance between human economic needs and finite natural resources. As the great Warring States Confucian Hsün Tzu (fl. 298–238 B.C.E.) noted, "All people desire and dislike the same things, but since desires are many and things that satisfy them relatively few, this scarcity will necessarily lead to conflict" (Knoblock 1990, 121). What is desperately needed is some way just to begin the global debate about how these issues are to be discussed and settled in a humane, just and sustainable fashion.

While much of the question and answer of ecology comes from the technological and economic spheres of human culture, there is clearly a religious dimension of the issue. A major part of that religious factor is the question of religious pluralism for all faith communities. How are we to work together as religious people to solve the ecological crisis? And of course, this will often directly lead the religious communities to ponder the whole question of religious diversity, the fourth of the paradigm shifts.

 Fourth, all of the other three transformative encounters lead inevitably to the question of religious pluralism in one form or another. We live in an age of self-conscious religious diversity created through the communication and transportation marvels of modern technology. For Christians this issue of diversity is thematized as the problem of religious pluralism or the demand for the articulation of an adequate and faithful theology of religions. From the Christian perspective, religions must find ways to learn to live together in order to survive the multiple crises of the late twentieth century. Perhaps the Christian churches need to understand the fact that pluralism is historically and perhaps even cosmically normative and not just some kind of passing phase. This will be one of the main points I will argue in this essay.

Unfortunately, much of the history of the interaction of religious communities has been disastrous and entirely lamentable, especially among the West Asian religions of Judaism, Christianity and Islam. The Jewish holocaust is only the last and perhaps the most frightening of the persistent human proclivity to be genocidal. We must find positive forms of religious interaction if for no other reason than that our military technology makes the shrinking globe unsafe for all people without some form of global political sanity. Hans Küng has argued that there will be no peace among nations until and unless the world's religions learn to live in peaceful cooperation directed toward the common good. "Peace among the religions is the prerequisite for peace among the nations" (Küng 1988, 209). The renewed Confucian-Christian dialogue serves as a test case for this encounter in terms of the reflection of fundamental intellectual positions and ways of being in the world.

Of course, the hope for dialogue could turn out to be yet another utopian dream. Sometimes, as the common saying goes, familiarity breeds contempt. Better understanding between religions will not solve all the ills of the modern world. Increased religious diversity may even cause new problems for parts of the world that were relatively homogeneous and peaceful for most of their histories. Religious diversity can provoke as much warfare as mutual respect, and on the balance, the violent reaction to other religions appears to be more the historic norm. What is needed is not a world wherein all peoples forgive past wrongs; but a world where civil dialogue can take place in order to negotiate difficult communal issues without resorting to violence. I believe that such a minimal hope is based on better understanding. Understanding does not necessarily mean appreciation, but it does mean that negotiation is possible between the antagonistic parties.

In many respects, all four of these issues mark paradigmatic cultural shifts inextricably related to the problem of cultural and religious diversity highlighted by the impact of modernism. If the last century saw the shock of "historicism" and the scientific worldview as inescapable for theological reflection, our sense of the inevitability of ideological and religious pluralism haunts Christian theology in this last decade of the twentieth century. The seemingly irreducible nature of religious pluralism assaults the classical Christian theological vision of unity and oneness. The mirror of the perfectly orthodox mind has been broken by difference and multifariousness. All Barth's men (and occasionally women, though feminist and womanist theologians are congenitally more disposed toward a positive view of pluralism) cannot put Humpty Dumpty back together again. While church historians are wont to remind us that this is not the first time we have lived in a pluralistic world, the challenge is global and not just regional or transitory. Modern self-conscious pluralism is a new theological challenge facing the church.

Christians are mesmerized by our images of difference, particularity, men from women, rich from poor, modern from ancient. This is especially poignant for a tradition that seeks to conform the minds of its adherents "to the mind of Christ." The pressing need is to find, if possible, a pluralistic and faithful exegesis of this crucial Christian theological imperative. If this is not done, Christians run the risk of encouraging a form of theological schizophrenia or fearful retreat to the dream world of past glories where one true form of faith was the norm, at least the norm that was exported by the great missionary movements of the sixteenth to twentieth centuries. The irony of the Christian claim to unity and uniqueness was often not lost on its East Asian recipients when they noticed the internal diversity of missionary presentations. For instance, this led to the continuing official Chinese differentiation of Christianity into its Roman Catholic and Protestant forms as the "The Lord-on-High religion" and the "Jesus religion." Christians may argue that they have one faith; the Chinese are less sure. In fact, we shall discover that the Chinese have been able to live with intellectual and religious pluralism much better than most cultures.

There is nothing wrong with unity as a theological goal as long as it does not become destructive of the intrinsic pluralism of the world by pretending that there is more unity than there actually is. Obviously, there must be some kind of unity for anything to exist at all, even for a pluralistic vision of reality. The myriad things, as the Confucians would put it, need the integrity of boundaries that mark off one thing from another thing. For human beings this is even more complicated. Part of my stronger philosophic claim is that this cosmological pluralism eventuates in a religious pluralism. Like all theological and philosophic claims, it needs to be defended by careful warrants and arguments. I will argue in chapter 5 that process theology and philosophy are committed to a pluralistic vision of reality. From the process perspective, any kind of monism, whether it be ontological, cosmological or religious, is wrong. It does not, however, suggest that all things, views or religions are of equal weight, truth or value. The pluralist merely notes that the world is incurably plural. The ordering of this pluralism is another matter entirely. The arena of Confucian-Christian dialogue provides a place for just such a demonstration of the larger theological and philosophic thesis of the importance of religious pluralism in terms of two distinctive traditions.

My working hypothesis is that these four themes as paradigm shifts are all serious questions for theology and will alter the shape of Christian opinion well into the twentieth century. However, all four issues as social movements are unnerving to various Christians in different ways and degrees. In this essay I will focus on just one issue, namely the question of religious pluralism as manifested in dialogue between Confucians and Christians. I hold the modern interfaith dialogue movement to be the legitimate child of the modern ecumenical movement. Interfaith dialogue began as Christians directed their theological and practical vision beyond the Christian family of churches. Having struggled to learn to live together as Christians, they are now confronting the parallel question of living with other thriving religious traditions. One major difference is that an acceptance of religious diversity will call for an even more dramatic transformation of Christian doctrine and practice than did the ecumenical movement of the first five decades of the twentieth century.[8]

One cannot overestimate the potential theological disequilibrium caused by a positive understanding of religious pluralism for many Christians. Such an affirmation amounts to a radical paradigm shift for Christology, apologetics and missiology (Kreiger 1991, 25–28), to mention just three of the more contentious challenges facing Christian systematic theology impacted by interfaith dialogue. And if this interest in dialogue was not disturbing enough, there are even those who are beginning to suggest that we need to revisit the notion of syncretism in terms of multiple religious participation between and among faith traditions. Not only are some Christians learning to live with Jews, Muslims, Hindus, Buddhists, Sikhs, Jains, Shintoists, Native Elders, Confucians and Taoists, they are beginning to learn *from* these people. Robert C. Neville (1991a, 163–64) articulates this issue by means of the image of moving from a religious home base out into new worlds of discourse in order to develop an enriched primary tradition on the basis of interreligious dialogue. For Neville, there are instances where the classical Neo-Confucians texts concerning sagehood have become the medium by which he can better understand the Christian tradition of sanctification.

Of course, a great deal depends upon how one understands the range and nature of previous paradigm shifts in Christian history—or even the fact of paradigm shifts.[9] Not all Christians agree that the content or structure of the Christian community of faith has or should change when confronted by new cultures and old religions. Oddly enough the orthodox and the modern fundamentalists agree that if the gospel is resolutely and properly proclaimed, then there is no reason to talk in terms of paradigm shifts. It is true that the cultural manifestations of the faith vary, but this does not indicate that something as drastic as a paradigm shift within the faith is necessary. It certainly does not mean that such a radical transformation is good. Not all change need be for the better. Some kinds of change may mark not a renewal but a final degeneration of a form of faith, a well-intentioned but totally misguided reading of the signs of the times and a loss of critical self-understanding of tradition. There are serious Christian theologians who argue that some of the radical pluralistic implications of interfaith dialogue announce just these kinds of negative changes for the churches.

Nonetheless, many conservative and liberal Christians agree with Paul Tillich that major ontic, moral and spiritual transformations have occurred within the churches, although not as basic changes to the essential faith of the gospel. Tillich outlined (1952, 57–63) his understanding of the three major paradigm shifts or periods of anxiety in Christian history when he argued that (1) the early church was driven by a concern for fate and death, whereas (2) the medieval church was dominated by ideas of guilt and condemnation. Tillich concluded that (3) the modern, post-Enlightenment church of the North Atlantic world is fixated on the existential questions of ultimate meaning, or any meaning at all in what seems a tychistic universe, empty and meaninglessness. If the internal questions of meaning were not enough for the post-Enlightenment churches of the North Atlantic world, there is now also the question of religious pluralism. Added to the questions of their own histories, the North Atlantic churches are beginning to wonder if they must now completely reevaluate their responses to other religions. Intellectual weariness compounds confusion without slackening for even one moment in a world driven by the winds of modernity.

Another way of deflating the theological value of these four paradigm shifts is to point out that they are essentially sociological or historical and not theological in nature. While it is true that the Christian Church was always responsive to the culture around it, the gospel does not sanctify any particular culture nor is it transformed essentially by the relative questions peculiar to a concrete historical culture. Respect for tradition and a lack of fixation on purely individualistic cogitations marked both Christianity and Confucianism in their classical periods. The questions raised by paradigmatic cultural transformations may be good ones; but they are never at the heart of the gospel from age to age. The classic early modern formulation of this was Luther's doctrine of the two kingdoms—that we should not expect more from the mundane world than is proper for it, and that the mundane world is never to be confused with the Kingdom of Heaven. We expect too much of any culture if we believe that it can give us the answers that belong properly to the revealed teachings of the church as embedded in normative tradition.

I do not mean to treat lightly the depth of pain caused by the paradigm shift generated by the modern awareness of religious diversity. A fine example of the theological unease caused by this pluralism debate can be found in Carl Braaten's (1992) study of the issue from a conservative perspective. Even though Braaten rejects the pluralistic option, he accepts the fact that this is one of the most important questions before the churches. As Braaten and everyone else affirms, a tradition would not be worth much if it were not believed to be, at all times and in all places, a way to the liberating truth expressed by its teachings, ritual and faith. All traditions purport to be paths to the truth, light and way, however distinctively they may particularize these themes. The problem arises when the assertion is made that one particular teaching is *the* embodiment of the truth, the light and the way for all times, places and conditions of people.[10] Within historic cultures dominated by a majority religious tradition this seems to have been the common human norm for understanding truth. Historically, the price which minority traditions paid for this majority view were often tragically immense. The sad history of Jewish-Christian-Muslim relations is a case in point, as was the first contact between the dominant European immigrant cultures and the ancient native traditions of North and South America.

Some scholars have argued that the landscape of the Chinese religious experience offers a counterpoint to the experience of Christendom as a search for unity. The Chinese, beginning with the introduction of Buddhism into China, have experienced the fact of religious pluralism perhaps more fully than any other major civilization. Paul Martinson (1987) points out that China has now experienced the reception of all the world's great families of religions, including the traditions of West and South Asia such as Judaism, Christianity and Islam, along with Buddhism, Taoism, Confucianism and Chinese popular religions.[11] Throughout major eras of their historical experience, the Chinese have lived with religious diversity and in some cases have even developed positive modes of interpreting this spiritual diversity. It is certainly the case that the unity of Chinese culture does not rest on all Chinese embracing only one religious tradition.

This Chinese (and East Asian) proclivity for a socially sanctioned religious civility has not always been deeply appreciated by the more conversionist or conservative wing of the Christian mission movement. For most Christians, that people can belong to more than one community of faith seems at best confusing and at worst, damning. Nonetheless, as I shall show in this essay, the question of multiple religious participation is beginning to emerge as a serious question of faith and practice in the North Atlantic Christian world.[12] The reason for this is the recognition of religious pluralism beyond just different Christian and Jewish denominations in the North Atlantic world.

I hasten to add that this general Chinese religious civility does not mean indifference to the question of truth. I will return to this question in chapter 6. Rather, it means in the Chinese case that there is nothing dramatic about accepting the fact that some people are Taoists, some Confucians, some Buddhists, some Muslims, some Christians. That you recognize the other traditions, however, does not mean that you think them to be the best way to interpret reality or to live life. For instance, anyone who believes this about the Neo-Confucian tradition should reread Ch'en Ch'un's (1159–1223) strictures against the Taoists and Buddhists of his day (Ch'en 1986, 168–73).[13] Yet, as de Bary (1988) so masterfully demonstrates, there is a dialogical impulse within the Confucian tradition in particular and most of East Asia's intellectual life in general that stands in necessary contrast to the dream of uniformity so often associated with classical Christendom.

One way contemporary theologians, such as John Hick (1989) and Leonard Swidler (1990), have tried to deal with this issue is to develop a doctrine of a 'relative absolute.' So far this idea has not gained many adherents. The notion of a relative absolute mocks the claims for the ultimate allegiance of trust at the foundation of religious commitment. But the ethical thrust (Driver 1981) of these new relativistic theological manifestos is important. Ideas have real impact in the world and we have a moral responsibility to develop ideas that liberate and neither enslave nor kill fellow human beings because of religious convictions contrary to those of the majority community. The need is to find a theology that allows us deep personal and communal conviction without destroying the human rights of others who think and believe differently. To paraphrase the Rt. Rev. Lois Wilson, a former co-president of the World Council of Churches and Moderator of the United Church of Canada, how can we praise Jesus and not curse the Buddha? And how do we not move from cursing to physically attacking the maligned other? If we are not going to lock ourselves into a world of intolerant majorities and frightened minorities, we must learn a whole new way for a theology that recognizes pluralism. Confucian-Christian dialogue is very useful at precisely this point because it puts Christians in touch with a tradition which has been ethically successful in dealing with the question of pluralism without becoming either relativistic or indifferent to competing truth claims.

THE PROCESS OPTION AND THEOLOGICAL DISCOURSE

What of Christianity? It hardly fares much better in the North Atlantic world than Confucianism in terms of self definition and confidence in the last decade of the twentieth century. As Whitehead wrote in 1933 about the Protestant churches,

> Protestant Christianity, as far as it concerns the institutional and dogmatic forms in which it flourished for three hundred years as derived from Luther, Calvin, and the Anglican Settlement, is shewing all the signs of steady decay. Its dogmas no longer dominate; its divisions no longer interest: its institutions no longer direct the patterns of life. (1933, 205)

How true! And how painful and applicable to all the families of Christ in the North Atlantic world![14] The best that can be said that is Christians live in boring theological times. There are no contemporary theologians of the public stature of the giants of the previous generation such as Barth, Tillich or Neibuhr. The larger secular world generally ignores the church except for scandal or humor. But this does not mean that there is no controversy within the churches. Christians are still good at being contentious; the problem is that no one is listening to the old arguments or really cares about what the church does or says. The only exceptions are those marginal Christians who continue to drop out of churches because it no longer serves any discernible need in their lives; they have made a negative choice to give up on what was once a grand tradition.

Part of the reason that no one listens to Christian preaching has to do, I am convinced, with the fact that most Christian discourse does not engage the range of complex and diverse experiences characterizing modern life. The simple fact is that we live in a pluralistic world—but without any coherent Christian theologies that try to explain this pluralism. From time to time W. C. Smith has referred to the fact that modern Christian theology makes a better stab at explaining the nature of the Milky Way than of the existence of the *Qur'an*, the *Gita* or the *I-Ching*.[15] I think that Smith is too sanguine about most Christian theologians really being able to say something intelligent about the Milky Way or modern science in general. I am sure that most theologians have very little useful to say about the other faith traditions. The reason for this is that they often know less about comparative religion than they do about modern science. This is becoming an issue of credibility given that many lay people have a greatly increased knowledge and appreciation of these traditions and their neighbors of other faiths. Simply repeating the neo-orthodox admonition that all religion is unbelief does not prove a very effective way of dealing with the present challenge posed in facing an increasingly pluralistic situation in religious demography.

An added complication is that nowadays people from all the different religious traditions of humankind mix in our great cities. When the girl next door is a Hindu named Maya and is the best friend of your daughter, the old notion of "outside the church there is no salvation" does not fit reality very well. Furthermore, reality can only be ignored by theology for so long before theology becomes irrelevant to religious life. To his great theological credit, Tillich, at the very end of his life, stated that if he were to do it over again, he would rewrite his great systematic theology in light of the question of religious pluralism. It is a minor tragedy for Christian thought that Tillich did not live another decade in order to be able to carry out his intention of taking other religions seriously in terms of Christian systematic theology. There was also something sad about the fact that graduate students at the University of Chicago in the mid-1960s probably knew more about other religions than their great master. Again, it was to Tillich's credit that he understood just where the problem lay: ignorance of other religions in their living, rich, diverse reality.

Many nominally post-Christian North Americans are not even hostile about Christianity; they just ignore it as something quaint. Or not even quaint. It has become something that is so out of touch with the realities of modern life, including religious pluralism, that it does not impinge on their lives at all. It now belongs to the cultural museum of the past. One may feel positively about it as a cultural form, one may dislike it, but there is nothing in it that speaks to one's condition. A common reaction to this is a strong desire on the part of church theologians to repeat old theological formulations and pretend that this is defending tradition. This defensive theory blames the problem on modern tradition and experience. Christians are advised to live in intellectual ghettos, repeating the great verbal formulations of the past, hoping that this will protect and transmit the faith to the younger generations. This may work for some but it does not suffice for many people within what used to be called the mainline churches, which are now rapidly becoming what can only be called "old line."

At this point my nostalgia is for a different past. It is for a past wherein the Christian tradition had something intelligent to say to the world. It is for a past when culture was taken seriously in all its dimensions by the church, and when theology felt challenged by the experience of the people. While I do not want to repeat the theologies of Aquinas, Wesley or Edwards, I do covet the fact that they were in touch with the high culture of their day and actually had something to say to their contemporaries. Theology was truly the work of the community reflecting on scripture, tradition, reason and experience. Nowadays we have a truncated tradition pretending to be scriptural, with a small measure of selected denominational tradition thrown in as if this will serve the demands of the people to be fed a gospel for a whole life to be lived abundantly in a religiously pluralistic world. Hardly any attention is paid to reason or experience when these serve to disturb the neo-orthodox slumbers of the old-line churches in North America. Does anyone really believe that the modern pluralisms of gender, race, culture or religion is going to disappear if we just ignore them long enough?

It will not come as a surprise that I have a theological candidate for the task of dealing with religious pluralism from a Christian perspective. As I have already made clear, I believe that process theology offers just such a way toward a modern fiduciary commitment to the canonical and classical texts of the Christian faith as well as a means to being open to religious pluralism. There is nothing mysterious about such a claim being made on the behalf of the process tradition. At the very heart of this tradition, as we shall see in chapter 5, there is an affirmation of the pluralistic nature of the cosmos. Along with the affirmation of pluralism, there is likewise a claim for the relational essence of the cosmos that makes conversation between religions possible and probable. There is nothing unique in this insight given that many theologians, professing varying degrees of allegiance to process theology, have been engaged in the interfaith dialogue movement for decades.

In chapter 5 I will employ Charles Hartshorne's doctrine of 'dual transcendence' to defend the claim that process theology offers a useful theological option for interpreting religious pluralism (Hartshorne 1976, 22–29). The choice of dual transcendence is proposed in order to focus more clearly on one highly suggestive theological paradigm shift generated from the modern experience of Confucian-Christian dialogue. The crux of this theological shift has to do with the question of transcendence-immanence in God-world relationships, which is one of the key concerns of Hartshorne's theory of dual transcendence. While this is a very cryptic way to state the issue, my thesis is that process theology allows for a faithful Christian understanding of the adjustments suggested by Confucian-Christian dialogue. These adjustments will be shown to be consonant with Christian tradition and the perceived modern imperative for interreligious encounter. Chapter 5 will deal directly with the technical question of dual transcendence and the Confucian of immanence of the will of heaven for mundane creatures.

My focus on the contribution of Charles Hartshorne and more specifically on the notion of "dual transcendence" needs a special comment. While it is true that A. N. Whitehead is the modern founder of the philosophic and theological process movement, few would deny the crucial role Hartshorne has played in the development of the theological side of the process tradition. Hartshorne would be the first to acknowledge his debt to Whitehead (1972, 1–7), although he has developed his own version of what he calls "neoclassical theism," which is, in significant ways, different from a strictly scholastic rereading of Whitehead. While a catalog of these differences need not detain us for the present, it is good to remember that Hartshorne does not merely repeat the words of the master.

Whereas Whitehead certainly touches on the areas of philosophy of religion and theology, he was not primarily concerned with reformulating Christian theology in terms of organic (his own term for what has come to be called process) thought.[16] Whitehead was fascinated with philosophic theology and religion in general as it pertained to the development and enrichment of his own organic philosophy. By extension, Hartshorne has, throughout his long and distinguished career, always been specifically concerned with theological issues qua natural if not church theology. He has tried to address all manner of classical theological doctrines and has suggested where process theology, or neoclassical theology as he calls it, offers positive correction to the classical Christian tradition (1964, 1967, 1984b). He is a resolute theist who further believes that his version of process theology is actually more consistent with the religious evidence of the Christian tradition than traditional systematic or philosophic theology has been.

Hartshorne has never been very much involved in formal ecclesial interfaith discussions although he has tried to make his theology responsive to more than just Western European versions of speculation on divine matters. For instance, he has often suggested a special affinity between Whitehead's philosophic vision and lineages within the Buddhist tradition (1967, 21–25; 1984b, 108–9). He has shown considerable interest in classical philosophic Hinduism and its doctrines of the divine reality (Hahn 1991, 235–69), but he has never been particularly interested in the Confucian tradition. Yet his stress on, among other things, the relational nature of the divine and the processive elements of reality provide comparative hermeneutic links to the Confucian Way as I will try to demonstrate in later chapters.

However illuminating I have found process theology to be in facilitating dialogue with Confucians, there are other fruitful approaches in the theological quest for an adequate comparative theology. For instance, I will also make use of a typology suggested by David Tracy's recent analysis of the styles and audiences of modern theological discourse (1981, 1987). I have found Tracy's tripartite division of theological discourse an especially useful heuristic tool for discussing dialogue as an intra-Christian topic. His distinctions of fundamental, systematic and practical (praxis) theology help us choose the proper mode of discourse for the complex conversation that needs to go on between Confucians and Christians and between those Christians who have talked to Confucians and those who have not. I will return to Tracy's methodology in chapter 2. David Lochhead (*The Dialogical Imperative*, 1988) also demonstrates, in something of an ecumenical *tour de force*, that one can even employ some of Barth's later insights into the universal working of the Holy Spirit for the encouragement of interfaith dialogue. Both Tracy and Lochhead agree that we live in a time when we need to transform some of the received paradigms of the Christian faith in order to make sense of the religious pluralism of the modern world.

THE PROBLEM OF THEOLOGICAL RECONSTRUCTION

The nature of the beast is that we live in a self-consciously pluralistic world where no one any longer really expects one religion to triumph over all the others—at least in the short term. This is the religious analogue to the growing secular recognition that no one socioeconomic system or culture is going to be the model for all nations. Just as more and more economies are seen as "mixed" economies, more and more cultures are seen as religiously diverse. Some people will lament this fact. They will dream of a time when this was not the case, and such dreamers will often be members of the majorities within a given culture and will not usually remember what it would have been like to have been an ethnic, racial or religious minority in a time of monocultural hegemony. Most minorities have very little desire to return to the good old days of religious or ethnic ghettos. What is hopeful is that many members of majority cultures are now beginning to sense the enriching, albeit disturbing, possibilities of a culturally acceptable pluralism.

In North America (at least the Canadian part of it), the term multiculturalism functions as a tentative affirmation of the possibilities of cultural pluralism (Bibby 1990). But again, it is important to note that this is only positive for some Christians and certainly *not* a positive term for many North American academicians who see it as a challenge to the values of cultural excellence that has dominated the Western academy since the rise of the modern universities.[17] There is a lively intellectual debate in many American universities about whether or not multiculturalism is something to be praised or avoided. And even if it is accepted that multiculturalism may be praiseworthy as an ideal, many scholars question if any society can achieve enough social coherence to provide a civilized life unless there is one dominant cultural tradition giving a sense of general direction, purpose and excellence to society.

The key notion, so often lacking in discussions of multiculturalism, is what to make of excellence as a general social condition of civilized social conduct in a multicultural context. Each particular culture has canons of excellence. The problem is that multiculturalism does not privilege any one canon; the real trick of an adequate multiculturalism will be the development of a pluralistic mode of public discourse wherein common norms of social excellence and conduct will be publicly articulated. Needless to say, such a dialogue is merely a present hope. The critics of multiculturalism have every right, indeed the obligation, to challenge not only the possibility but also the feasibility of such a pluralistic social vision. Can one really hope to find cross-cultural norms of discourse, civility, and excellence?[18] Whether or not this hope of a multiculturalism of excellence is possible or not, interfaith dialogue is an essential element of the discussion, for it is only when people talk about their religion that they reach the depths of what it means for them to be human.

Now may be a *kairos* moment for the Christian family to admit that there are other families in the world that God cares for and seeks to nurture as distinct religious traditions. This is a hard learning and it has the potential for splitting the church. Nonetheless, the sociological and historical problem is that this is what the logic of the present moment demands. We can reject the religious logic of multiculturalism in the same fashion that we can reject a creative approach to the teaching of diverse cultures in the academy. We can say honestly that those who are outside the Christian family are damned, however much we deplore the fact, or we can begin to develop a theology that reflects on what God intends through the multifarious nature of human religious tradition and experience. As Geoffrey Parrinder (1987) has suggested, we need a third reformation, a reformation of insight that will allow us to perceive God's gracious presence in the reality of the other faiths. In short, I will argue on the basis of process theology that we need to become true monotheists when confronted by the experience of other religious communities.

This experience of radical religious and cosmological pluralism is the crucial nexus of my theological reflections although I fully understand that Christians will not start here in their analysis of the modern condition.[19] Some will want to claim a careful reading of scripture, tradition, reason or other forms of experience as their point of theological departure. My reason for beginning with the experience of religious pluralism as a sociological and historical reality is that I believe it is in the existential and demanding experience of religious pluralism that interfaith dialogue begins. It strikes me that nothing in modern traditional biblical, systematic or apologetic theology drives us in this direction; rather it is the impact of actual religious diversity in our cities and universities that fuels interest in dialogue. The guilds of systematic theology and biblical studies are only now beginning to awake to the reality of religious pluralism induced by the dream of Christendom.

Nor should we forget the impact of the modern technologies of travel and communication in this intellectual paradigm shift. Joseph Needham, in his monumental study of the history of Chinese science begun in 1954, has repeatedly made the point that modern science and technology, as opposed to traditional technologies and science, have become truly ecumenical in the secular sense of the term. Needham has argued that anyone can become a modern scientist if she or he has the brains and the proper training. The same point can be made for technology, which some theologians treat as religiously neutral in the sense that any tradition can make use of its fruits. Nonetheless, Khomeini did not ride back to Teheran on an Persian horse but rather on an American Boeing jet. The problem, which is certainly well understood in Teheran, is that some of the effects of modern technology are not so culturally neutral as they may seem at first.

My own case is illustrative of the point in question. When I grew up in Norman, Oklahoma, in the 1950s, I had a very limited understanding of the reality of cultural, racial or religious pluralism. In the days prior to the Civil Rights movement there were few African-Americans in Norman, or anyone else apart from white Baptists and Methodists, for that matter. My whole young sense of religious diversity was limited to the awareness that there were some people called Roman Catholics and Lutherans, along with a few Presbyterians. I did not meet a Jew until I was well into my secondary education. This is hardly a representative sample of what I now have experienced as the religious, ethnic and cultural diversity of humankind. Yet all of this has changed. Under the influence of the nightly national news (and CCN all day long), a boy or girl growing up in Norman will surely have an expanded awareness of the religious diversity of the modern world. A girl or boy in the American Midwest or the prairie provinces of Canada may actually even know someone of another ethnic or religious group. She or he may have a friend of African-American descent, or a Jewish playmate, or play ball with a Hindu, a Sikh, Buddhist, a Jain, a Muslim or even a youth whose family belongs to one of the Native American communities of faith.

However, just having a sense of the cultural or religious diversity of the world is not the same things as having anything like an informed understanding of the nature and history of these other groups. The nightly dose of television news, for instance, has not done a very good job in educating majority-tradition North Americans about the living reality of Islam. Nor has it made many of them aware of the continuing influence of Confucianism in East Asia. But in contradistinction to the Western hostility to Islam, there is little overt hostility, as of yet, to the Confucian *tao* even if there is little understanding of it either. It is encouraging that the North Atlantic world is showing concerted signs of interest in other parts of the world. There has always been a curiosity and wanderlust in the people of the North Atlantic world that drives them to move beyond their own physical and intellectual shores. But on the other hand, all this positive incipient intercultural dialogue may be changing with the rise of the economic might of Japan and the other "little dragons" of the Pacific Rim. There is a growing awareness of the impact of Confucianism on the industrial cultures of East Asia and beyond. Many people are not very happy with the economic prowess of the Japanese or others on the Pacific Rim. What happens when China, and it surely will, joins the rest of the Pacific Rim in terms of economic modernization, boggles the imagination.

In the midst of all this theological and social transformation, a process theology articulating a radically pluralistic cosmological worldview will run against the grain of much of the classical Christian theological search for the presence of divine unity and the oneness of being and action—all understood as happening salvifically *within* the Christian church. Classical theology has sought unity, the absolute truth as expressed in the one faith taught by the catholic and apostolic church. In practice the church probably never has lived up to this ideal, but this does not mean that the ideal was or is not important. Yet I confess that I find the world incurably plural, and hence my fundamental philosophic and theological categories thematize this pluralistic conviction. I agree with Whitehead "that the true method of philosophic construction is to frame a scheme of ideas, the best that one can, and unflinchingly to explore the interpretation of experience in terms of that scheme" (Whitehead 1978, xiv). I will try not to flinch in the face of pluralism, and the mirror I will hold up to reflect the 'other' discovered in dialogue will be the Confucian tradition as embodied in the Neo-Confucianism of the Sung dynasty and the modern New Confucian movement.

THE CONFUCIAN TRADITION

The notion of Confucianism itself is an ambiguous term, signifying a vast range of conceptual territory as we shall see in chapters 3 and 4. Just what "Confucianism" do we mean to dialogue with? I will make the following preliminary set of distinctions drawn from the historical development of the Confucian tradition: first, the term Confucianism stands for the entire range of the tradition so defined by self-professing Confucians beginning with Confucius (c. 551–479 B.C.E.), Mencius (c. 372–289 B.C.E.) and Hsün Tzu (fl. 298–238 B.C.E.). We should remember that the term Confucianism is a Western neologism, created when Europeans invented the idea of religions as something every culture has as part of its spiritual makeup. I use Confucianism to express generally what the Chinese (and Koreans, Japanese and Vietnamese) take to be the meaning of *ju-chia* or the Confucian School and *ju-chiao* or Confucian Learning, and what the post-Sung Neo-Confucians defined as *tao-hsüeh* or the Study of the Way.[20]

The second subdivision of the historic tradition important for modern interfaith dialogue is Neo-Confucianism, another Western neologism. The Chinese equivalent, no doubt, is *tao-hsüeh*, including all the various Sung, Yüan, Ming and Ch'ing schools in China, plus their Korean, Japanese and Vietnamese extensions. In many respects this is the family of Confucian schools alive today throughout East Asia. The introduction to chapter 3 will provide a short historical outline of the development of the whole Chinese Confucian movement. As Whitehead noted, no tradition ever recovers from the shock of a great thinker

(1978, 11), or in this case, a group of great thinkers in the Northern and Southern Sung as canonized by Chu Hsi (1130–1200). In fact, it is Chu Hsi's own voice which has shaped much of East Asian civilization from the Sung to the present— both in terms of his own school and in terms of those who demurred from it. We will examine Chu Hsi more thoroughly in chapter 3.

The third sub-division of the Confucian tradition is "New Confucianism" (Chang 1976). This term defines a group of modern scholars who have sought to help revive, redefine and reform the Confucian tradition in the twentieth century. Just as Whitehead is recognized as the founder of the modern process movement, Hsiung Shih-li serves as the foundational figure for most of the scholars of the New Confucianism. These scholars write within the hermeneutic circle of a chastened Neo-Confucian sensibility, but also with a great deal of familiarity with Western philosophy and theology. The main contemporary representatives of this movement are T'ang Chün-i, Ch'ien Mu, Hsü Fu-kuan and Mou Tsung-san. There are a number of younger scholars, often students of these men, such as Liu Shu-hsien, Cheng Chung-ying, Julia Ching, Tu Wei-ming, Antonio Cua, Yü Ying-shih, Ts'ai Jen-hou and others who are also able expositors of the New Confucianism within the Chinese intellectual diaspora.

I will focus my discussion upon two key representatives of the New Confucian movement from the first and second generations, Mou Tsung-san and Tu Wei-ming. I do so because I believe that one must be able and willing to dialogue with the living representatives of the other tradition in order to allow them to define, describe and commend their way. Mou is especially interesting because of his metasystematic reformulation of the Confucian tradition; Tu appeals because of his sensitivity to the social dimension of the Confucian tradition that he thematizes as fiduciary community. Taken together, Mou and Tu express perennial Confucian concerns for self and community in dialogue with other global philosophies and religions.

The main reason for the choice of Mou Tsung-san and Tu Wei-ming is that I consider these two scholars, who stand in a teacher-student relationship, to ably and effectively represent the New Confucianism. Mou Tsung-san is, no doubt, the most philosophically astute and provocative member of the now senior generation of the New Confucians and is so recognized by all the rest. Not everyone agrees with Mou's positions, but they all take his work with the utmost seriousness.[21]

Even more recently, Tu has undertaken the task of trying to explicate and renovate the modern meaning of the Confucian tradition both in the Chinese intellectual milieu and for interested Western intellectuals. Tu has sought to make the Confucian sense of society as fiduciary community come alive as a present possibility for humankind. In the last decade Tu has published a number of books in English that seek to describe, commend and reform the Confucian Way by means of a "fiduciary commentary" on key texts and personalities of the cumulative tradition. In terms of interreligious contact, Tu is also extremely interested in defining the religious dimensions of the Confucian Way by means of dialogue with Christian theologians.

Throughout his long and distinguished career, Mou Tsung-san has sought to analyze and reinterpret the Confucian Way for the modern world. His contributions to the history of Confucian thought are justly famous, as is his dedication to the promotion of comparative philosophy and intellectual history. Although not a central focus of his research project, Mou has also been interested in the religious dimensions of Confucianism, which makes him relatively unique among his generational cohorts. Mou has tried to show that the Confucian exploration of human nature and mind is a profoundly religious quest, given his definition of the religious life. His synoptic statement of these themes is neatly summarized in two short works, *Chung-kuo che-hsüeh te t'e-chih* [The Uniqueness of Chinese Philosophy] and *Chung-kuo che-hsüeh shih-chiu chiang* [Nineteen Lectures on Chinese Philosophy].[22] I personally believe that Mou's research project is one of the most important modern statements concerning the religious nature of Confucianism, and is even more important because it is made from within the tradition by one of the most famous of the New Confucians. Along with Tu Wei-ming's reflection on the notion of "fiduciary community," Mou's understanding of Confucian religiosity and transcendence will be central to the argument of this essay.

THE RECEPTION OF CONFUCIAN-CHRISTIAN DIALOGUE

In the Anglican tradition the term 'reception' is often used when an important or controversial topic is commended to the church for study and reflection (Rusch 1988). By urging that the topic be received, the appropriate court of the church indicates that it feels that its report or suggestions can be faithfully considered a Christian response to the issue at hand. The notion of reception does not make absolute claims for its suggestions; reception humbly notes that these are the kinds of ideas or actions which a Christian can sincerely and prayerfully consider in light of the life and witness of the faith. The designation 'reception' suggests that it is one viable option—one which does not foreclose discussion or suggest that it is the only possible way a Christian may approach the issue at hand. I think the term 'reception' quite accurately indicates where most Christians find themselves when thinking about interfaith dialogue and relations.

As I have stressed again and again, Christians are in the midst of a great paradigm shift in terms of a growing awareness of the persistent religious pluralism of our world. This has come about primarily through the massive demographic changes that marked the end of the Second World War and the close of the colonial period. One of the great and unfinished tasks of Christian theology is to come to terms with other individuals and communities of faith, now often resident in the heart of what was traditionally the homebase of Christendom.

The struggle to understand religious pluralism is often a contest between our deepest ethical motivations and our loyalty to our inherited theological structures, at least as they have been expressed in the last three centuries or so for the Protestant West (Hutchinson 1987). Our Reformation, Catholic and Orthodox traditions try to teach us respect for all human beings created in the image of God. This respect for humankind places upon it certain dialogical demands that are often difficult enough when they are exercised among Christian groups and the situation becomes even more demanding and perplexing when other faith communities appear on our horizon of awareness. It is clear that we are to love God and our neighbors; what is to happen practically and theologically is not so clear when the neighbor turns out to be a Muslim, a Buddhist, a Native Elder, a Jew, a Confucian or others. So we receive a new duty through the wondrous workings of modern immigration patterns. And yet we also feel that our theology should not just be a gospel of decency and gentility, however noble these virtues are within the Christian tradition.

As Whitehead pointed out decades ago, we are still desperately awaiting a new reformation (1933, 205–21). We rummage around in our past and in the cumulative traditions of others in order to find a way to reconcile our deepest ethical prompting with our inherited theological tradition—which speaks in terms of the one way, the truth and the uniqueness of the life, death and resurrection of Jesus of Nazareth. It is not likely to be an easy topic! It will take time and patience and a willingness to explore numerous avenues of concrete dialogue. All Christian parties will need charity of discernment in order to be able to sense what God will for the church. No better credo for the ecumenical interfaith dialogue movement exists than the admonition of Pope John XXIII: "In essential matters, unity; in doubtful matters, freedom; in all matters, charity."

Ha.'

THE PERILS OF SYNCRETISM
AND MULTIPLE RELIGIOUS PARTICIPATION

Within the general matrix of the developing debate on religious pluralism, the question of syncretism and multiple religious participation is one of the most difficult to be faced by the Western proponents of interfaith dialogue. This question will be the main topic of chapter 6. On the one hand, no one actually consciously argues for the creation of new religions in formal dialogue circles; but on the other hand, it is clear that one of the outcomes of dialogue is the enrichment and transformation of the original position. Such an outcome can and has been labelled syncretism. It does little good to point out that one person's syncretism is another's creativity. The same kinds of moves cluster around the notion of whether or not a person can participate with integrity in more than one religious tradition. This has never been considered a really serious option in the Western religious traditions. But just this sort of multiple religious experimentation is what seems to be happening.

The Chinese religious experience makes this multiple participation, or what can also be called dual religious citizenship, less problematic. It does seem to be the case that something like multiple participation in different religious traditions has a long and successful history in East Asia. One of the interesting points is that none of the three great traditions of China has been absorbed into the other two. In China we still find today Taoists, Confucians and Buddhists, along with Muslims and Christians, in growing numbers. The lesson seems to be that each tradition has a combination of essential features or a root metaphor that gives it a stable and recognizable trajectory through history.

It is at this point that process theology may also be of assistance. With its emphasis on cosmological pluralism and intrinsic creativity for each creature, including the divine reality, it provides suggestions as to how to deal with the notion of mutual transformation, enrichment and growth without the loss of essential features of a tradition. I will argue that process theology is resolutely pluralistic and therefore does not find religious pluralism particularly baffling in terms of its fundamental intellectual commitments.

Process pluralism also provides the basis for an understanding of what Charles Hartshorne calls "dual transcendence." Dual transcendence demonstrates how the divine reality is linked to the emergence of each creature that comes to be and also explicates how the emerging creatures can enrich the divine reality and in turn contribute to the emergence of other novel creatures. Given the doctrine of dual transcendence there is nothing cosmologically astounding about mutual transformation between and among religions. As with Lao Tzu, the modern process theologian holds that one of the marks of the living being is to be supple, soft and receptive. The mark of the dead is that it is hard, closed and unreceptive. Perhaps one of the marks of a living religion has always been receptivity to new ideas; that this idea of receptivity now has become self-conscious is one of the key features of the interfaith dialogue movement.

Whereas Confucians and Christians have not, historically speaking, had much to do with each other in the past, this mutual isolation is now rapidly giving way to mutual stimulation both intellectually and economically. It may even lead to mutual transformation and reformation. Only time will tell whether this is a good or evil thing. I believe that it can be a good thing. Further, it is important for scholarly Christians and Confucians to do their part in clarifying the issues at hand for their traditions. Scholarly debate is surely not the entire story, but it does play its own necessary role. It is especially useful in helping to frame the concepts used in discussing the issues involved in dialogue. It is to those issues that we now turn.

2

Religious Pluralism and the Theological Situation

Yet some have wondered how it is that the Universe, if it be
composed of contrary principles—namely, dry and moist, hot and
cold—has not long ago perished and been destroyed. It is just as
though one should wonder how a city continues to exist, being, as
it is, composed of the most opposite classes—rich and poor, young
and old, weak and strong, good and bad. They fail to notice that
this has always been the most striking characteristic of civic
concord, that it evolves unity out of plurality, and similarity out of
dissimilarity, admitting every kind of nature and chance.

Aristotle, *On the Universe* 5.1–6[1]

HISTORICAL REFLECTIONS

Every interfaith relationship or dialogue is generated out of a unique historical
context, raises particular practical religious and theological questions, and
demands a range of methodological and interpretive tools in order to explicate
its attending historical, theological and methodologically interrelated ramifications. The renewed Confucian-Christian dialogue illustrates these interlocking
themes of history, theology, and methodology perfectly.

Confucianism is a remarkably protean word to encompass in dialogue.
What does Confucianism mean, if anything, beyond being a modern English
neologism? For some scholars this is a very serious question. They query whether
there is anything really identifiable in the cumulative East Asian experience
corresponding to the modern Western discussions of the Confucian tradition.
For the purpose of a preliminary discussion, Confucianism defines a living East
Asian and now global tradition. It is a rich tradition in China, Korea, Vietnam,
Japan and the East Asian diaspora which traces it roots to the teachings of
Master K'ung, latinized by early and learned Catholic missionaries as Confucius.

43

All Confucians trace their sense of lineage to Confucius even though they stress that there was much proto-Confucian activity in ancient China prior to its articulation by Master K'ung.

The renewal of Confucianism in its sixth stage (see chapter 3 for a discussion of the phases of the Confucian tradition) by the New Confucians such as Mou Tsung-san and Tu Wei-ming coincides with the decision of the ecumenical Christian churches to promote interreligious dialogue by means of various bilateral and multilateral dialogues. One very good reason for encouraging Confucian-Christian dialogue is the favorable historical climate for dialogue between the two traditions. For the most part, Christians have been impressed with the ethical sobriety and philosophic wisdom of the Confucian tradition, even if there was considerable debate well into the 1970s and 1980s as to whether or not Confucianism was and is a religious tradition. There is consensus now that one can define and describe Confucianism as a tradition with strong religious dimensions.

It would also be naive not to recognize that the renewed interest in the Confucian roots of post-Confucian East Asia is based on the rise of Japanese, Korean and now Chinese economic power. Whereas I will argue that there is a theologically legitimate reason for interreligious dialogue separate from the sociological realities of modern life, I fully realize that many Western Christians are probably willing to take Confucianism seriously only because of Hondas, Sonys and Hyundais instead of any change of theological heart. As is so often the case, religion functions as the handmaiden of economics and politics, in this case of the East Asian rise to international prominence.

As a counterpoint to this renewed modern interest, early Confucian-Christian interaction, represented by the Roman Catholic missions of the sixteenth to the eighteenth centuries in China and Japan, was also highly favorable to dialogue (Young 1983; Mungello 1985; Whyte 1988, Gernet 1985; Standaert 1988; T. Lee 1991). Compared with their unanimous rejection of Taoism and Buddhism (and Shamanism and Shinto in Korea and Japan), the Jesuits, if not the Franciscans, manifested a great deal of practical and intellectual respect for the Confucian tradition. For instance, after some early experiments in wearing Buddhist priestly garb, the Jesuits made the decision to don the robes of Confucian scholars. They did so not only because they realized that this was the most effective way to reach the dominant literati class but also because they had become impressed by the Confucian tradition. Just how successful the early Roman Catholics were in this regard is now undergoing careful reexamination.

The early Jesuits interpreted the Confucian Way as being similar to Greek philosophy in the West. While Confucianism was definitely not sufficient for salvation, it did serve as preparation for the propagation of the Christian gospel. Confucius and Mencius could take their place along with Plato and Aristotle in the gallery of worthy pagan philosophers. The Chinese texts were considered as "classics," not scripture and hence could be appreciated by the Christian, not rejected out of hand as were Buddhist and Taoist texts. As I noted above, given the universally hostile reaction of the early Christian missionaries to almost every other aspect of the spiritual life of East Asia, this assessment of the value of the Confucian tradition was no mean concession on the part of the Jesuits. Often this meant that the Jesuits interpreted the Confucian Way as a philosophy and not as a purely religious movement.

Likewise, in the nineteenth century some of the first Protestant missionaries held an equally high opinion of the Confucian tradition. For instance, James Legge, the great missionary translator of the Chinese classics, felt that the Confucian sages were honorable and decent men. As Legge said of Mencius, "Never did Christian priest lift up his mitred front, nor show his shaven crown or wear his Geneva gown, more loftily in courts and palaces than Mencius, the Teacher, demeaned himself" (1960, 2:52) Needless to say, this was not a highly popular opinion for a Protestant missionary to hold. Yet even Legge (1960, 1:416), when it came to what Mou Tsung-san will call the cosmological heart of the Confucian tradition, could make little sense of that section of the *Chung-yung* [Doctrine of the Mean] where Heaven, earth and humanity form a creative trinity to enhance the ceaseless work of the Tao. Sadly, Legge called this very important Confucian religious teaching an unintelligible extravagance.

In both cases, the early Jesuits and Protestants missionaries, the respect felt for the Confucian tradition was reserved for the earliest canonical sources and not the later tradition of the "literati." Whereas the Jesuits and scholar-missionaries such as Legge were drawn to the ethical purity of the *Analects* and the *Mencius* as texts, they were not so sympathetically inclined towards the followers of Chu Hsi, Wang Yang-ming, Liu Tsung-chou or Tai Chen. The Western missionaries believed that these later Confucians had been corrupted by a perverse materialism and atheism that effectively obscured the clearly theistic import of the earliest Confucian classics from them. This was, according to the Western missionaries, a tragedy both for these individual literati and for Confucian China as a whole. They saw, as one of their tasks in preaching the gospel, the need to remind the Chinese of the theistic roots of their own tradition. This is a theme that we will address in later chapters of this study.

THE LACK OF HOSTILITY BETWEEN
CONFUCIANS AND CHRISTIANS

Another point to remember is that Confucians and Christians have never managed to slaughter each other for religious reasons with the sustained gusto of Christians, Jews and Muslims in their long and unfortunate interreligious history. While many Confucians were not well disposed towards what they saw as yet another imported heterodox tradition, there were rarely religious crusades or campaigns to eradicate the faith in spite of sporadic hostilities between the two communities.[2] The notable exception to this general rule was the relationship of Confucianism and Christianity in nineteenth-century Yi dynasty Korea. There, active persecution did occur, although it can be argued that neither tradition was infected by the virus of sustained conflict sufficient to produce a congenital aversion towards the other. Part of the reason for the early conflict had more to do with internal Korean political and ideological conflict than any profound antagonism between the two traditions.[3]

With the rise of the ecumenical interfaith dialogue movement in the 1960s, this rather promising history of interaction was revived and augmented, even in Korea where there is now a very strong Christian presence. One of the rather dramatic shifts in religious history followed from the promulgation of *Noster Atatae* by Vatican II. This short document marked a sea change in perceived Roman Catholic attitudes towards the other religious communities of humankind. In the early 1970s the World Council of Churches followed suit and established the Sub-Unit on Dialogue With People of Living Faiths and Ideologies (shortened in the 1980s to Dialogue With People of Living Faiths). The dialogue movement sponsored by the Roman Catholic Church and the World Council of Churches had begun in earnest by the mid-1970s. Year after year new bilaterals and multilaterals were established by the Roman Catholic Church and the member churches of the World Council of Churches. The old history of conflict bequeathed many unresolved questions whereas the modern inclination for institutional dialogue offered new possibilities for conversation.[4]

THEOLOGICAL ISSUES

One of the main theological questions that emerged from the first formal international dialogue in Hong Kong in 1988 was the question of the religious status of the Confucian tradition. This was often put in terms of trying to clarify the particular Confucian understanding of transcendence and immanence. In chapter 5 I will contend that the process theology movement allows for a Christian appreciation of the Confucian insistence on the unity of transcendence and immanence. Within process theology, Charles Hartshorne has called this the question of dual transcendence. At the first two international dialogues in 1988 and 1991 it was agreed that the notions of transcendence and immanence should be put on the agenda for future dialogues. From a Christian perspective this was the way into a discussion of the nature of divine things.

Following the conversation about dual transcendence came the even more challenging question of multiple religious participation or the question of dual citizenship. At the Second International Confucian-Christian Dialogue, the question was asked whether it is possible to be both Confucian and Christian. This is an especially unsettling question for the Christian participants because it is often assumed that it is a question to which there must always be a negative answer. For instance, one cannot, by traditional and orthodox definition, be both Christian and Jewish or Muslim or Buddhist. The problem, however, is more difficult when we examine our own scholarly and personal appropriation of other traditions. What is the boundary between appreciating another tradition as a scholar and beginning to appropriate selectively parts of the new tradition into one's own theology?

Some Confucians pointed out that this was not as devastating a question in the East Asian context as it was for those shaped in the Christian West. In the classical Christian context, any suggestion of dual citizenship or even multiple participation would be met almost immediately with the charge of syncretism, and if persistently pressed as a positive theological option, by charges of defection and ultimately, heresy. From an East Asian perspective, this is less clearly negative. Many serious East Asian intellectuals have adumbrated the notion that it is perfectly acceptable to embrace, or at least to borrow extensively from, more than one religious tradition. In Ming China there had been respected scholars who advocated the unity of the three ways of Confucianism, Taoism and Buddhism (Berling 1980). Nonetheless this call for *san chiao ho-i* (the unity of the three religions) is highly suspect even to liberal Christian ears. If possible, what would it mean for the integrity of the faith?

The question of multiple participation is not frivolous, nor are the objections to it inevitably reactionary or obscurantist. The challenges to multiple religious participation often go to the heart of the vision of what it means to be religious, to be committed in faith to a tradition and to seek perfection, sanctification, salvation or liberation by means of such participation. One way of putting the issue is to note that all this talk about multiple religious participation seems to reduce religious practice to something like idle browsing through a modern supermarket. If you do not like the meditations of your own tradition, then you can happily borrow something from the Tibetans, the Japanese, the Sufis or others. If you are unhappy with the conceptual bindings of modern Western cosmology, then you are free to dabble in the delights of various Neo-Confucian reveries on matter-energy and its primordial patterns of axiological principles. But this process may be hopelessly dilettantish and can lead in the end, with the best of intentions, to the excess of what is now called New Age Religion.

The counterargument to the supermarket vision of religious participation points out that religions have integrity in themselves and that tradition, narrative and orthopraxy are essential to being part of that religion and not another. The argument is made against the pluralists within the dialogue movement that pluralism qua theology is a modern heresy in the making if you can create your religion to taste and still call it Christianity or Confucianism. Religions are not just different brands of cereal. Aloysius Pieris (1989) has labelled such instrumental or functional use of selected elements of a tradition "commercialism" and strongly condemns the continued abuse of East traditions by a not too subtle form of Western religious colonialism, now intent on exporting meditation rather than the raw materials for industrial or economic exploitation. Having created a very nervous North Atlantic civilization, based partially on the plundered wealth of Asia he argues that the West is now seeking spiritual and emotional salvation and release through the meditation "technology" of Eastern gurus, sages and roshis.

This argument demands a careful response from the perspective of a pluralist who believes that such interreligious borrowing may be in order. One of the first questions that needs to be raised is whether someone (a Christian in this case) who believes in modern multiple participation can still call him or herself a Christian theologian. They may believe that they are still Christians, but does their obvious bending of the tradition allow them the added title of "theologian?" For instance, the Roman Catholic Church no longer allows Hans Küng to use the title of Roman Catholic Theologian because of what it takes to be his false teachings, but has not denied Küng's Christian identity, faith or priesthood. By analogy, do pluralists speak for the Christian community of faith in any meaningful sense? And if not, what does that mean for their theological pretensions? I will return to this issue later.

Perhaps nowhere else than in the question of multiple participation does one more keenly sense that we are living in the middle of a religious paradigm shift. Just asking such a question even three decades ago in World Council of Churches circles would have been almost unthinkable. If it were thinkable, it would not have been voiced openly for fear of ridicule or expulsion from the ranks of respectable Christian thinkers. Even now such thoughts have a tinge of heresy about them, not to mention the dubious odor of New Age religiosity in all its facile and shallow eclecticism. Yet something important is happening here. More and more people are experiencing the fact that they are influenced profoundly by more than one religious tradition. They still belong to one tradition; they are not converts and see themselves still in a fiduciary relationship to their tradition, but they now see a wider world of religious revelation before them. With the kaleidosope of many religion in front of their eyes they cannot go back to a monochrome world even though they find it difficult to describe their new vision and defend it against the hallowed charge of syncretism.

METHODOLOGICAL CONCERNS

The first problem that we face is that there is no consensus on what makes for good cross-cultural comparison. Methods are interpretive devices generated within specific cultures and there is always the lurking suspicion that the analogies which any methodology discovers may obscure more than it enlightens beyond its culture of origin.[5] This is a fear with a name: apples for oranges. Yet, in the face of such methodological hesitations, people do communicate over cultural barriers: we buy Toyotas in Boston and the Gospel is preached in New Delhi. In fact, the spread of the great "world" religions such as Buddhism, Islam and Christianity presents the spectacle of complex cultural achievements moving around the globe while still being recognized as part of one religious family, however transformed they might be in the cross-cultural translation. But, as the Buddhist experience in China teaches, this is rarely an easy or a quick process.[6]

Nonetheless, theologians, cautious due to the complexity of the problem, are developing an interest in other religious traditions. But when they do show such interest, how do they approach their subject matter? David Tracy (1981) has provided us, correctly, I believe, with an outline of how theology is done these days in the North Atlantic world, at least in academic circles interested in the life of the church. There are of course other possible models, for we live in theologically diverse age. There is no grand or universal orthodoxy, although one is always hesitant to make such a statement in front of Eastern Orthodox colleagues who still sustain a much more robust sense of historical continuity with their living theological traditions. For instance, the characteristic Eastern orthodox emphasis on the role of the Holy Spirit in dialogue is certainly a fruitful way for Christians to address the issue. One can only hope for more sustained Eastern orthodox participation, especially in the dialogues with the living religions of East Asia.

Tracy notes that we now divide theological discourse into the fundamental, systematic and praxis modes. First, fundamental theology is carried out primarily in the academy and is often closely related to philosophy of religion and allied disciplines in religious studies, the history of religions and the social sciences. This kind of discourse seeks to be fundamental in that it does not initially warrant any one tradition or canon of sacred texts as normative for discussion.

Second, systematic theology is the theology of a particular confessional family of churches or a church. It privileges a particular tradition and works within the specified realm of discourse of that tradition; it can and does quote holy scripture and tradition to make its points. For instance, Methodists cite the Wesleyan quadrilateral in all debates, affirming the proper place of scripture, tradition, reason and experience for theological deliberation.

Third, praxis-oriented theology is directed to the transformation of the individual within a particular society. This form of theology is most often identified with political theologies, including liberation theology and some forms of feminist speculation. It is not merely a form of practice. Praxis theologians believe that theory and practice are so interconnected that neither can be neglected although constant attention must always be directed to the living situation and the effects of ideology on the lives of the people involved. Praxis theology is invariably pragmatic.

In terms of our present concern, I believe that the dialogue movement begins in the praxis of pluralistic societies and not in the theological academy, although it certainly has also begun to flourish in the academy. Interfaith dialogue begins when people of different religious traditions meet, talk, sometimes cooperate, argue and sadly, make holy war with each other. Then and only then does it become part of academic concern. At that point academic dialogue can become very important in authenticating the activity for members of the faith communities. In time, it often becomes part of the two other disciplines of systematic and fundamental theology. The flood of recent books and articles concerning interfaith relations demonstrates that it is becoming a most lively topic for systematic and fundamental theologians.

Tracy's analysis is also helpful in directing us to our proper audience for each of the three modes. I find that much confusion is avoided if we are clear about which of the three types of theology engages our attention at any given moment. As we shall see, there are different modes of disputation for fundamental, systematic and praxis theology. For instance, dialogue usually begins

in the praxis of everyday life, for good or ill—theological conversation follows
the dialogue of life. Each side learns that it cannot use its favorite forms of
authoritative argumentation in the early stages of the conversation with the
people of the other religion. For instance, sometimes Christians are surprised
that a Hindu or Buddhist is not impressed with an apt quotation from the
New Testament. Fundamental theological discourse does not accept the scripture
of any one tradition, and in fact, may not even accept the notion that scripture
is relevant at all. Such would be the case for dialogue with many aboriginal
peoples who do not have a formal written scripture. Yet one quickly discovers
that conversation is often possible, albeit on more neutral ground.

This is often a problem within the Christian traditions too. The quarrels
between liberal and conservative Christians demonstrate the point nicely. Both
sides will often quote scripture, but their understanding of these quotations
will be radically different. Conservative and liberal Christians live in
paradigmatically different intellectual worlds, even if they profess the same historic
faith. Actually, some familiarity with the Confucian tradition is useful here.
All Confucians claim the same basic origins, but the tradition has been
transformed throughout history. In fact, the great Sung revival form was given
a new name in Western scholarship, namely Neo-Confucianism. Outsiders to
Christian debates could well label some forms of modern Christian thought
Neo-Christian with as much justification as the early Western scholars who
invented the artificial term of Neo-Confucianism. Yet rarely does any great
reform movement want to acknowledge such originality. If they do claim such
a radical break, it usually means the creation of a new community. Examples
would be Christianity itself, along with such traditions as Buddhism and more
recently, Sikhism or the Baha'is. If you remain intentionally within the faith
of the mothers and fathers you learn to speak in terms of systematic theology.
You master the idiom of continuity, all the while transforming the structure
of the tradition.

An illustration of this phenomenon appears in Tracy's exposition of
fundamental or foundational theology. He points out that this is primarily the
theology of the global academy where no single tradition may warrant its own
tradition, texts or revelations. It is the arena in which persons of good will
must seek a common vision of at least what constitutes a proper truth claim
if not the truth itself. It points to a world beyond the borders of just one
community and given the religiously pluralistic complexity of our modern world,
it axiomatically directs our attention to the foundational questions of interfaith
dialogue. Tracy's fundamental theologians can be likened to the scouts of an
advancing wagon train (or the good ship Enterprise in Star Trek mythology).

They go where their tradition has not gone before and report back to the main body of believers. The definition of the tradition, therefore, is a result of a complicated three-way dance between Tracy's fundamental theologians and his other two partners, the systematic and the practical theologians.

One major difficulty in the dialogical dance is called the problem or question of relativism: we are never, ever, going to speak to each other using the same language or view the tasks at hand from the same cultural perspective. If we are pluralists, we may never be able to affirm a unity of perspectives or an all-embracing ordinal location as Justus Buckler has defined the notion in his metaphysics of natural complexes. To be a finite creature is to have a particular ordinal location in a multiplicity of orders and we can never have precisely the same location in any order of being or knowing or acting as another finite creature. Nonetheless, the role of scholarship and humane letters is to allow us to develop forms of communication that permit, as far as is humanly possible, the recognition that we are talking about apples and oranges when we are looking together at the same fruits.

Therefore I find much of the present serious academic discussion of dialogue focused on the metadialogical or methodological issues of the foundations of discourse itself. This is the case for such sophisticated methodologists such as Tracy, Watson and Dilworth. For instance, even the choice of language is never a neutral one. I am sure that Buddhist-Christian dialogue would be markedly different from the same bilateral dialogue if it were conducted in Japanese rather than in English. It is interesting to note that the first international Confucian-Christian dialogue, 1988, was conducted in both Chinese and English; papers were also read in Chinese and Korean at the second conference in 1991. One salient feature of this multilingualism was the ability to confirm that we were all talking about the same things even in different languages. And of course, at this point in the Confucian-Christian dialogue, a great deal of time was taken, correctly, to clarify linguistic conventions.

Yet fundamental dialogue is something more than just getting the right translations among cultures and religions, even if this is crucial for future intercultural communication and a worthy goal in and of itself. Fundamental discourse stipulates no tradition as the norm for dialogue and seeks to find a way for each partner to recognize the other and have that recognition affirmed by the partner. No one expects the Confucian to become a Christian, but the Confucian has every right to expect that the Christian's explanation of Confucianism seem plausible. W. C. Smith (1981) has argued that dialogue demands that the outsider's account of the religious phenomena be recognizable to the insider, with proper weight being given to the fact that the insider realizes that the outsider is giving an external account. This is a difficult although not impossible task, and in fact, goes on all the time. Take the example of a good professor of comparative religion, who is often able to give a better and perhaps even more attractive interpretation of another tradition to a target audience than an adherent of the other community of faith. The professor has an informed understanding and appreciation both of the target audiences and what makes sense to them and a facility for interpreting the other religion. The professor as outsider does not have the right to define the contours of the other tradition, but may be able to describe that tradition in meaningful terms within the parameters of his or her own culture.

For the modern ecumenical Christian engaged in interfaith dialogue the most difficult audience is that of the systematic theologians. This is the group that, for all religions in their intellectual modes, can be called "the folks back home." Systematic theologians are the guardians of the very forms of orthodoxy and the self-definitions of the contours of the community. For dialogue to flower this group of scholars will need to be persuaded that what goes on in praxis and what is proffered from the academic dialogue on foundations somehow coheres with a faithful renewal or revision of inherited systematic theology.

Theological resistance to dialogue from systematic theologians can be broken down into two major forms for heuristic purposes. The first group are those confessional theologians intensely concerned with the preservation of cumulative religious tradition. As stated above, these are the guardians, formal and informal, of orthodoxy. Their general concern is to preserve the historic continuity of the community of faith. Actually, there is often nothing intrinsically antidialogical about the guild of systematizers; the problem is that their interests often lie elsewhere and they are fascinated by a different set of questions internal to the theological history of the Christian tradition. And of course, there are those systematizers who, on principle, reject dialogue as a faithful form of Christian life.

Biblical scholars are another example of systematic theologians who are often simply disinterested in dialogue issues. This is a very influential group and they have their own norms of scholarship, professional advancement and peer audience. Given that interfaith dialogue does not, in the first instance, begin with questions about Christian scripture, why should any aspiring or established biblical scholar become interested in the field? Without putting too fine a point on it, writing about dialogue will probably not get a young scholar tenure in the North Atlantic world. Biblical scholars are sometimes interested in dialogue in order to explicate certain problematic passages that seem to preclude any Christian interest in dialogue; or they are called upon to provide enough proof-texts to warrant the whole enterprise.

The second group is the guild of denominational or historical systematic theologians, those charged with the exposition of the confessional teaching of the churches. This group often defines itself as "church theologians." This is not usually the kind of group that appreciates the perspectival or relativistic approaches to Christian tradition advanced by some of the bolder proponents of dialogue. Why should they? Their job, as historically understood, is to deploy the particular language of a tradition to define that tradition. From the perspective of a Christian systematic theologian, why should they have to grapple with the intricacies of Buddhist dharma theory in order to expound the gospel? At best there is an apologetic interest and the ethical imperative not to bear false witness against the neighbor.

Systematizers are confessional theologians because their stock–in–trade is the cultural and linguistic particularities of a specific tradition. As Lindbeck (1984) has argued so well, they are masters of one definitive religious language game, with its own vocabulary and rules of discourse. To introduce new vocabulary and new rules changes the game, and one of the main functions of systematic church theologians is to umpire a specific game, not to change the rules of that game in the middle of play. That would be bad form and bad faith. They are trained to win arguments and make points using privileged documents, dogmas and approved philosophic traditions.

The issue of particularity is crucial for systematic theologians or philosophers as confessional intellectuals for any particular tradition. It is a difficult task. On the one hand, there is the pressure to defend the tradition in its particularity as it has been articulated in the historic tradition. This means mastery and fidelity to a grammar of discourse, a style of life, an ethical path, a body of canonical literature or collection of tales—the list can be multiplied but the point is clear. This is the knowledge of the member for the members. But on the other hand, there are also the intersystematic claims that this specific religious path is a path of salvation for all peoples (at least for most of the historic traditions). So systematic theologians must be adept at the apologetic skills that make a plausible case for the application of the particular claims of their tradition to the universal soteriological life of humankind. The problem is that people outside the confessional tradition are not initially likely to be moved by arguments that are based on the warrants, texts, stories and arguments from a specific tradition that they do not share, hence there is almost always a need for intercultural apologetics. But apologetics is only a subdiscipline of the systematic craft and is not always essential to it in a culture already imbued with a history of a particular theological tradition.

Although it may seem odd to some, my affirmation of process theology is a form of cross-cultural apologetics in the grand tradition of missionary faith, or at least the cosmological side of faith and philosophic discourse. Process theology is a Western form of thought and does not stand outside of history any more than does Mou Tsung-san's reformed Confucianism. Its claim for being a species of fundamental discourse is based on the fact that it points to what it takes to be common experience and not the specific tradition of any one religious community. I fully recognize that this is a suspect move in these times of such highly charged hermeneutics of suspicion. Nonetheless, I will argue in abstract metasystemic terms for the use of the foundational notions of form, dynamics and unification for the analysis of reality.[7] I believe that the analysis of any thing or event of our cosmos will reveal a balance of three constituent elements: (1) the formal, (2) the dynamic and (3) the unifying aspect of all that we can know, feel, sense, intuit—in short, the total of all that is possible for human reflection. For cosmological purposes, I derive this short list of analytic elements from reflection on Whitehead's category of the ultimate as outlined in *Process and Reality*. As Whitehead (1978, 21) put it,

> 'Creativity,' 'many,' 'one' are the ultimate notions involved in the meaning of the synonymous terms 'things,' 'being,' 'entity.' These three notions complete the Category of the Ultimate and are presupposed in all the more special categories.

This is one of the most controversial and oft-quoted Whiteheadian statements, and has caused just as much exegetical grief as Chu Hsi's interpretation of Chou Tun-i's opening sentence in the *Diagram of the Supreme Ultimate* about the relationship of the Supreme Ultimate and the Non-Ultimate.

Behind my cosmological categories of form, dynamics and unification rests an incurable Christian penchant for trinitarian speculation. Or, as Tillich would have put the matter, these Whiteheadian-inspired categories can also be equated with love, power and justice, yet another trinitarian way to go about foundational theology. For instance, I agree with David Dilworth (1989) that the Christian philosophic tradition, following the Book of Revelation, proclaims a world where everything is always made new. I therefore find it completely appropriate as a Christian theologian to thematize the notion of creativity as part of a process theology in line with the great history of the Christian faith. This notion of creativity will be defended in chapter 5 by means of a selective appropriation of Whitehead's and Hartshorne's cosmology. I also believe that it can be defended on Christian theological terms both as fundamental and systematic discourse.

While my primary debt to process theology is paid to A. N. Whitehead and Charles Hartshorne, I will also rely on the work of a group of scholars heavily implicated in the development of the process movement even if they no longer see themselves as orthodox process thinkers. By this I mean the work of such scholars as Robert Cummings Neville, David L. Hall and Roger T. Ames. While none of these three scholars accepts the label of process theologian or philosopher, they have all contributed significant work in the area of axiology, comparative philosophy and religion, and philosophic sinology. Along with the work of such scholars as Steve Odin (1982) and John Keenan (1989) in Buddhism, they demonstrate the emergence of new school of comparative philosophy and theology. Neville, Hall and Ames are also all interested in the study of Confucianism as a living, important philosophic and spiritual system.

I believe there is a cognate to this Christian, deep tripartite structure to be found in Chu Hsi's mature synthesis, although the content of the vision is radically different, as would be expected. When Chu Hsi analyzes the world in terms of *li, ch'i,* and *hsin,* there does seem to be, on prima facie grounds, good reason for observing a certain formal similarity between the trinitarian process and organic philosophy of Whitehead as I have defined it and the Neo-Confucian vision of Chu Hsi. This similarity between process thought and the Neo-Confucian synthesis has been noticed before (Yu 1959) and I will explore its meaning in later sections of the essay.

Over twenty years ago people asked me why in the world I was bothering to study a dead religion such as Confucianism. Surely, the argument ran, Confucianism has been shattered forever by the impact of the West and finally buried for good by Mao's Great Proletarian Cultural Revolution. I told my colleagues that Confucianism hardly seemed dead to me or to many Confucian scholars and that the rumors of its demise were greatly exaggerated. The economic success of the large and small dragons of the Pacific Rim has stopped all such questions in the last decade, although no one is certain what precise cultural role Confucianism will play in the development of modern East Asia. (Tu 1992). Confucianism is now perceived as a viable intellectual and religious tradition in the process of renovation along with the other great religious traditions of humankind.

Furthermore, I believe that thinkers such as Chu Hsi and Wang Yang-ming are globally important both intellectually and spiritually. For instance, Chu and his disciple Ch'en Ch'un (1159–1223) have taught me a great deal about philosophic matters and have provided me with an alternative vision,

a vision that has allowed me to view my own tradition from new and exciting
perspectives. And where I cannot follow Chu, Ch'en, Wang Yang-ming, Liu
Tsung-chou, Tai Chen and a host of other Neo-Confucian masters in the
particulars of their thinking, they have aided me immeasurably in looking afresh
at my own theological and intellectual heritage. This appears to me to be at
least one of the marks of a successful dialogue.

COMPARATIVE THEOLOGY

The term comparative religion (Kilgore 1991, 30, 51–52) was used by Dean
William Fairfield Warren to describe the teaching of Asian religions at the Boston
University School of Theology in the mid-nineteenth century. In honor of
my predecessor's early attempt to encourage better understanding of Asian
thought and culture, this study could have been called a work in comparative
theology.[8] It is a mark of the strangeness of the dialogue movement that we
lack a common name for the theological study of the relationships between
religions.

In the field of Buddhist-Christian dialogue, a fine example of this kind
of comparative religious study and cross-cultural theology is found in John P.
Keenan's *The Meaning of Christ: A Mahāyāna Theology* (1989). Keenan argues
that the Christian theologian is free to employ any philosophic system in order
to better illumine the meaning and practice of the Christian faith. Keenan applies
his own theory through the application of a modified Mahāyāna Buddhist
Yogācara philosophy to traditional Christian topics. I cite his work as an example
of the creative potential to be found in the cross-referencing of religious traditions.
One can also point to the work John Cobb, Jr. has done over the last three
decades in promoting Buddhist-Christian dialogue.

Just because it has been the case that the Christian tradition was formulated
first in terms of the dominant intellectual currents of the Greco-Roman world
which included Greek philosophy and Rabbinic speculation, this does not mean
that all theology must be cast in this light. For instance, Robert E. Hood (1990)
has made just this case most forcefully in terms of the varied African-American
and African Christian traditions. Just as post-Enlightenment North Atlantic
theologians have sought to present alternative metasystematic articulations of
the faith through such modern movements as process theology, Christian
feminism or political theology, there is nothing un-Christian in attempting a
similar expansion of the Christian intellectual horizon through the appropriation
of Confucian categories.

Such an attempt at reformation would be in line with the modern ecumenical call for the globalization of theology. I contend that globalization does not mean just teaching about the other traditions. It is fundamentally an exploration of what the Christian faith becomes if articulated boldly from a Confucian perspective, or more conservatively, in conversation and cross-referenced with Confucianism. It will be for Confucians to make or reject a similar assessment of dialogue for their tradition. Yet, if such modern Confucians such as Mou Tsung-san, Liu Shu-hsien and Tu Wei-ming are to be believed, such a movement is already underway under the banner of the New Confucianism. And this means the reformation of Confucianism and Christianity in Boston as well as in Beijing, Hong Kong, Taipei, Seoul, Tokyo, Kyoto or Singapore. As it has become clear that no culture can monopolize the Christian gospel, likewise no single intellectual tradition, however rich, can make a similar claim to having cashed out all the ramifications of the Christian faith tradition.

Furthermore, we live in a self-consciously hermeneutical age, where analysis of meaning has become a key intellectual function of the theological community (Watson 1985, 5–9). One way of reading the present situation is to see the various religious traditions as a collection of global texts expressing the interaction of the divine reality with humankind. As an aside, I hope that my Buddhist colleagues will be able to understand what I am trying to say in terms of the divine reality although no Buddhist would ever put it in this quasi-theistic way. We are rapidly moving from a world where we read one text to one in which we read many texts. Whereas the history of our various traditions was usually self-referencing and self-warranting in terms of one canon, our era demands a theological cross-referencing hermeneutical art for all human canons.

THE CONTEXT OF CONFUCIAN-CHRISTIAN DIALOGUE

I believe that Christians have arrived at dialogue with Confucians for at least two reasons, although there are other kinds of possible motivation. I will not try to speculate on why Confucians are involved in dialogue—that is for them to explain in the course of conversation. The first reason for the Christian is practical and has to do with the growing awareness of pluralism in all its permutations around the globe generated by the dramatic population shifts that have occurred since the end of the Second World War. One of the aspects of this new self-awareness is that Christians have become more and more aware that they share the world with people from other religious traditions, even in what used to be the almost entirely Christian nations of the North Atlantic world.[9] Although Christians have known that there were other religions for a long time, there is now a certain urgency to the question of pluralism because of the transformed religious demography of all our major urban centers in the North Atlantic world.

At its roots I believe that there is nothing particularly theoretical about this new awareness of religious pluralism. Most of it comes from the immigration of peoples around the world. An excellent example would be Toronto, Boston or San Francisco where we now find all the historic faith communities of the world are well-represented in the metropolitan areas. If you are a Christian theologian, you cannot avoid the question of religious pluralism as you move about the city. Much the same thing can be said about any other major city of the world. So if traditional Christian systematic theology does not inspire interest in interfaith dialogue, a ride on the Toronto, Boston or San Francisco subway will.

Some will argue that the recognition of religious diversity only makes a virtue out of the necessity of acknowledging the changing demographics of North America, a belated recognition of the loss of missionary nerve that led to the truly amazing expansion of the Christian world from the early 1800s to the 1990s. It is interesting to note that dialogue only found its way onto the agenda of the World Council of Churches when the issue was raised by the churches of Asia, where the question is that of being a minority community in the midst of a larger majority community or communities. What began with a pressing question in the nineteenth century for European and North American missionaries has now become a question for the churches of North America and Europe. Without this great modern movement of peoples theologians would not have taken up the question at all.

We must also remember the role of Vatican II in making the question of interfaith dialogue a legitimate one for the Roman Catholic Church, and by extension, for the whole ecumenical movement.

The second reason for the rise of the interfaith dialogue movement has to do with the ongoing intellectual and religious paradigm shift in Western thought discussed in chapter 1. In theological terms this change (Küng 1988; Knitter 1985) has been described as a move from classical Western views of a static, dualistic, mechanistic and substantive reality to the emergence of a new relational or processive paradigm.[10] The process theological perspective of this essay expresses many of the chief concerns of the new relational and processive revolution. In fact, Charles Hartshorne's exposition of 'dual transcendence' tries to explain what transcendence means for God in a relational and processive cosmos. But this anticipates the discussion about the theological roots of the modern dialogue movement.

I have begun this section with the practical side of the dialogue movement because I believe that this is why dialogue has become such an important contemporary theological issue. As the Christian Conference of Asia has put it, dialogue arises out of the "dialogue of life," the concrete interaction of women and men day by day. The content and structure of contemporary North Atlantic theology previously had no internal imperative to think about the other religions as anything other than targets for conversion sought by mission programs. Of course, there were notable exceptions to this general observation. At the end of his career Paul Tillich (1963), working with the great University of Chicago historian of religion Mircea Eliade, was beginning to grapple with the question of the permanent role of religious pluralism in Christian thought. In the more distant past, there is always the example of *De Pace Fidei* by Nicholas of Cusa, the patron saint of the modern dialogue movement (de Cusa 1962, 195–237). Nonetheless, given the persistent conversionist tone of most modern theology, there was no theoretical need for dialogue to match the practical impact of the world's changing demography.

This modern Christian theological concern for dialogue must strike the Confucian community as a singular Christian problem. It is well to remember that there is nothing at all strange in the Chinese tradition about interreligious dialogue. There has been a great deal of positive social, religious and intellectual interaction among Confucians, Taoists and Buddhists in China over the centuries, often with significant transforming results. Of course, as we shall see with Chu Hsi and Ch'en Ch'un, there were also shape disagreements too. Even within the Neo-Confucian tradition there was much debate about how much Buddhism and Taoism was borrowed by major figures such as Chu Hsi and Wang Yang-ming.[11]

 As we observe the beginning of the modern era of formal Confucian-Christian dialogue, we must remember that dialogue is conducted between persons, not abstract entities. Beyond the contact of individuals in conversation there is really no "dialogue" between Confucianism and Christianity. Nonetheless, it is the hope of most official dialogues that the participants are committed to their traditions and are therefore spokespersons for it, however formally or informally such roles are to be taken. Further, ecumenical religious dialogue is something more than a purely formal academic discussion, however engaging and necessary academic rigor is for the general health of a bilateral dialogue. Dialogue is not just a conversation of scholars about ancient texts, though this careful preparation does have a role to play in any serious dialogue. Knowledge of faith, belief and practice is a prerequisite for any dialogical encounter and scholars have an obligation to help promote candor and historical insight in these conversations.

Formal dialogue implies that the participants are also, in some sense, representatives of their traditions in that they identify with those traditions and seek to express the substance, style, attitude, doctrine, sensibility and so forth, of their tradition. In short, dialogue presupposes some sense of community as the participants speak about their faith, express its ideals for action, and honestly recognize its imperfections and historical foibles. Intellectual honesty and public expression of opinion are joined with an affirmation of participation in an ongoing religious tradition. It is this sense of religious identity that helps to distinguish dialogue from other forms of academic exchange about religion.

Having said all this about the faith of the participants of dialogues, I must add an important caveat. None of what was said above should be construed as denying a place for scholars who do not personally identify with the tradition they are discussing. Often someone from outside a tradition or even someone who does not belong to any religious tradition at all can see things within a tradition that have been missed by those within the tradition. Just being a member of a faith community does not necessarily mean that one is an expert on the history or intellectual foundations of the tradition; nor does membership in a religious community even imply that one is pious or practicing in any meaningful sense. All formal membership means is that one defines the contours of life from within that specific tradition, however successful or pious or self-conscious the defining is. A scholar beyond the tradition may know certain things about the tradition better than most members.

Perhaps this is just a quibble over terminology. I reserve the term 'interfaith dialogue' for conversation among committed members of a religious tradition. Such a definition in no way suggests that independent scholars do not have a role to play in the discussion and teaching of religious history. What I assert is only that, by definition, they are doing something other than interfaith dialogue when they are talking about interreligious matters. For instance, while a tradition can only be *defined as a tradition by a member*, it can definitely be understood, discussed and taught by any reasonably qualified person. Such an affirmation strikes me as both theologically sound and ethically inclusive. If our religious traditions cannot accept critique from those outside the immediately family of faith, then probably something has gone seriously wrong with the tradition. As Lao Tzu teaches us all in the *Tao Te Ching*, the mark of being alive is to be supple and open to new influences, whereas to be on the path to death is to become rigid and closed.

DEFINITIONS OF DIALOGUE: VATICAN AND GENEVA

In order to be precise about what 'interfaith dialogue' means from a formal Christian perspective I will quote from the statements of the Vatican and the World Council of Churches (WCC) about the nature and aims of dialogue. This should put to rest any lingering fears that the passion for dialogue merely represents the enthusiasm of a few marginal theologians. The various published statements present the considered reflections of the largest Christian organizations and can hardly be considered marginal. For instance, *The Attitude of the Church Towards the Followers of Other Religions (Reflections and Orientations on Dialogue and Mission*, prepared by the Vatican Secretariat for Non-Christians (Pentecost 1984), states:

> This new attitude has taken the name of dialogue. This term, which is both the norm and the ideal, was made known to the church by Paul VI in the encyclical "Ecclesiam Suam" (6 August 1966). Since that time, it has been frequently used by the Council as well as in other church teachings. It means not only discussion, but also individuals and communities of other faiths which are directed at mutual understanding and enrichment. (para. 3)

In a joint Vatican paper, *Dialogue and Proclamation*, prepared by the Pontifical Council for Interreligious Dialogue and the Congregation for the Evangelization of Peoples, 1991, these views are reaffirmed and expanded upon in relationship to proclamation as Christian witness.

> *Dialogue* can be understood in different ways. First, at the purely human level, it means reciprocal communication, leading to a common goal or, at a deeper level, to interpersonal communication. Second, dialogue can be taken as an attitude of respect and friendship, which permeates or should permeate all those activities constituting the evangelizing mission of the church. . . .Third, in the context of religious plurality, dialogue means "all positive and constructive interreligious relations with individuals and communities of other faiths which are directed at mutual understanding and enrichment." (*Dialogue and Proclamation*, para. 9, 124)

The theological reason for dialogue is that "the council (i.e., Vatican II) reaffirms the traditional doctrine according to which salvation in Jesus Christ is, in a mysterious way, a reality open to all persons of good will" (*Dialogue and Proclamation*, para. 15, 125).

Dialogue and Proclamation (para. 41, 129) suggests at least four possible forms of dialogue. First, there is the dialogue of life. This is the dialogue of learning to be a neighbor to people of other faiths. Second, there is the dialogue of action. Here Christians and people of other faiths seek common struggles of human rights, political liberation and economic justice. Third, there is the dialogue of theological exchange. There is a real need for traditions to better understand each other, which means study and theological reflection. Fourth, there is the dialogue of religious experience. Beyond social action and theological exchange, there is often a dialogue of the heart, of prayer and meditation as important aspects of dialogue. Again, the rationale for such dialogue action is that "the Holy Spirit, the Spirit of Christ, is present and active among the hearers of the good news even before the church's missionary action comes into operation" (*Dialogue and Proclamation*, para. 68, 132).

A similar concern for dialogue is also part of the WCC's theological agenda. In 1979 the World Council of Churches published the *Guidelines on Dialogue with People of Living Faiths and Ideologies*. The WCC report states:

> No more than "community" can "dialogue" be precisely defined. Rather it has to be described, experienced and developed as a life-style.... Now and then it happens that out of our talking and out relationships arises a deeper encounter, an opening up, in more than intellectual terms, of each to the concern of the other... but we are particularly concerned with the dialogue which reaches across differences of faith, ideology and culture, even where the partners in dialogue do not agree on important central aspects of human life. Dialogue can be recognized as a welcome way of obedience the commandment of the Decalogue: "You shall not bear false witness against your neighbour."... It has been the experience of many Christians that this dialogue is indeed possible on the basis of mutual trust and a respect for the integrity of each participant's identity. (*Guidelines*, 1979, 10)

The *Guidelines* go on to state:

> The aim of dialogue is not reduction of living faiths and ideologies to a lowest common denominator, nor only a comparison and discussion of symbols and concepts, but the enabling of a true encounter between those spiritual insights and experiences which are only found at the deepest levels of human life. (*Guidelines*, 1979, 13)

John Cobb, Jr. (1984) has written an excellent analysis of the content and style of WCC statements on dialogue. Based on Cobb's analysis it should not surprise us that the WCC statement is the more tentative in its entirety of the two. Cobb is probably correct in assuming that this is about as far as the highly diverse collection of churches within the WCC can go at this time in affirming dialogue. Even to quote what the Vatican says about the positive features of dialogue in the Pentecost 1984 statement would not be acceptable to the more conservative denominations and confessional families in the WCC, especially in regard to the social and collective nature of religious identity. The WCC is only willing to acknowledge that people *seek* God in the other traditions; the WCC reserves judgment about whether members of the other faith communities will find the richness of the divine reality in their traditions qua religious teachings.

THE DIALOGICAL NATURE OF CONFUCIANISM

Wm. Theodore de Bary (1988) has suggested that the notion of dialogue as intercultural cross-referencing can be applied to the development of the various cultures of East Asia. For instance, he believes that the model of dialogue is crucial to the internal constitution and development of Confucianism. So besides the modern definitions of dialogue operative in Christian ecumenical circles, de Bary (1988, ix) suggests that dialogue has broad secular and philosophic implications for East Asia.

> I should like to explain my use of the term "dialogue." There I use it to convey a sharing or exchange of ideas in the broadest sense, including even the effects of ideas and institutions upon each other, as people have reflected on choices to be made in crucial historical situations.... Not everyone will be comfortable with such a loose use of the word, but in discussing East Asian civilizations in general terms, I have found no better way to describe the process of historical interaction among the great systems of thought and major institutional configurations in East Asia.

De Bary goes on to demonstrate how this notion of intercultural and civilizing dialogue finds its expression at the very inception of the self-conscious Confucian movement.

> Confucian dialogue proper, as the dialogue anyone could hope to enter into personally, starts with the opening lines of the *Analects* of Confucius: "To study and in due season to practice what one has learned, is this not a pleasure? To have friends come from afar, is that not a delight? To remain unembittered even though one is unrecognized, is that not to be a noble man?" (*chün-tzu*) (1988, 2)

Embedded in the very fabric of the Confucian Way de Bary finds an important manifestation of the dialogical imperative, therefore it is highly appropriate that the modern ecumenical Christian dialogue movement reengages the

Confucian tradition as a partner. No better form of interaction would be more fruitful or faithful for either tradition as living communities of faith.

As we shall see in chapter 4, Mou Tsung-san and Tu Wei-ming are interested in the dialogical nature of Confucianism as it confronts the modern world. Tu has committed himself to the formal process of Confucian-Christian dialogue, as have a number of other New Confucians such as Liu Shu-hsien and Cheng Chung-ying. Mou, Tu, Liu and Cheng are excellent examples of thinkers who manifest the ongoing concern for dialogue de Bary has noted as a part of the East Asian Confucian tradition. It is only now, as Confucius noted so long ago, that the friends come from even farther afield than in Confucius' own day. The friends of the New Confucians truly come from the ends of the earth.

THE QUESTION OF CONFUCIAN REPRESENTATION

In formal dialogues the pattern has been for the Christian participants to be appointed by their church, confessional family or other ecclesiastical agency. Of course, there are many dialogue situations where there is no such demand for this level of formal recognition, but most of the major Christian churches and councils have units or secretariats who have this kind of representational responsibility as part of their institutional mandate. For the most part, these interfaith concerns arose naturally and almost spontaneously from older ecumenical relationships. Dialogue offices are often seen as the foreign service of the churches.

The first modern formal dialogues sponsored by the Roman Catholic Church and the World Council of Churches with the Jewish and then Muslim communities reinforced this special perception of representation. Each side was eager to send only those whom it trusted in terms of religious maturity and institutional stability to the table of dialogue. It is an axiom of Jewish-Christian-Muslim dialogue that the right of self-definition resides with the community, which alone defines who does or does not speak for it. Nor is this often a practical problem because there are a number of international and national Jewish, Christian and Muslim organizations that effectively function in this fashion. There is a very interesting theoretical question that subtends the more pragmatic issue of institutional representation. Is any community of faith adequately represented by its formal bureaucracy at any given time? Often bureaucracies may not, in hindsight, be seen as the most profound guardians of the true faith, but then, they do almost always control the necessary funding for any international dialogue.

None of this is so clear in the case of Confucianism in East Asia and within the Chinese, Korean, Vietnamese and Japanese diaspora. Here it is a very pressing question about who speaks for the modern Confucian tao. Tu Wei-ming has argued that it is often inappropriate for a person even to claim to be a representative of the tradition. It is better, Tu believes, for others to recognize the person as Confucian that to make the claim for him or herself. Once the person has been recognized as a Confucian it is his or her duty to explain clearly what the tradition means, to try to understand what this has meant historically and what it might imply for conduct today, and last, but least, to commend this description and understanding as something applicable to human life.

The point about the difficulty in recognizing Confucian spokespersons has been cogently discussed by de Bary (1988) in his history of the development of East Asian civilization. "Confucianism, alone among the major world traditions, has today no church, no clergy, and indeed no institutional voice whatever to represent it" (1988, 109). However, de Bary is quick to point out that this was not always the case in China, Japan, Korea or Vietnam: "In traditional times, as we have seen, Confucianism has three main institutional strongholds: the family, the school, and the state" (1988, 109). He demonstrates that all of these Confucian strongholds have been drastically modified in mainland China and elsewhere in East Asia. In short, Confucianism, institutionally speaking, has become a "homeless" and disenfranchised tradition. But de Bary is careful to indicate that it has been in this kind of position before and has the internal resources to deal with such institutional exile. One only has to think of the Ch'in dynasty and the long period of relative decline between the Han and the Northern Sung to sense how the Confucian tradition will deal with its modern vicissitudes. Furthermore, de Bary points out how many Confucian values, such as an emphasis on universal education, echo throughout the life of modern East Asia. It will remain to be seen how these persistent pan-Confucian themes will find self-conscious expression in what de Bary calls the "post-Confucian era" in modern East Asia.

All of this makes for a fascinating and difficult answer to the question of representation from the Confucian side. A simple way around the problem is to recognize those who profess to be Confucians and are so recognized by others who can speak for the tradition. Yet, even with all of its problems, there are many able Asian intellectuals who do affirm some rather profound appropriation of the Confucian tao as their form of religious affirmation; they seek to express the Confucian Way in their lives and in their scholarship, however austere this affirmation may be. The structure of the Confucian tradition has been transformed dramatically in the past and has gone through as many paradigm shifts as has the Christian tradition, and there is no doubt that we witness such a transformation again today.

THE THEOLOGICAL CHALLENGE
OF DIALOGUE WITH CONFUCIANISM

Interfaith dialogue provides examples of many kinds of challenges. Even a brief survey of contemporary world events illustrates how explosive interfaith relations, if not dialogue, can be. The continuing tensions in Israel, the occupied territories and Jerusalem; Sri Lanka; Northern Ireland; Burma; the Gulf region; and the conflict over the purported birthplace of Rama in India, and others, illustrate the range and scope of the problem. These examples of conflict give the lie to the notion that interfaith relations are merely of academic interest. In fact, it would be a vast improvement if all interfaith relations were "merely academic." Whatever the faults of academic discussion, whatever lack of perspective, whatever the arcane research topics and personal foibles academicians may have, they do have the virtue of rarely physically assaulting or killing each other while engaged in dialogue. When communal religious tensions run high a little academic dialogue may not be a bad thing.

Beyond the problems caused by the all too physical confrontation of religious communities, there are also challenges and perils to be faced on the intellectual front. A concrete case of this intellectual challenge grew directly out of the first and second international Confucian-Christian dialogues held in Hong Kong in 1988 and Berkeley, California, in 1991. At least one question raised in that context of these two formal dialogues was a challenge of historic proportions to the Christian participants. In its most stark formulation, some Confucian participants asked if a person could be a Confucian-Christian, which is to say, a person so formed by the Confucian and Christian traditions that she or he saw herself or himself as having a dual citizenship in both traditions. Of course, this raised the hallowed Christian concern for syncretism, a term to be stringently avoided by Christians, or so it seems.

Can the question of dual citizenship raised in Confucian-Christian dialogue be avoided once dialogue has begun? Perhaps the question points to a real fact of modern life. Just as a Bostonian can enjoy the art of bonsai, so too can he or she enjoy or be transformed by the Confucian tradition. It being the case that we live in a world of multiple religious commitments, what does this mean for our understanding of the Christian faith? Can we even consider a person with dual loyalties a citizen of either of the historic faith communities?

These are weighty personal and communal questions, bearing directly on the future of a tradition as tradition. Just to ask about the possibility of such an understanding of the Christian faith raises questions of authentic membership in the community. It conjures up all the traditional problems concerning the question of syncretism that have so bedeviled the ecumenical movement in the modern period (Gort 1989).

3

The Religious Dimension of Confucianism

CONFUCIAN REFLECTIONS ON TRANSCENDENCE

This will be a long chapter because it seeks to achieve two objectives. First, it provides a short introduction to the history, philosophic themes and religious dimension of the Confucian tradition. Although no short introduction will ever do justice to a tradition as intellectually and historically rich as Confucianism, some disussion of the history of Confucianism, with special reference to the religious dimensions of the tradition, is necessary so as to understand contemporary Confucian-Christian dialogue. While evidently the Confucian tradition is not an organized religion on the model of the Christian church, it is clear to some modern Confucians that they have become interested in interreligious dialogue because of the diverse religious elements of their tradition's spiritual dimension. I hope that the introduction will illustrate why such a Confucian interest in interreligious dialogue meshes with key aspects of the tradition itself.

Second, I will try to demonstrate why anyone involved in contemporary Confucian-Christian dialogue must have some working knowledge of the Neo-Confucian phase of the tradition. As I will show, it is the Neo-Confucian or fourth phase of the evolving Confucian tradition that still defines the Confucian response to the modern interreligious invitation to dialogue. Given the limitations of space, it is simply impossible to review the entire history of Confucianism with an eye to its implication for dialogue theory. But if one has to begin somewhere in the middle of the story, Chu Hsi's Southern Sung synthesis is the perfect place to commence because he stands at the beginning of the Neo-Confucian tradition as it understands itself today. Hence this whole chapter will serve as a preface to the Confucian side of the dialogue.

THE ROOTS OF THE CONFUCIAN TRADITION

Theologians and historians of religion inevitably try to return to the roots of a tradition in order to define its essential characteristics and its historical trajectories. Both groups of scholars, when pressed, usually argue that in order to understand any tradition one must at least describe the purported beginning of the tradition, the axial moments when revelation or truth shine forth and are so recognized by those who continue to follow the way of the early masters. As we have noted before, Confucianism defines a whole range of internally diverse Chinese and East Asian schools of thought, ritual, scholarship, action and practice including the school and teachings of the literati (*ju-chia* and *ju-chiao*) as well as the Teaching of the Way (*tao-hsüeh*).[1] From the eleventh to the nineteenth Centuries this Neo-Confucian tradition was also known in China by the names of various schools such as the Teaching of the Way (*tao-hsüeh*), the School of Principle (*li-hsüeh*), the School of Mind (*hsin-hsüeh*) and the School of Han Learning (*han-hsüeh*). Confucian history covers more than 2,500 years of scholarship, study, action, ritual practice and meditation beginning with Confucius' own attempt to revive the classical culture and wisdom of his own day.

It is only fair to note that the claim that Confucianism is a religion is controversial. Even though a great deal of work has been done on the religious dimension of the Confucian tradition in Asian and Western scholarship (Taylor 1990a, 1990b), many scholars still resist defining Confucianism a religion. The probable cause for such scholarly qualms is that Confucianism does not resemble the great West Asian religions of Judaism, Christianity and Islam, the religious traditions that serve as the norm for defining what religion is in terms of the Western scholarly understanding of religion. What is much less controversial is the claim that there are distinctive religious dimensions to the Confucian tradition. On the basis of the recognition of these religious elements in the Confucian tradition, a strong case can be made for reevaluating our ways of defining religion in order to make room for the clearly religious aspects of Confucianism in East Asia and the East Asian diaspora. The international scholarly community has an opportunity to expand its conceptual understanding of human religious nature by attending to the religious aspects of Confucianism.

What this strong claim for the religious dimension of the Confucian tradition does not do is assert that all aspects of the Confucian tradition are religious in nature. Confucianism is an internally complicated cultural artifact with different cultural manifestations, only some of which are clearly religious in nature. It is equally true to argue that Confucianism is also a philosophic tradition as well as a historical, poetic, artistic, economic and political set of related movements. There were clearly ancient, medieval, early modern and modern Confucians who were tone-deaf to the religious dimensions of their tradition although they defined themselves as Confucians in terms of their scholarship as well as their political and cultural concerns. These nonreligious Confucians have as much right to claim membership in the Confucian Way as do those who sense the spiritual dimensions of the tradition. Yet it is more and more clear, on the basis of modern understandings of religion, that there is a profound religious dimension to the tradition. If this religious dimension is ignored then a significant part of the historical and modern story of the Confucian Way is neglected to the detriment of true humane scholarship.

In defining Confucianism it is important to remember that Confucius (551–479 B.C.E.) did not see himself as founding a new tradition. Just as the case of Moses at Sinai, there was much history in the Confucian tradition before Confucius talked with his disciples about preserving the way of the ancient sages. Like Judaism in West Asia, Confucianism traces its tradition back to the primordial beginnings of Chinese civilization. It was only later that scholars recognized Confucius' personal and defining contribution to the evolution of the Confucian Way. So while Confucius would not have made the claim himself, the tradition has come to believe that his life normatively defines the contours of the emerging Confucian tradition among the other competing ways of thought in ancient China, for instance, those later known as Mohism, Taoism and Legalism. Nonetheless, it is also still important to note that the term Confucianism is a Western scholarly and missionary neologism for which there is no precise Chinese equivalent.

Confucians have always followed Confucius in seeking to define their tradition. They do not revere Confucius as a founder of a religion in the sense that Buddha initiated Buddhism or Mohammed began the great movement of Islam. What is sought by the Confucians is the faithful appropriation of the tradition of the primordial sages. Whatever else it may be, Confucianism is a movement in search of sagely wisdom. Confucius believed that the early sage rulers of China were exemplars of this tradition and that it was his task to transmit this wisdom to his generation. This search for and active participation in tradition have marked the Confucian Way as the way of the scholar. Along with whatever other roles the Confucian might play—wise minister, contemplative mystic, grand historian, dedicated military leader, sublime poet— scholarship and the arts of the scholar are essential to the Confucian mission. One simply cannot be a Confucian without a strong commitment to and the achievement of learning as defined by the growing tradition.

The most inclusive defining characteristic of Confucianism, embodied in its scholarly transmission of the Way of the Sages, is its embrace of all the various East Asian traditions inspired and dedicated to the thought and practice of Confucius as the First Teacher. In trying to sense a roughly accurate definition of any tradition, it is interesting to see what kinds of titles are conferred on the founder. In this regard, we observe that the title of First Teacher has always been the proudest and most uncontested title for Confucius. Such a title speaks volumes about the self-perceptions of Confucians. While all great religious traditions have a role for the scholar, Confucianism defines itself universally as a scholarly tradition. So, while some Confucians are not particularly interested in the religious dimensions of their tradition, all Confucians are united in being scholars of the entire tradition, both religious and secular.

While it is historically true that the Confucian Way has been dramatically transformed in transmission through time and across cultures in East Asia and now beyond the shores of the Pacific, its modes of action, ritual, piety and scholarship have always remained faithful to the way of life first expressed by Confucius in late Chou China. Confucius and the other early masters of the Chou dynasty have continued to define the normative parameters of the tradition. This does not mean that Confucianism has remained an unchanging reiteration of the same message from generation to generation. The Confucian teachings of the great Sung master Chu Hsi (1130–1200), Yi T'oegye (1501–70) of Korea's Yi dynasty, Kaibara Ekken (1630–1714) of Japan's Tokugawa Shogunate and Mou Tsung-san of contemporary Hong Kong and Taiwan were and are all different yet mutually recognizable as Confucian. The Confucian movement is indeed a mansion with many rooms.

MAJOR THEMES OF THE CONFUCIAN WAY

Confucianism, in all its various East Asian and diaspora manifestations, focuses on the question of the ultimate values for human life. No doubt it is this question of ultimate values that gives the Confucian Way its religious dimension. The Confucians always ask, "What makes life worth living as civilized human beings? What are the personal and familial virtues as well as the proper civic ordinances needed to create a humane civilization worth transmitting from one generation to the next?" As we have stressed before, because Confucianism stresses questions of the meaning of the ultimate life values, it includes what in Western intellectual history are considered questions of philosophy and religion. Of course, as we also noted, it includes reflections on the arts, government, family and social rituals and much, much more in terms of personal and social self-cultivation.

There are very good reasons for the Sung Neo-Confucians to talk about this pattern of learning as the Learning of the Way. When Confucianism is a creative and vital force in any cultural context, it demands a total vision of personal and social life.

Confucians never begin their quest for authentic humanity de novo. Confucians always rely on their historic tradition to enlighten them as to what is appropriate conduct in the present age. For instance, as we noted before, Confucians have been adept at adding layers of meaning to old terminology rather than creating entirely new semantic worlds to inhabit in the search for the truth of human life. Hence it would be impossible to conceive of any Confucian who was not interested in at least four dimensions of being human in the world as defined by the cumulative tradition:

1. *Jen* as the virtue of humanity and the cardinal virtue of all the other virtues, individual and social;

2. *T'ien-ming* as the universal Mandate of Heaven, the primordial creativity of the cosmos that provides a model for the special human virtues in the context of a living history and civilization;

3. *Hsin* as the heart-and-mind of humanity, both destined and inclined to lead a moral life, the veritable seat of human intelligence, will and passion, the nexus of the experiential unity of thought, action and meditation;

4. *Hsing* as human nature and the nature of all that is within the cosmic drama of human life, the creative source and goal of the quest for values that informs the life of all seeking to become profound persons.

For example, the Confucians, in their search for the meaning of life, have probed the transcendent dimensions of what it means to understand the Will of Heaven. The Sung and Ming Neo-Confucians of the fourth stage are best known for their careful attention to the questions of ultimate meaning framed by their response to the Buddhist religious and metaphysical challenge. While the classical Confucians helped to define the tradition's approach to ontology and cosmology, it was the Neo-Confucians who sought to fathom the workings of the primordial creativity of the Tao as it is governed by the ceaseless alternation of the yin and yang forces of the universe. In their patterns of personal cultivation, the Neo-Confucians sought to find a balance between the Great Ultimate in its guise as the Mandate of Heaven as the source of being for all beings and the infinite ground of all being as expressed in the figure of the mystical Non-Ultimate. They always explored what it meant to be a human being seeking the highest good. They sought to get the Way for themselves in service to all other human beings.

Two key features of the pan-Confucian concern for ultimate life values are found in (1) the realization of the intersubjective, relational and creative qualities of human nature and (2) the quest for an autonomous morality directed by the insights of the Confucian sages and worthies. However, although the historical tradition of the sages palpably plays a key role in Confucian self-cultivation, we must note that no amount of historical learning can replace the process of "getting it for oneself" that lies at the heart of the matter. To be autonomous as a moral being does not mean merely living within a tradition or history; it means that this history becomes a living core for the person who accepts it as helping to define her or his own creative appropriation of the Tao. It is likewise crucial to recognize the intersubjective nature of this quest. The Confucian is never a person alone with the Tao as some kind of abstract universal. The Confucian is always and everywhere a person among persons, a human being seeking to be of service to the wider world of humanity.

The true Confucian seeks to situate him or herself in the midst of cosmic creativity by means of an effective moral and social unity of lived experience. The traditional symbolic expression of this fusion of cosmic creativity, social reform and individual virtue is disclosed in Confucius' concept of *jen* as humaneness as the highest human virtue. Although Confucianism lacks a stark visual presentation of its core vision such as the cross for Christians, there is always the story of Confucius as one burdened by Heaven with a vision of the Way which inspired countless generations of Confucians to begin their quest for sagehood. As Confucius taught, although the Way is long and heavy, it is the responsibility of everyone to seek it nonetheless. Not to seek human virtue would be to deny our full humanity. Hence the true symbol of Confucian life is the scholar or disciple seeking ultimate humane values.

The Confucian search for the values of civilized humane life is always bracketed between a cosmological understanding of the cosmos and individual reflections on the meaning of creativity for each person. Cosmic, social and personal moral creativity is expressed as the unceasing Way of Heaven. This cosmic and ethical concern for others is thematically expressed by means of the classical inventory of specific Confucian personal and social virtues. The most famous list from Mencius and the Han scholars consists of the five cardinal virtues: *jen* as humanity or humaneness, *i* as righteousness or justice, *li* as proper ritual action or rites, *chih* as wisdom in thought and action and *hsin* as faithfulness. These five virtues are then correlated to various familial and social situations in terms of the Confucian analysis of proper social hierarchy.

Along with these five prime virtues, the Confucian tradition always emphasized the need to realize these virtues in the depths of a person's being. Merely knowing what virtue was never counted for real virtue. A person must achieve virtue in order to be counted a worthy human being. In order to live these virtues, the Confucians highlighted the role of *ch'eng* or self-realization in action and wisdom as the proper way to make concrete the five cardinal virtues. And while the Confucians often recognized that individual families may be tragically flawed, the tradition argued for the irreducible role of the family in the generation of humane human values. If a person could not be a proper wife or husband, father or mother, parent or child, brother or sister or a good friend to friends, then the Confucians held out little hope for that person being able to be an effective moral agent in the larger world. It was only upon these basic family concerns that society can be organized in a harmonious and civilized fashion. Therefore, the family is always the first educational and social matrix for Confucian virtue and social action.

The Confucians always universalized primordial family ties in order to justify their sense of social hierarchy. Reciprocity (*pao*) and deference to proper authority and wisdom were key methods for ethical socialization. The Confucians believed passionately that virtue could be learned, practiced and studied, and there were always models in the classical writings of the sages even if one's own parents were not moral paragons. The Confucians were also aware of the tension between the emotional particularities of the family and their commitment to a broader social arena. The Confucians struggled to find a balance between the threat of nepotism and the recognition that we learn to be humane within the context of the family, if we learn this lesson at all. The Confucians were quick to point out that each person moves chronologically between different roles in the family, from being a child to being a parent, and finally to becoming a respected elder. Each station in life demanded appropriate ethical conduct and self-discipline in order not to abuse power within the natural hierarchy of the family. Each person, once having reached an age where comprehension was possible, needed to be guided by the five virtues of humaneness, justice, ritual, wisdom and faithfulness in every social setting.

THE CONFUCIAN CLASSICAL CANON

Another distinctive, although not unique, feature of the Confucian tradition has been its appeal to and veneration of a canon of classical texts. Much of the learning and piety of the Confucian tradition has been lavished on the careful study of and commentary on these classic texts. These texts include works of poetry, history, divination, ritual and philosophy. The number of texts included in the formal list of the classic canon has grown over the centuries. However, it is important to understand that this expansion of the canon from five in the early period to the more robust thirteen of the later scholastics does not imply that additional revelations came to later generations. What it meant was that additional and equally old texts were recognized as being of canonical status as time went on. The addition of the *Book of Change* (*I-Ching*) is a good example of this expansion of the Confucian canon. Of course, what counted as a canon within the canon changed over time as well.

For instance, Chu Hsi is justly famous for selecting four rather small texts as the definitive Four Books—the *Analects* of Confucius, the *Mencius*, the *Great Learning* and the *Doctrine of the Mean*—as representing the essence of the Confucian Way. Chu's selection became the basis for all Confucian education and was an official part of the imperial examination system from 1313 until the early twentieth century. Chu's commentary on the Four Books even became recognized as something of a minor classic in itself.

Along with the official canon of the thirteen classics, there was also an influential group of philosophic writings that were esteemed as definitive for a correct understanding of the tradition. For instance, even though Hsün Tzu's work did not become one of the official classics, it was read carefully by all the generations of Confucians. In the Han dynasty, Tung Chung-shu contributed works that helped to define the second great stage of the Confucian story. Along with his selection of the Four Books, Chu Hsi and his good friend Lü Tsu-ch'ien compiled and edited the famous *Reflections on Things at Hand*, a text made up of their selection of passages from the Northern Sung masters. *Reflections on Things at Hand* itself became a classic of Neo-Confucian thought and a gateway to reading the established canon in the style of the Chu Hsi school. In the Ming period, the great scholar, general and critic of Chu Hsi, Wang Yang-ming (1472–1529), wrote the *Instructions for Practical Living* in order to provide his school with a counterproposal to Chu Hsi's interpretation of the tradition. In the period of the School of Evidential Learning, Tai Chen wrote *An Evidential Study of the Meaning of Terms in the Mencius*, returning the fifth stage of the Confucian movement to its fascination with its earliest sources such as Mencius and showing how it differed from Chu Hsi and Wang Yang-ming.

It is interesting to note that each Confucian master assigns the various key symbols of the canonical tradition such as *jen* to specific texts, texts that then act almost like patron saints for the idea in question. For instance, Mou Tsung-san has argued that the notion of *jen* finds primary expression in the

Analects of Confucius as well as in all the other early classical philosophic works of the canon such as the *Mencius* and the Doctrine of the Mean. The cosmological aspects of the tradition, such as the notion of the Mandate of Heaven or the Supreme Ultimate, Mou uncovers in the *I-Ching*, the Doctrine of the Mean and the *Analects* yet again. For Mou, the key text for understanding the mind-heart as the experiential unity of human life is found in the Mencius. And for the fundamental exposition of human nature, Mou discovers that the Doctrine of the Mean and the *Mencius* serve to define this aspect of the Confucian Way. Almost every important Confucian, regardless of historical stage, does much the same thing in showing how a favored series of canonical texts contain the essence of the tradition.

In this fashion the Confucians transmitted their interpretative expansion of tradition from generation to generation. It is fascinating to see New Confucians such as Mou Tsung-san and Tu Wei-ming continuing this pattern in some of their own works. The tradition is a burden that scholars gratefully carry with them in order to make sure they are heading in the right direction of true wisdom. Confucianism, always transformed and renewed, lives in the constant study of the classics and their application to those things near at hand to all people, the search for a civilized life and culture.

EPOCHS OF CONFUCIAN LEARNING

Having noted the persistent Confucian concern with scholarship and the correct transmission of the way as the primordial Way of Heaven, it is appropriate to present a brief outline of the epochs of Confucian learning in the Chinese branch of the tradition. No other global religio-philosophic tradition is so interested in its own history; some of the earliest books of the Confucian canon are histories of early Chinese civilization and many of the greatest Confucian scholars are remembered as historians of the highest order. Often modern Western Christians like to say that theirs is a historical religion based on the life of Jesus confessed as the Christ. But no one, not even post-Enlightenment historically-minded Christians, can outshine the Confucian reverence for historical learning as a basis for the development of tradition. While one might well begin the study of Christianity with a review of the creeds of the Church universal, any study of Confucianism must begin with a historical narrative of the tradition.[2]

Since its thematization by Confucius in the Chou dynasty, Confucianism has undergone at least six major paradigmatic transformations. The first great epoch was that of the classical and foundational era beginning with Confucius, shaped by ~~Mencius (371–289~~ B.C.E.) and concluded by Hsün Tzu (fl. 298–238 B.C.E.). Given the historical bent of the tradition, it is also well to remember that the classical Confucians relied on a broad range of historical, poetical, commentarial and ritual texts later given the title "classics." The number of recognized classics has varied from five to thirteen as the canon was expanded over the centuries. Nonetheless, it is crucial to remember that the expansion merely added ancient material to the canon until all the early texts important to the Confucians were included in the package. Although the notion of canon was fluid, this did not mean that new classics were written or revealed. Only commonly accepted ancient texts from the times before Confucius were included. If fact, legend has it that Confucius himself was the first great historian, commentator and editor of the Confucian classics.

In terms of the classical philosophers of the Confucian Way, Confucius, Mencius and Hsün Tzu are remembered as the great early masters of the tradition. However, we note that although all the later Confucians read Hsün Tzu, he was considered a controversial figure because of his philosophic arguments with Mencius, who was often called the Second Sage. However, no one ever doubted Hsün Tzu's Confucian credentials even if, especially after the Sung dynasty, he was never recognized as orthodox when compared to Confucius or Mencius. Hsün Tzu's great error was to hold that human nature was evil or at least prone to error. Along with the formation of the classical Confucian canon, Confucius, Mencius and Hsün Tzu also defined the ongoing intellectual discourse of the tradition by thematizing the conceptual apparatus of Confucianism in terms of historically sanctioned ethical discourse.

While the tradition expanded over the next 2,500 years, the key philosophic, social and religious concerns and concepts have remained remarkably stable. The Confucians demonstrated a genius for expanding the semantic and intellectual range of key early concepts and terms in order to diversify and increase the range of the tradition as it moved out from its north Chinese home into the broader world. For instance, the critical early Confucian concern for humanity as defined by *jen* (humaneness) as the cardinal virtue can still be found as a central issue for Mou Tsung-san in Hong Kong and Taiwan as well as for Tu Wei-ming teaching at Harvard University. However, this takes us ahead to Mou and Tu as representatives of the sixth stage of the development of the Confucian tradition.

The second stage of the development of the Confucian Way came with the rise of the Han dynasty (206 B.C.E.–220 C.E.). The distinctive contribution of the Han Confucians was the formulation of the state-sponsored imperial Confucian orthodoxy that was to dominate the Chinese political scene in one form or another till the revolution of 1911. On the one hand, many Confucians were profoundly nervous about the use of Confucian symbols for political control. But on the other hand, there was always the desire of Confucians to serve the common good. This service was intimately tied to the state from the Han dynasty on. Along with the political theory of the Han Confucians, this was also an era of careful scholarship, commentary and historical compilations. We need to remember that all the texts we now have from classical China were lovingly collected, edited and commented on by the Han Confucians as a profound labor of devotion to the preservation of the past.

Two of the most representative Han Confucians were Tung Chung-shu (c. 179–104 B.C.E.) and Yang Hsiung (53 B.C.E–18 C.E.). The Han Confucians have never had the elevated reputations of the classical thinkers. Theirs was the task of collecting and preserving the tradition as well as working out a compromise with the power of the imperial Chinese state. In terms of the political role of Confucianism, the contribution of the Han scholars ensured the continuation of the tradition in a remarkably stable form till the twentieth century. Given that it was a compromise with the state, there have always been grave questions about whether the Han Confucians gave too much to the state and preserved too little for their tradition as an independent force to balance the power of the government.[3]

After the fall of the Han, the Confucian tradition entered its third middle period extending to the end of the great T'ang dynasty (618–907 C.E.). It is important to remember that this long medieval period was the golden age first of what has been called the Neo-Taoist revival of the Wei-Chin period (220–420 C.E.) and the rise and success of Buddhism in China under the T'ang. While it is apparent that Confucianism never disappeared from the Chinese scene, it is accurate to say that the most acute religious and philosophic Chinese minds were involved in the reception and elaboration of the Buddha dharma in China. The rise of the great Chinese T'ang Buddhist schools such as T'ien-t'ai, Hua-yen, Ch'an and Pure Land mark one of the most remarkable chapters in the religious history of humankind. The great South Asian religion of Buddhism was transformed in creative ways into one of the three great religions of China, and from China the glorious T'ang Buddhist heritage was transmitted to the rest of East Asia. It was this great high T'ang Buddhist intellectual heritage that formed the backdrop for the fourth epoch of Confucianism. This Buddhist transmission of the distinctive fruits of T'ang Buddhism continues today as East Asian Buddhism has spread to the North Atlantic world.

The two most famous of the T'ang Confucians were Han Yü (768–824) and Li Ao (fl. 798). According to the tradition, Han and Li preserved and defended the Confucian tradition as it came to grips with the challenge of Buddhism. Along with typical Confucian concerns for government service, family ritual and historical writing, Han and Li also began to frame the Confucian response to Buddhist religious and philosophic discourse. While the great period of the Sung Confucian revival would only come in the eleventh century, there were few themes and concerns that Han and Li did not share with the Neo-Confucians proper.

The fourth stage of the Confucian saga is the great Northern and Southern Sung (960–1279) revival of Confucian learning and piety know in the West as Neo-Confucianism. The Sung scholars actually did have a special term for their school, namely the Learning of the Way. This is the period that culminates in the grand scholarly synthesis of Chu Hsi (1130–1200), who is often called the Aquinas of China. Given that this is the form of Confucianism we will address in the later sections of this chapter, we will not review its achievements in any detail at this point. Suffice it to say that the Neo-Confucian period, however we choose to subdivide it, extends from the eleventh century to the beginning of the twentieth century. Chu Hsi's form of Confucianism, along with the writings of the other Southern and Northern Sung masters, spread into Korea, Vietnam and Japan. Various forms of Neo-Confucian thought eventually came to dominate the intellectual life of East Asia, replacing the previous ascendancy of Buddhism in all these countries.

From the Confucian perspective, the Neo-Confucian traditions are viewed as second only to the great classical founders. From a Confucian viewpoint this praise is as high as can be given. To be seen as ranking with Confucius, Mencius and their followers is to be acknowledged as reconstituting the tradition of sagely learning. If Confucius and Mencius defended the Confucian Way during the intellectual and spiritual turmoil of the late Chou, Chu Hsi and his Northern Sung masters renewed the tradition by attacking the Buddhist schools with an effective Confucian response. While there have been great developments in the tradition after Chu Hsi, no one can deny the pivotal role he and his colleagues played in the early modern reformation of the tradition.

The most important Ming Neo-Confucian to challenge Chu Hsi's interpretation in the fourth stage was Wang Yang-ming (1472–1529). Wang is remembered as the founder of the School of Mind as well as a great teacher, poet, civil servant and victorious general. He was best known for his philosophic challenge to Chu Hsi wherein he rejected the notion that principle can be found by the examination of things external to the mind. Wang further elaborated a doctrine of the unity of knowledge and action based on the notion that principle is found within the mind. Wang, through a practice of intense personal self-cultivation, rediscovered what he took to be the true Confucian method of spiritual insight based on *liang-chih* as the innate knowledge of reality as manifested in the mind of the sage. His teachings also spread throughout East Asia and became influential in Korea and especially in Japan. Much contemporary Confucian political reform in East Asia owes a great debt to Wang's vision of a socially reforming and engaged Confucianism.

The fifth stage of the Confucian story is really a subset of the Sung and Ming Neo-Confucian narrative. It is often called the School of Evidential Learning or the School of Han Learning and was the last important Confucian movement prior to Western contact. Its great leaders were scholars such as Wang Fu-chih (1619–92) and Tai Chen (1723–77). These Ch'ing dynasty (1644–1911) scholars challenged what they saw as excessive Sung and Ming interest in metaphysics and abstract thought. According to this school, both Chu Hsi and Wang Yang-ming were excessively idealistic, almost Buddhistic in their attention to self-cultivation as a spiritual discipline. They believed that Confucianism had to be of some concrete use to the people and the government. Therefore they stressed historical research that often resembles modern social science as well as studies in the various applied sciences in terms of its potential application to social policy. All of this empirical and detailed work they believed to be more in tune with true Confucian social and political concerns rather than with the quasi-Buddhist metaphysics of Chu Hsi and his host of followers. Yet Wang and Tai's critiques only make sense against the background of Neo-Confucian discourse. As with all Chinese developments, the writings of the School of Evidential Learning was transmitted to other parts of East Asia to become part of the international Confucian tradition.

The sixth stage of the Confucian story is dramatically different from the previous two stages. With the arrival of the Western colonial empires in the sixteenth century, Neo-Confucianism, along with all other aspects of Chinese intellectual, political, economic, religious and artistic life was severely disrupted. This disruption continues today as Chinese intellectuals seek to come to grips with the interruption and confrontation with the West just as their Sung ancestors grappled with the medieval Buddhist challenge. But the differences between the Buddhist and Western challenge are as profound as are the similarities. The Buddhists never arrived with an overwhelming military, political and economic challenge.

In the midst of China's search for a modern identity, the Confucians have responded with their sixth paradigm shift. This modern movement is called New Confucianism and often traces its roots to the work of the philosopher Hsiung Shih-li (1885–1968) at Beijing University. The New Confucianism finds expression in the work of contemporary scholars seeking to describe, understand and commend the Confucian Way as a humane and viable contribution to the creation of a new world civilization. It continues the work of its Sung, Yüan, Ming and Ch'ing ancestors but with a focus that is now global and not just concerned with the East Asian context. Given that New Confucianism is a reformation in process, it is impossible to state clearly what its final special contribution to the development of the Confucian Way will be.

For instance, both Mou Tsung-san and Tu Wei-ming are important representatives of the New Confucianism. Tu Wei-ming has described the New Confucianism as a third wave or epoch (Tu 1986) of the Confucian tradition, and a wave of the tradition that will be as important to it as a tradition moving out from its East Asian homeland as were the classical founders and the Sung Neo-Confucians. Along with Hsiung Shih-li, Tu and other modern scholars such as T'ang Chün-i, Hsü Fu-kuan, Ch'ien Mu, Carsun Chang and Wing-tsit Chan have all contributed to the development of this modern form of Confucianism. These men, and their students, are the actual Confucian partners in the renewed Confucian-Christian dialogue. It is likewise important to note that the development of the Confucian tradition in its modern form continues in the work of Japanese and Korean scholars who continue to define the multinational characteristics of New Confucianism. We will return to a special consideration of the contributions of Mou Tsung-san and Tu Wei-ming in chapter 4.

As heirs of the first five stages of the Confucian narrative, the New Confucians, constituting a sixth stage, seek to achieve a number of goals in the reformation of the Confucian Way. First, as scholars they seek to explain the tradition in all its diverse and multinational richness. They are committed to the highest standards of the emerging ecumenical life of the modern mind. Second, they all also seek to understand what they have described in their scholarly accounts of the history and meaning of the tradition. For Confucians, it is not merely enough to describe the tradition from the outside; the person of true humanity must be able to understand and even embody the tradition. And third, the New Confucians believe that they must commend the tradition to those outside of it as have Confucians from the very beginning of the tradition. In one sense, this Confucian commitment to commending what they have found of value is the missionary element of the tradition. They believe that what they have described and understood is worthy of being considered part of the material and intellectual base for the new ecumenical world order.

When thinkers such as Mou Tsung-san and Tu Wei-ming are taken to represent Confucianism's sixth phase, the argument is often made that Mou and Tu only represent a modernized, sophisticated, Westernized and one-sided reformulation of Wang Yang-ming's idealistic version of the *tao-hsüeh*.[4] Neither Mou nor Tu speaks for the whole range of the tradition, especially its classical humanist discourse as found in Confucius, Mencius and Hsün Tzu. Whatever kind of religious, spiritual or transcendent dimension Mou and Tu discover and defend as part of the Sung and Ming development of the tradition is taken to be a mirage for the tradition when taken as a whole. The issue of Confucian representation will be addressed primarily in chapter 4. It is now time to turn our attention to Chu Hsi's contribution.

THE RISE OF EARLY MODERN CONFUCIAN DISCOURSE: CHU HSI'S METASYSTEM

While it is clear by now that I do not agree with Hall and Ames' thesis that the early Confucian tradition lacks any transcendent dimension, I do appreciate several of their comparative philosophic insights in *Thinking Through Confucius*.[5] Nowhere is this more evident in their reflections on *ontologia generalis*, *scientia universalis* and *ars contextualis* (1987, 199–200, 246–49). Hall and Ames' neologism *ars contextualis* points directly to the question of trying to characterize the Chu Hsi tradition from a Western philosophic position—a difficult task as we have seen. While Chu Hsi does have intellectual genres roughly analogous to the classical, medieval and modern Western notions of cosmology and ontology, the fit is never close enough to get rid of the nagging suspicion that these Western philosophic disciplines do not describe what Chu Hsi and the Sung-Ming Neo-Confucians were seeking to create in their most characteristic modes of discourse.

Hall and Ames raise the issue of the fundamental characterization of classical Chinese thought in terms of their depiction of the Western cosmological tradition. They argue (1987, 199) that

> In the Western tradition, cosmology has carried two principle connotations. First, *ontologia generalis*, general ontology, which is concerned with the question of the be-ing of beings. The second sense is that associated with the term, *scientia universalis*, the science of principles.

They point out that historically in the West, most philosophers have tried to unite these two types of disciplines although one foundational science has usually been given priority over the other in the work of each philosopher. For instance, Martin Heidegger is well known for his pursuit of general ontology whereas Whitehead is famous for his interest in cosmology. Hall and Ames state that

the principle(s) of beings is subject matter of *scientia universalis*, whereas
the subject matter of *ontologia generalis* is the being of principles (*archai*)—
that is, the being of the original and originating entities comprising that
which is. (199)

The challenge presented by Chinese thought in general and Confucius
in particular is that neither of these Western foundational disciplines really
defines what is going on in Chinese speculation on the nature of being. In
order to overcome this difficulty, Hall and Ames (1987, 358 n. 7) define the
term *ars contextualis* as the way Confucian

> sensibility may be said to presuppose the activity of contextualization in
> which any element in a context is assessed by the contribution it makes
> to construing the context, and alternatively the contribution made by the
> context to the constitution of that element.

As John Henderson (1991) has pointed out, whatever else the Confucian
and Neo-Confucian traditions of the fourth and fifth stages may be, they are
resolutely hermeneutic, commentarial and hence contextual in reading the world
as a series of texts, historic and personal, which need to be construed in order
to understand reality. Hall and Ames (1987, 248) argue that Confucius does
not present us with a general theory of the principle of being or even a universal
ordering of the sciences of the world. Rather, Confucius has

> an aesthetic understanding, an *ars contextualis*, in which the correlatively
> of "part" and "whole"—of focus and field—permits the mutual inter-
> dependence of all things to be assessed in terms of particular contexts defined
> by social roles and functions.

While Hall and Ames theorize that Confucius' axiology as *ars contextualis*
is a generalization of the activities of thinking and becoming a person, Mou
Tsung-san, as we shall see, suggests an even more profound sense of the Confucian task, that is, the embodiment of what Mou calls "concern-consciousness."
Hall and Ames (1987, 248) reiterate the same sense of intersubjective concern
consciousness when they state that

> Confucius' cosmology is generalized sociology, a vision of the manner in
> which human beings emerge from within a social context grounded in
> tradition, while remaining open to novel articulations insofar as these might
> be called for by the *ming* (mandate or decree) of present circumstances.

No doubt Mou Tsung-san would want to invert the Hall and Ames thesis and
argue that what we have in good sociology is nothing but a specification of

ars contextualis as the Confucian understanding of cosmology and ontology. In any event, in terms of Neville's reformed process cosmology this is a profound axiological approach to thinking and acting—the constitution of a world where the concern for values is the search for ultimate human life values. Or so I will construe Mou Tsung-san's vision of the Confucian Way in chapter 4.

OUTLINING CHU HSI'S TAO

Before we begin an examination of Chu Hsi's idea of transcendence, it is necessary to outline the basics of his metasystem as an *ars contextualis*. Without some basic understanding of Chu's fundamental intellectual axioms, it is impossible to comprehend his vision of the transcendent (or anything else in his thought). As I have noted before, the various concepts of Chu's mature thought suggest the triadic thematization of the notions of form, dynamics and unification.[6]

Obviously, one cannot apply the triadic typology of form, dynamics and unification mechanically to any sophisticated religio-philosophic discourse except in a highly abstract fashion. The typology is a heuristic device designed to illumine certain aspects of Chu Hsi's thought. For instance, Donald Munro (1988) has demonstrated that Chu also often frames aspects of his thought in terms of dyads of yin-yang balanced forces. Just as process thought offers one viable alternative for Christian reflection on religious pluralism, the triad of form, dynamics and unification is only one way of trying to get at the deep grammar of Chu Hsi's mature and always vivid vision of the Tao. There are other ways of trying to delineate Chu Hsi's hardwires, to borrow the language of computer science, of the system. Another example would be the careful historical analysis of Chu Hsi's interaction with other philosophers in the Southern Sung as outlined by Tillman (1992b).

The Formal Elements

We now need to explore those essential elements of axioms of Chu Hsi's thought which serve to define what Chu takes to be the "really real." First, there are Chu Hsi's formal terms that define what Chu Hsi asserts to be the traits of sapiental discrimination, the principles of everything that can be described as different from something else. These principles or *li* are his rational principles of analysis for any object or event in our collective universe. The most conspicuous of these are principles (*li*) as the formal elements of boundary and separation within the vital world of *ch'i* or configured matter-energy.[7] To these one might safely add the Supreme Ultimate (*t'ai-chi*) in that it provides the lure by which the principle of a thing informs the process of actualization. The Supreme Ultimate also affords a description of order as found in the Tao as the Way of Heaven. These formal terms all indicate the reality of defining norms but do not necessarily imply any form of actuality. They exist but are not specific prior to the concrete process of actualization. They are not definite things or events in themselves; they are the sources of potentiality for actualization. For example, they provide the norms by which ethical actions can be judged, and are hence the potential models for all human conduct. They are formal principles which are real but are not creative prior to the process of actualization.

This kind of interpretation of the formal traits has been defended and documented at great length by Mou Tsung-san in his monumental study of the rise of Neo-Confucianism (for instance, Mou 1968–69, 1:58), although the language of form, dynamics and unification is mine and not Mou's. We shall return to Mou's interpretation of the matter in chapter 4. The formal traits are the "mere" reasons of the universe, not the concrete people, events, moral choices or things of the lived world of human experience. Yet these *li* become ever so real when they are realized in the context of human life, choice, decision and action. They become the real stuff of human history as the ideals of Neo-Confucian civilization.

Dynamic Elements

Second, the dynamic trait concerns the actualization of person, event or thing. Since Chu Hsi is most concerned with human conduct in its moral aspects, the key terms here deal with his moral anthropology and are derived from Confucian speculation of the ethical issues of human relationships and cultural achievements such as ritual action and the arts. The obvious concepts expressing the dynamism of human life are (*hsin*/mind, (*hsing*/human nature and (*ch'ing*/feelings or emotions). It is well to remember that mind especially has a dipolar quality to it. There is both a dynamic element but also the capacity to recognize and realize form as principle. As with so many other aspects of Chu Hsi's thought, one cannot suggest that it is some kind of simple dualism. Whatever dyads exist are always balanced and have the capacity to transform themselves by means of the yin-yang forces. Hence the dynamic mind mediates the formal side of human nature and the dynamic drive of emotion and passion.

And of course, the ever present concept of *ch'i* or dynamic matter-energy provides the concrete basis of the creative activity of the dynamic side of Chu Hsi's metasystem. These dynamic terms refer to the manifestations of human life through self-cultivation that produces moral excellence. They all denote the activities and dispositions of human beings either subjectively or as intersubjectively observable processes in the conduct of normal human life. The mind, for example, refers both to the agency and the norm (principle) that is the seat of human personality as well as the mechanism by which the other faculties are regulated. Thus, as Chu so often said, the mind fundamentally unites human nature and the natural human emotions as a dynamic process.

Unifying Elements

Third, there are the unifying traits represented by such crucial Confucian notions as *ch'eng* or self-actualization and *jen* or humane action. The human mind also plays a unifying role in its mediation of principle as human nature and human emotion or passion. These unifying terms have a descriptive and axiological content because they refer to the process by which things come together in some particular state. Unifying terms carry strongly positive connotations— they are ideal states or moral virtues that a person should seek to emulate. While a person can be described in terms of principle or matter-energy, the process by which the principle is unified in actuality is called *ch'eng* or self-actualization. *Ch'eng* is more than a description of what this process should be and points to the ideal foundation of all actuality. It moves the Confucian in the direction of unifying the ideal actualization of principle in the formation of a person of virtue and a participant in the creation of a just social order. (Li 1973, 1:350) *Jen* or humanity differs from *ch'eng* in that it describes the ideal moral virtue as the intentionality of an individual that gives unity of humane purpose to all human conduct.

Chu Hsi framed his metasystem as an *ars contextualis* in terms of the traits of form, dynamics and unification. This tendency can be observed in each of the three realms of discourse and is also characteristic of all three sets of terms when taken together. As we shall see, Chu Hsi liked to pose questions about the world in dyadic forms that find their mediation or resolution through a third term that does not belong directly to either term of the dyad. As Munro (1988) has pointed out, there are tensions in the way Chu Hsi tried to resolve some of these problems, such as discerning the proper Confucian understanding of the balancing of private family concerns with social solidarity.

THE AXIOLOGICAL BASIS FOR CHU HSI'S
MORAL METAPHYSICS

As we have seen above, Chu Hsi has one indispensable term for his vision of the formal or normative traits as the transcendent order of the world: *li* (principle). *Li* was so crucial that Chu's legacy has been called the school of principle even though he was as concerned with *hsin* (mind) as anyone in the Neo-Confucian tradition. His exposition of *li* was more than a mere description of an ordering principle for the world; it was an articulation of the way the world ought to be, a world that would transcend the failings and injustices of the present order. In trying to explain *li*, Chu Hsi engaged in a profound attempt to frame a moral metasystem grounded in the self-transforming and self-transcending axiology of creative being and meaning. For Chu Hsi the language of morally shared concerns becomes the language of metasystem, the root metaphor of the whole edifice.

What distinguishes this axiological approach from other philosophic beginnings is that "axiological cosmology emphasizes the sense of subjectivity referring to what is unique to the identity of individuals in contrast to what is externally derivative" (Neville 1974, 49). A philosophy founded on axiology mixes together the language of ethics, aesthetics and even natural observation as the basis for its analysis of what is. Valuation is perceived as the foundation of reality: the world is incurably moral and interrelated by means of the shared values of becoming and being which are the foundations of any creature altogether. The language of morally shared concern becomes the language of a moral metasystem; it is the discourse of *ars contextualis*.

For Chu Hsi, to answer *what* constitutes the formal, normative nature is to describe *how* a person makes choices about the world. Questions of metasystemic analysis become, to borrow Mou Tsung-san's insightful phrase, questions of moral metaphysics. The essential feature of moral metaphysics is that it rests on axiological premises. This topic will be discussed more thoroughly in chapter 4 when we return to Mou's exposition of the Confucian religious dimension. To be real is to make harmonious and humane moral decisions, to make an effort to be in right relation to the world as a sage person.

THE THEORY OF LI

In Chu Hsi's thought, *li* as the formal trait of any thing at all is unitary in its creative purpose as relational agent or norm. Yet in this respect it can also be considered plural, since it is viewed from the perspective of other creatures, each with its own unitary nature (*hsing*) that makes it unique and allows it to have a perspective on reality. It is just this point that bothers Mou Tsung-san so much about Chu Hsi's School of Principle as we shall see in chapter 4. Chu Hsi's notion of *li* seems to rob *li* of its creative drive and Mou takes creativity very seriously. If principle is primarily limitation or a rule of definiteness it cannot also be creativity itself. *Li* would then, following Mou, lose its creative power and could not be the focus of Neo-Confucian transcendence, which Mou takes to be a defining characteristic of the mainline of the unfolding of Neo-Confucianism. As we shall see in chapter 4, Mou does not define Chu Hsi as the main branch of the Neo-Confucian.

Chu Hsi, in one of his clearest statements about *li* embedded in his subcommentary *Further Comments [Huo-wen] on the Great Learning* states the following. "Arriving at the things of the world, what is called *li* is that each one has reasons why it is what it is and the norm by which it ought to be so" (Chao, *Shu-ssu tsuan-shu*, 16; hereafter cited as *SSTS*) It is interesting and important to notice the context of this comment. The definition of principle appears right after the point in the text of the *Great Learning* where the eight steps for bringing about the unity of the empire have been introduced. Of course, for Chu the key to this process of self-cultivation leading to social transformation can only be understood as the examination of things by means of discerning their principles. We must be clear that these principles can only be found in the actual events of the intersubjective world of common human experience.

The dual nature of these principles points to another aspect of principle commonly overlooked. What is referred to as principle is the reason why of a thing, something capable of being cognitively known. However, it is also true that principle is the normative judgment about what these patterns are as they become realized through the appropriate active choices of the definite, actualized creature. Principle must be actively sought, for it is active in and of itself, appropriated and embodied by the student who seeks to know. It is the goal for choice as well as a subject of knowledge. It is a pattern that forces the person to attend to certain noncognitive issues.

As Chu's *Huo-wen* subcommentary on the *Great Learning* unfolds, the meaning of principle is made even clearer as the fact of perfecting the person, not merely of increasing the factual knowledge of the person. As Chu Hsi puts it, "to study without being aware, how can this be called the way to study?" (*SSTS*, 28). Chu goes on to make it clear that the process of study is not by rote. He rejects any simplistic appeal either to the cultivation of one thing or to the total unqualified incorporation of the whole universe into the student's mind. The best method is to work on the process of study, even though there is no way of picking out exactly what kind of subject matter will necessarily enhance the chances of realizing principle (*SSTS*, 29). Only when the whole person is cultivated does there come a time when there is a state of awareness equal to what Chu Hsi feels is the comprehending power of the sagely mind.

It is interesting to note, in terms of comparative philosophy, that Chu Hsi uses the Buddhist term *wu* for enlightenment to describe the state of perfect awareness (*SSTS*, 29). In yet another level of subcommentary added to Chu's *Huo-wen*, it is said that in this state of enlightenment all things of the world are truly in the person, that is, in the mind of the person. This, however, is not a Neo-Confucian capitulation to Ch'an Buddhist theory or praxis, for the state of awareness dawns only during the process of self-reflection (*fan-shen*), and must not be confused with activity in the world. This enlightenment experience leads back to the world through the power of empathetic understanding. It is like the situation in which there are many roads and paths to a country, but once you have found your own road, "then you can [know the others] by analogy and comprehend the remainder" (*SSTS*, 29).

Chu Hsi's doctrine of principle provides the basis for choosing the definition of one's own personhood, one's own limits and perfections, but the choice is not solely based on principle. The choice to act this way or that way is made by the embodied mind and not by principle even as a recognized normative pattern demanding attention by the person or any other abstract concept—abstraction does not act in the *tao-hsüeh* worldview. Chu Hsi's theory of principle points to other parts of his system and makes the axiological implications of his way clear. We must now examine the role of mind/*hsin* in terms of ethical discrimination and action.

THE DYNAMICS OF MIND (*HSIN*)

The agent of the emerging person who actually "knows" these principles is the mind (*hsin*). The history of the protean and crucial development of Chu Hsi's notion of mind has yet to be written. In fact, within the entire range of the Neo-Confucian tradition, the notion of *hsin* probably has the most complex, convoluted and contentious historical and philosophical development of any key Neo-Confucian term. One's relation to the development and role of the notion of mind often defines a thinker's place within the tradition. The seminal research of Mou Tsung-san, Ch'ien Mu, T'ang Chün-i, Wm. Theodore de Bary, Donald Munro, Hoyt Tillman and Liu Shu-hsien over the last four decades have fully demonstrated just how complex the history of mind is in the Confucian tradition, and how inadequate the old division of the tradition into the *li-hsüeh* (School of Principle) and *hsin-hsüeh* (School of Mind) is in light of the reality of the ongoing Confucian quest for realizing and understanding the mind. As Ch'ien Mu (1971, vol. 2) has pointed out so conclusively, there is no philosopher more interested in the mind than Chu Hsi. Mou Tsung-san (1968–69, vol. 3) and Liu Shu-hsien (1982) have also documented the crucial role the concept of mind played in Chu Hsi's philosophic transformation from a disciple of the Northern Sung philosophers into a master in his own right.

As often the case, Ch'en Ch'un (1986) provides us with a systematic summary of Chu Hsi's reflections on mind in his *Neo-Confucian Terms Explained*.[8] In discussing the historical origins of Chu's mature definition, Ch'en mentions two primary sources for Chu's concept of mind. First Ch'en quotes Ch'eng I, Chu Hsi's favorite Northern Sung thinker, to the effect that the mind is one thing or a unitary process (Graham 1958, 63). This is the quiet or unperturbed aspect of the mind. Second, Ch'en quotes Chang Tsai's famous statement that the mind controls the nature and feelings. According to Ch'en, no one since Mencius has better defined the mind than Chang, but Ch'en reserves his highest praise for Chu Hsi's own synthesis of Ch'eng I's and Chang Tsai's theories. "Wen-kung [Chu Hsi] said: Nature is the principle of mind; feeling is the function of the mind; mind is the director of feeling and nature. This explains it very clearly" (Ch'en 1840, 1:16b; hereafter cited as *PHTI*; 1986, 60).

Ch'en Ch'un is also very eager to distinguish Chu Hsi's theory from the Buddhist and Taoist concepts of mind. "What the Buddhist school calls nature only seems like what the Confucian school calls the mind. They take this human mind's empty consciousness and call it nature" (*PHTI*, 1:16b; 1986, 60). What Ch'en is implying is that there is always nature as principle in the mind, and therefore mind is conscious, but not just conscious of its own consciousness. It is conscious of having principle as nature within, always defining its essential reality. According to Ch'en, when the Buddhists say that the mind is completely undifferentiated consciousness, this is a fallacy. The mind fuses or directs the union of principle and feeling, and this creative act is anything but a void state or achievement. Consciousness for Ch'en would always be consciousness of something. In the beginning of ethical reflection, for example, it would be the recognition of the four Mencian incipient seeds of virtue (humanity, righteousness, ritual and wisdom) (*PHTI*, 1:16b–17a) or this consciousness can also arise from meditation on the structure of *ch'i* (*PHTI*, 1:14a).

However, the mind is not just a manifestation of principle, because a person receives an allotment of *ch'i* to help form the mind in the unceasingly creative matrix of the Neo-Confucian cosmology. As Ch'en Ch'un says, "Principle and *ch'i* unite in such as way that they become this mind" (*PHTI*, 1:13b). The special quality of mind as *ch'i* is the power of consciousness of other things; of the directional nature of consciousness. We can only be conscious of things that are definite and differentiated from other things.

Ch'en, following Chu Hsi, attests that the lucid consciousness of the mind serves to direct the life of the person and is not itself an object of pure contemplation (*PHTI*, 1:13b–14a). It is not hard to see why Mou Tsung-san is very unhappy with this definition for it seems to Mou that this way of looking at the mind comes perilously close to repeating Hsün Tzu's definition of mind as "empty, unified and still" (Watson 1967, 127). Chu and Ch'en's notion of consciousness, according to Mou, seems to mean the ability to recognize distinctions in the configured world and not the transcendent power of moral creativity that Mou argues is the essence of the mainline Confucian tradition.

According to Ch'en Ch'un, the mind can be analyzed in terms of essence (*t'i*) and function (*yung*). Its essence is to make the assembled principles concrete or manifest and its function is to respond to the perceived things and events of the world. In its essential state it is like a scale that is well balanced. Of course, this balance is only achieved by interaction with the world, so the process is a continuous one of constant interaction. When the mind is properly balanced, and when there is contact with the world, the response of the balanced mind is correct. This is the proper functioning of the mind. For Chu Hsi, the capacity of the mind to respond to stimulus occurs because the mind is a "balanced" scale that can function by responding to the world. The question of how the mind can become balanced belongs to Chu Hsi's theory of self cultivation.

Ch'en Ch'un also describes the mind as "alive" (*PHTI*, 1:15a). One reason that the mind is alive is that it is composed of the ever active and dynamic *ch'i*; it is more than merely aimless activity however, because the mind unites both *ch'i* and principle. The liveliness of mind, its responsiveness in the most profound sense, comes from the interaction of principle and *ch'i* that is held to be the mind's most important function (*PHTI*, 1:15a). This is why Mencius said that Confucius affirmed that the mind could be held fast and also lost (*PHTI*, 1:15a; *SSTS*, 501 for Chu's comment on Mencius). The mind's activity in the world is not the locus of error per se; it is only when the mind becomes unbalanced that it becomes prone to error. For Ch'en cultivation of the mind must be practiced because of this synthetic and creative nature into order to keep it balanced. The essence of a good mind is only realized through an extensive process of self-cultivation and study (*PHTI*, 1:15b).

Ch'en Ch'un also affirms that while the mind is physically small, its capacity is unbounded (*PHTI*, 1:15b). There is no principle it cannot appropriate, nor any event or thing it cannot theoretically control. But it takes the effort of *hsüeh* (study) to bring the mind to completion. When the mind is truly cultivated, there should be nothing left unrealized, no unbalanced response to the world. At this point, Confucian rationalism passes over into religious faith, a quest for self-actualization and self-transformation.

There is no better definition of this program and anticipated results than Chu Hsi's short essay "Treatise on the Completion of Mind (*Chin-hsin shuo*)" (Mou 1968–69, 3:439–47):

> The completion of mind is knowing nature. "Knowing nature is knowing Heaven" [quote from Mencius, see *SSTS*, 521]. We say that a person can complete the mind when the person knows nature and this capacity to know nature is to know Heaven. Now, Heaven is the spontaneity of principle and the source from which humanity is born. Nature is the essence of principle that a person receives to become human. The mind is the way a person controls the self and fully sets forth this principle. "Heaven is great and boundless," [Wang 1974, 27] and nature receives [this boundlessness] completely. Therefore the essence of a person's fundamental mind is itself expansive and without limitation. Only when it is fettered by the selfishness of concrete things, hemmed in by seeing and hearing pettiness, does it become concealed and incomplete. A person can in each event and in each thing exhaustively examine their principles until one day the person will penetratingly comprehend them all without anything be left out: then the person can complete the broad essence of the fundamental mind. The reason for a person's nature being what it is and the reason for Heaven being Heaven is not beyond this and is connected in its unity.

The mind can be explained by what it does as well as by a description of the ethical and ritual habits it develops by acting in a manner consistent with the burden of the classical Confucian canon. If one seeks to know the mind as an object, one may make the Buddhist mistake of seeing the mind as true emptiness. How can one cultivate something that does not exist for itself and then use it to think about the self itself, when it really is nothing but the activity of cultivation and reflection? The mind, apart from the effort of self-cultivation within the matrix of a realistically plural cosmos, is inconceivable for Chu Hsi. To know the mind is to know how it acts in the world, to understand its choices, but not to be ultimately bound or constrained by them because the process never ceases nor does creativity ever abate.

In summary we note the following points. The mind is essentially an active, living process; the mind controls both the essential and functional parts of human nature, the normative and the actual, the unmanifested and the manifested. "Nature has not yet moved while the emotions have already moved. The mind incorporates the already moved and the not yet moved" (Li 1973, 1:332). Chu Hsi wants to make it clear that this is not merely an abstract process. The role of the mind is to be master of nature and the emotions, to be something creative that unites the two.

> The mind means master. It is master whether in the state of activity or in the state of repose. It is not that in the state of repose there is no need for a master, but that there is a master only when there is movement. By master is meant an all-pervading control and command existing in the mind itself. The mind unites and apprehends nature and the emotions, but it is not united with them as a vague entity without any distinction from them. (Li 1973, 1:333; Chan 1963, 631)

Chu Hsi believes that the answer to the question of how the mind relates to the world can only be discovered in the practice of self-cultivation and made worthwhile through the manifestations of the virtues appropriate to this great effort of self-cultivation.

As we noted in the introduction, the study of self-cultivation involves us in the analysis of another of Chu Hsi's most important concepts, *ch'eng* as self-actualization. However important self-actualization theory is in Chu Hsi's synthesis, the exploration of this topic deflects us from our main theme, Chu Hsi's understanding of transcendence. Yet any careful reflection on the nature and function of the mind requires that we attend to two other key metasystematic terms, *ming* and *t'ai-chi* in terms of Chu Hsi's Confucian sense of transcendence.

THE PIVOTS OF BEING: *MING* AND *T'AI-CHI*

As we have already noted, Chu Hsi and his school generally organize their metasystem by means of a triadic structure of the traits of form, dynamics and unification. In the Chu Hsi school metasystem we have seen how *li* acts as the normative trait and how *ch'i* provides the dynamic ground for the cosmos. I am acutely aware that I have not discussed *ch'i* or matter-energy in much detail even though it as essential a component of the cosmos as *li*. This omission is the result of the fact that my primary interest is to discover Chu Hsi's Neo-Confucian sense of transcendence. As we shall see, the transcendent dimension for the Neo-Confucians is most often identified with *li* or principle, *ming* or decree and *t'ai-chi* or the Supreme Ultimate. I believe that this is an accurate reading of the Chu Hsi school understanding of the transcendent elements of reality. Whether we should continue to exclude matter-energy from this list of transcendent referents rests with further research on the role of *ch'i* in the Neo-Confucian tradition in general and in the Chu Hsi school in particular.[9]

In Chu Hsi's moral anthropology the relational or unifying aspect is *hsin*/mind. As we have seen, the best image Chu Hsi and Ch'en Ch'un can find for the mind is that of the director of nature and feelings, representing the normative and the dynamic aspects of their thought. As Ch'en puts it,

> Mind has essence and function. Setting forth all principle is its essence; responding to the myriad affairs of the world is its function. Quiet and unmoving, this is its essence; stimulated and engaged, this is its function. Essence is called nature, and we refer to it in terms of quiescence. Function is called feeling, and we refer to it in terms of movement. (*PHTI* 1:14b; 1986, 57–58)

The two terms that Chu Hsi and Ch'en Ch'un chose for their meta-systematic explanation of the unifying trait were *ming* or command/decree and *t'ai-chi* or the Supreme Ultimate. Both of these are necessary for the coherence of their system and as markers for the particular sense of Confucian transcendence. From the perspective of process theology, the reason for Chu and Ch'en's creative expansion of their tradition by means of two different terms is clear. According to Whitehead, on the one hand, the world is characterized by the category of creativity, the constant and foundational advance into novelty (1978, 31–32). This is the processive trait of the world. However, on the other hand, there is always another aspect of the world that has to be considered: the world is a stubborn reality of past actual entities, at least for mundane creatures (1978, 101–2). The world is a mixture of the coordinated activity of the settled past and the final creativity of the emerging actual entities as they choose how to react to their relevant past.[10] The reality of the past places a certain obligation upon the emerging creature. Some choices are impossible, even if we would like to make them. There is a stark tone to the world in which we are commanded to be what we are. There are both creativity and constraint at work and the Neo-Confucians were also well aware of this duality of the cosmos. In terms of moral anthropology, Chu Hsi used the mind-and-heart to represent these two aspects of the living creature.

For Chu Hsi and Ch'en Ch'un, all creatures are free to respond to the normative lure for perfection—they can actualize their own natures and yet, they are conditioned by their relevant past. Neither side can be ignored in a full portrait of being for the Neo-Confucians. Without the two aspects, there would be nothing for the Neo-Confucians, nothing at all. In this respect, Chu Hsi and Whitehead agree that without both process as cosmic creativity and reality as the settled past, there would be no cosmos.

Thomas Metzger (1977, 127–34) has perceptively pointed out that *ming* is a much neglected concept in Neo-Confucian studies. "One is almost tempted to compare it to a stranger who has stumbled into a gathering where he has no functional role to play" (Metzger 1977, 128). The reason for this, at least in the modern period, has to do with which parts of their tradition the New Confucians have chosen to emphasize and present to the world as their orthodox cumulative tradition. Such thinkers as T'ang Chün-i and Mou Tsung-san, only two of the most prominent of the New Confucians, stung by the criticism that Confucianism necessarily represents a reactionary view of life, have emphasized the long-neglected "creative" roots of Confucian thought. As Mou Tsung-san has repeatedly stressed, the essence of the tradition is "active" or "creative" reason (Mou 1974, 184–202). Therefore, in some respects, *ming* in its more "commanding" role has been allowed to remain an unaccentuated part of their renewed Confucian tradition. Yet for Chu Hsi and Ch'en Ch'un, *ming* is just as important a term as the Supreme Ultimate, which functions as the lure for the creative advance into novelty. As we shall see, both T'ang and Mou have some very decisive comments to make on the role of *ming* in Chu Hsi's thought (Mou 1974, 206 n. 1).

According to T'ang Chün-i (1974, 597), Chu Hsi has three basic meanings for *ming*: (1) as the Tao of Heaven, (2) as the *ch'i* allotted to individual people and (3) that which unifies *li*, the Tao and *ch'i*. T'ang thinks that this last meaning of *ming* as the unifying agent is Chu Hsi's special contribution to the development of *ming* theory. As we have seen, the mind also acts as a unifying agent. Therefore, it is unmistakable that *ming*, like mind, operates as a "pivot," a mediating element between the normative and the dynamic aspects of the cosmos. Because of this, Chu Hsi argues that *ming* connects elements of determinism (the settled past of actual creatures) and tychism (the freedom of the person) in the process of self-actualization (T'ang 1974, 598).

Chu Hsi is explicit on the issue of the unifying role of *ming* as a balance of the normative and dynamic traits of reality. For instance, one of his students asked him why *ming* has both a normative and a dynamic aspect. Chu Hsi replied that while it was true that these meanings were not completely compatible on the surface, however, and this is Chu's main response, if Heaven were not at least partially *ch'i* itself, it could not command a person because the person is also constituted by *ch'i* (Li 1973, 1:297). Chu Hsi was aware that there is a "tension" between the two readings but he concludes that this is a necessary and fruitful tension. It does not thwart the relationship between humanity and Heaven. On the contrary, Chu seems to think that it facilitates their mutual interaction.

Ch'en Ch'un has a typically well organized summary of the various shades of meaning of *ming* in his philosophical glossary. He begins by stating that "*Ming* is command" (*PHTI*, 1:1a). It represents the forceful, ordering aspect of the power of Heaven, Earth and humanity. It is what forces us to make our choices. Because this definition of *ming* as command is the first one Ch'en offers, it should demonstrate that he took the compelling side of reality seriously; it is not something gratuitous in the cosmos. *Ming* is the great, unceasing, orderly and productive activity of the cosmos. As *ch'i* becomes individuated, the "command" that divides and gives all things their essential nature is the decree of Heaven (*PHTI*, 1:1a).

Yet this command must be used for some purpose. As we shall see, *t'ai-chi* provides the goal towards which the power of Heaven properly lures people. It is a lure for the perfection that is possible because *ming* balances *li* and *ch'i*. In terms of principle, Ch'en defines *ming* as follows:

> Its real principle is not beyond configurational energy (*ch'i*). No doubt the two *ch'i* flow out of it without ceasing from the past right down to the present. But it cannot be an empty *ch'i*: it must have a master, which is said to be its principle. Principle is in the midst of it like a pivot. Therefore the grant transformations of Heaven and Earth flow forth, never ceasing for a moment. (*PHTI*, 1:1a–1b; 1986, 38)

Ch'en has another definition of *ming* as principle that is derived from the first. Since *ch'i* itself begins in an undifferentiated state, it must have a director or master, in short, some kind of organizing principle. This director is *ming*, which is, as Ch'en points out, like a pivot. This is highly suggestive of the role of mind; this is the *ming* that Confucius said he knew when he was fifty (*SSTS*, 161; Waley 1938, 88). In this mode, *ming* is clearly identified with human nature, which is the normative aspect of a person in Chu and Ch'en's moral anthropology (*PHTI*, 1:1b). The mention of the fact that Confucius "knew" *ming* when he was fifty shows how *ming* can be a form of enlightenment about the way things really are. The realization of *ming* implies a complete comprehension and appropriation of Heavenly principle that in the perfected state is the actualization of one's true nature (*PHTI*, 1:1b).

For Ch'en Ch'un, these two facets of *ming* in relation to principle demonstrate a two-stage process of articulation. In the first state, *ming* flows forth from Heaven as a command, a principle of what things ought to be. This is discussed in terms of the unceasing nature of *ming* as the director or pivot of the transformation of yin-yang. But *ming* is not blind fate. There is an element of conscious choice involved. People on the road to sagehood must learn to "know" their own fates, to comprehend why Heaven has decreed a certain portion for them. The sage must understand the vector quality of the universe, the direction of unceasing creativity. Therefore, *ming*, when it has been properly understood, is not merely an element of blind compulsion, but takes on an element of the lure for perfection which is best represented by the life of the sage.

To borrow an insight from Whitehead, the Supreme Ultimate serves as the normative principle of the subjective aim of the person, while the principles of other things, even when they are fully comprehended, are objective disciminanda for the mind of the sage. Therefore, the self-creativity of any particular person is intimately connected with this person's appropriation of *ming* and *t'ai-chi* as the person's essential nature. In one sense, *ming* refers to what the person is commanded to be by Heaven and the other creatures, whereas *t'ai-chi* is what the person ought to strive to be because of this unique perspective on the world. In this way, the Supreme Ultimate is to be discriminated from all other objective and subjective species of principle.

Generally speaking, the Supreme Ultimate has two main meanings for Chu Hsi. The first is the most important, and when it is distinguished from the second, part of the confusion about the term becomes evident. Foremost, the Supreme Ultimate is an axiological concept in that it thematizes the highest normative synthesis to be found in any creature. It represents the perfected goal of each person in the universe and also the perfection of the whole universe as Tao.

The second meaning defines the function of the Supreme Ultimate as the norm of perfection of the yin-yang forces. It is the essence of this activity, while *ming* is the function of the actualization of the creatures. As Chu Hsi states, "*Li* is the *t'i* of Heaven; *ming* is the function of *li*" (Li 1973, 1:309). This is the usage that seems to cause problems for later interpreters. When Chu talks about the Supreme Ultimate in this functional mode, he often has recourse to such metaphors as a person riding a horse or the trigger of a crossbow. The first metaphor, the rider on the horse, caused some later Confucians to wonder if it might not be the case of a dead principle riding a live horse, which would imply the contradiction of a directionless flow of energy to the universe. They considered this directionless *ch'i* an unorthodox stance (Ch'ien 1971, 1:279–82; Gedalecia 1974, 443–47). The second metaphor, the trigger of a crossbow, has been explicated most ably by David Gedalecia in his dissertation on Wu Ch'eng (1249–1333) (Gedalecia 1971, 117–23).

However, Chu Hsi's main teaching is missed if we continue to talk about the Supreme Ultimate doing something or how it rides about the dynamic *ch'i* or triggers the activity of the universe. In and of itself, the Supreme Ultimate does none of these things because it is principle and not some kind of embodied function. Activity per se is symbolized in Chu's metasystem by *ming*. For Chu, to ask for the reasons for any kind of activity is to ask about the kinds of things that act and not about the terms that we use to describe these actions and agents. The Supreme Ultimate is a term for explaining how things act and not the action itself, except as this action is considered in abstraction from the creative act, which is plainly impossible for Chu Hsi. For Chu, the Supreme Ultimate is definitely something, but this does not mean that it is something abstracted from the concrete reality of the world.

> Someone asked about the Supreme Ultimate. The Master said: The Supreme Ultimate is only the supreme good and perfected principle of the Tao. Each person has a Supreme Ultimate and each thing has its Supreme Ultimate. Chou Tun-i has said that the Supreme Ultimate is the most perfect and best manifested virtue of Heaven, Earth, humanity, and the myriad things. (Li 1973, 6:4916)

The most important characteristic of the Supreme Ultimate is that it is instantiated in every creature and may be brought to completion by the process known as *ming*.

Chu Hsi respects the axiological pluralism of the world, the process of selection and choice that constitutes reality. He claims that the Supreme Ultimate is both in each thing as its normative principle and is also the generalized principle of the universal creativity. "The Supreme Ultimate is the most exalted good and supremely perfect principle of the Tao" (Li 1973, 6:4916). For Chu, the essence of the Supreme Ultimate is that it functions as a goal for the decision of the creature to be self-determined. It is a goal or lure that the emerging creature should seek in order to actualize its potential for realizing its essential nature. As T'ang Chün-i points out, there is a very close connection between the Supreme Ultimate and the theory of *ch'eng* as self-realization in Chou Tun-i, a connection that was not lost on Chu Hsi. For Chou and Chu, the Supreme Ultimate finds expression only in the ethical self-perfection of the sage that is best understood by a reference to *ch'eng* (T'ang 1974). By pointing to the perfection of the Supreme Ultimate as an ethical goal, Chu Hsi is affirming a fundamental axiology, a creation created and conditioned by true values. It is also a fundamental axiology that has features analogous to what Hartshorne calls his doctrine of dual transcendence.

Ch'en Ch'un points out that the essential nature of the Supreme Ultimate is to be understood in terms of the perfection of the self. To explain this, Ch'en uses the phrase *tzu-yüan* (self-perfecting). He illustrates his point with the metaphor of a large drop of quicksilver that is broken and scattered into a host of little beads of quicksilver. The roundness of the little pieces is dependent on the previous perfection of the larger unscattered piece. Ch'en argues that if there were the slightest hint of imperfection in the Supreme Ultimate, it would be a defective principle and not worthy of the name Supreme Ultimate (*PHTI*, 2:11a–11b). As he puts it in another section, there is nothing that can be added to the Supreme Ultimate that can make it any better or more illustrious (*PHTI*, 2:11a–11b).

Another of Ch'en Ch'un's definitions of the Supreme Ultimate derives from the first. The creatures manifest the Supreme Ultimate as a goal for perfecting the entire universe. Therefore Ch'en states:

> The Supreme Ultimate is the primordial extension of principle. One cannot express it in terms of *ch'i*. In the ancient classics, the term Supreme Ultimate is only to be seen in the *I-Ching*'s *Hsi-tz'u* commentary where it says, "The *I* has the Supreme Ultimate." The *I* or change is the transformation of yin-yang. The principle of the transformation of yin-yang is the Supreme Ultimate. (*PHTI*, 2:8a; 1986, 115)

He also says that "what is the pivot of the myriad transformations, the basis of the variety of things, this is what explains the meaning of the Supreme Ultimate" (*PHTI*, 2:9a). This explanation of the meaning of the Supreme Ultimate in no way contravenes the first set of meanings that we have already explored. It shows the connection of the Supreme Ultimate as the essence of principle as contrasted with *ming*'s role as the function of creativity. It simply takes the ethically perfecting nature of the Supreme Ultimate for granted and shows how this nature becomes explicit in the cosmic process of generation.

The Supreme Ultimate is the principle of the Tao that unifies the normative and dynamic traits of any particular thing. Something is needed to act as the goal or lure for creativity, a *t'i* for the principle of Heaven. "The Supreme Ultimate is not separated as one thing. It is yin-yang and is *in* yin-yang. It is the myriad things and *in* the myriad things: it is only one principle, and therefore called the Supreme Ultimate" (Li 1973, 6:4916). For Chu Hsi, the Supreme Ultimate stands in the universe and in things as the pivot of creation. It is a concrete lure that provides the goal for the function of *ming* to create definite and harmonious value.

The normative side of the Supreme Ultimate functions as a goal of the creatures as they seek to manifest ethical values. Even though it is not actual in and of itself, Chu Hsi thought that any description of the actual world had to rely on the Supreme Ultimate as an essence of *ming*'s ordering process. For

Chu, the Supreme Ultimate plays a vital role in the constitution of everything that is. It is the normative goal for *ch'i* in the same way the mind manifesting *jen* was the unifying aspect of human nature and feeling. Chu's definition of the Supreme Ultimate as the essence of Heaven points to the relational and transcendent aspects of his system.

By now I hope that I have demonstrated the transcendent dimension of Chu Hsi's metasystem, especially in terms of the notion of the Supreme Ultimate. In the next chapter we will return to Mou Tsung-san's and Tu Wei-ming's modern Confucian reformation and defense of Confucian religiosity. Although Mou and, to a lesser extent, Tu, are harsh critics of Chu Hsi, I believe it is now clear that the debate between Mou and Chu is a profound struggle between Confucian masters seeking to take responsibility for the Way. Nothing could be more Confucian, and nothing more unambiguously demonstrates the profoundly transcendent dimension of their quest. Both Chu and Mou have a profound understanding of the transcendent and religious dimensions of the Confucian Way.

One intriguing aspect of this Neo-Confucian sense of transcendence is that it has such close analogies to certain features of modern process theology. Perhaps this should not be surprising given that both movements were and are reformations of their respective intellectual histories and were and are fascinated by the role of change and the humane creation of enduring values in the world. One could argue that both are profound axiological versions of a global *ars contextualis*. This heuristic correlation will be a theme for remaining chapters of this essay. The discussion of this dimension of Confucian-Christian dialogue is also a preliminary contribution to the question of the emerging global philosophy and theology of comparative religions as it seeks to develop a methodology appropriate not only to the cultures and religious of West Asia but also congruent to the traditions of East Asia. One of the future contributions of Confucian-Christian dialogue will be the generation of a more adequate methodology for discussing the religious dimension of human life in the twenty-first century.

4

Mou Tsung-san's Defense of Confucian Religiosity and Tu Wei-ming's Appeal to Fiduciary Community

MOU TSUNG-SAN'S DEFINITION
OF CONFUCIAN RELIGIOSITY

The exhaustive examination and explanation of the religious dimensions of the Confucian Way has never been a main thematic preoccupation of any member of the sixth phase of the Confucian tradition, a group of scholars now known as the New Confucian movement.[1] In fact, as we have seen in the previous chapters, an intense interest in the religious dimensions of the tradition never defined any of the major figures of the Neo-Confucian movement at all. The Neo-Confucians did not understand themselves in the fashion of a West Asian religious community because the theistic question was not a central intellectual challenge within their tradition. One of the things that gives reading about the early Jesuit-Confucian encounter a special charm is the fact that this is really a case of two ships passing in the night. Sometimes the more prescient among the early Jesuits and their Confucian friends knew that something odd was going on, but the Confucians had other more pressing matters afoot that needed attention. This makes Mou Tsung-san (1909–   ) and Tu Wei-ming's interest in the religious elements of their tradition all the more intriguing.

Because Mou Tsung-san is the one major representative of the first generation of the New Confucians who explicitly deal with the religious dimension of the Confucian Way, I will concentrate on those points of his revisionist narrative of the tradition dealing with the definition and defense of Confucian religiosity.[2] As I have noted before, there is a consensus in scholarly circles about the merit of Mou's contribution to the renewal of Confucian scholarship in terms of his systematic philosophic project. There is a wide and growing recognition that Mou is philosophically sophisticated and creative in his attempt to restate one line of the Neo-Confucian vision in a way that demonstrates a synthesis of Confucian and Western philosophic discourses. One of Mou's great strengths is that he articulates major issues in Confucian philosophy and religion in terms of comparative religious and intellectual history, including constant reference and attention to classical and modern Western as well as Chinese Buddhist and Taoist intellectual history. Moreover, Mou has not written exclusively as a detached intellectual historian, rather he has manifested a desire to reform and develop the Confucian *tao* Way for modern sensibilities. Mou seeks to describe, understand and commend the Confucian tradition as one worthy of respect and influence in the global culture of the modern world.

Mou Tsung-san truly represents the emergence of an East Asian global philosophy. In this regard he resembles the Japanese Kyoto school except that he is Confucian rather than Buddhist in commitment. While some Western intellectuals make a parlor game out of wondering if it will ever be possible for thinkers from one culture to understand another, Mou demonstrates, as do the Kyoto school thinkers, that it is not only possible, it has already been done. For instance, Mou has had a constant dialogue with Kant from the beginning of his career. One can only hope that more of Mou's students will write in English so that the richness of this religio-philosophic position will become better known in the North Atlantic world.

In addition to a review of Mou Tsung-san's reformed Neo-Confucianism, I will also review Tu Wei-ming's suggestive contribution to the discussion of the religious dimension of the Confucian tradition in the second part of this chapter. No one has better articulated in English the New Confucian position on this matter. Furthermore, Tu has an excellent exposition of the spiritual foundations of the Confucian sense of fiduciary community as the goal of humane social interaction. In many respects Tu's notion of the fiduciary community is analogous to the Christian sense of the beloved community. Both are ideal types of human community, normative forms that express the highest aspirations of the communal spiritual quests of Confucians and Christians. In all these areas Tu builds upon and expands key themes in Mou's New Confucianism.

To sketch Mou's position on Confucian religiosity I will make primary use of two published collections of lectures on Chinese intellectual history, with special reference of those parts dealing with the Confucian tradition.[3] The first set of lectures, *The Uniqueness of Chinese Philosophy*, was first delivered in the 1960s and republished with a new introduction in 1974 in Taiwan. In the 1974 introduction Mou is careful to note that this is a very short outline of Chinese thought and is therefore not overly subtle. He urges anyone interested in the details of his arguments to see his more complete scholarly works, especially the series of interrelated books examining Confucian intellectual history beginning with *Hsin-t'i yü hsing-t'i* (Mind and Nature), his great series of studies on the rise of the Neo-Confucian movement. While it should be noted that the main topic of most of Mou's extensive corpus is the Chinese tradition, he does devote large sections of his various studies to comparative issues of the Buddhist tradition in China along with an examination of modern Western philosophy.

The second and more extensive collection are the *Nineteen Lectures on Chinese Philosophy* published in 1983. In the preface to the *Nineteen Lectures*, originally delivered at Taiwan National University in 1975, Mou points out that these lectures are an expansion of material presented in *The Uniqueness of Chinese Philosophy*. Whereas the first set of lectures primarily addresses the Confucian tradition as the dominant expression of Chinese intellectual history, in the *Nineteen Lectures* Mou seeks to deal with the full range of the philosophic content of the Confucian, Taoist and Buddhist traditions in order to provide a richer understanding of Chinese intellectual history.

For our present purposes *The Uniqueness of Chinese Philosophy* and *Nineteen Lectures* are excellent points for departure because they illustrate Mou's understanding of the entire development of the Chinese religio-philosophic world. Mou begins the Tainan, Taiwan, lectures by noting that if we use modern Western definitions of philosophy or religion, then China seems to have very little of which fits either philosophy or religion.[4] Nonetheless China certainly has a long tradition of reflections on the meaning of life and the values that make life worth living. Mou believes that the main emphasis of Chinese thought resides in the balance of intersubjectivity[5] and autonomous morality (1983, 69–81). As a "moral metaphysics," Chinese philosophy and religion are grounded in what Mou calls "concerned consciousness," a fundamentally axiological reading of the world and human life. He believes that the Confucian sense of "concerned consciousness" is a root metaphor for all the various schools of Chinese thought, comparable to the Buddhist concept of great compassion (*karuṇa*) and the Christian notion of love (*agape*). In this Mou is certainly following the axiological vision of the transcendent also shared by Chu Hsi.

The style of Mou's narrative is very much in tune with classical Neo-Confucian presentations of the tradition. In many ways it is a profoundly commentarial approach to the renewal of Confucianism. It is couched in terms of comments and references to material that Mou considers the major texts of the classical philosophic and sagely traditions of Confucianism, Taoism and Buddhism. John B. Henderson (1991, 215–216) has noted the continuity of Mou's intellectual style with the entire commentarial, exegetical and hermeneutic traditions of China. Henderson argues that China's interpretive traditions, just as the case with Jewish and Christian biblical, Islamic koranic and Western Homeric studies, did undergo a profound movement away from classical commentarial assumptions and methods after contact with post-Enlightenment Western traditions. Nonetheless, Mou fixes his focus on a version of the canonical Confucian Way by means of an intricate exegesis of key texts in the Confucian tradition such as Chu Hsi's "Letters to the Gentlemen of Hunan" and discussions of the notion of *jen*. While these letters of Chu Hsi may not be known beyond scholarly circles, Mou points out that they are the definitive texts wherein the Sung Neo-Confucian masters established their unique contribution to the Confucian Way.

MOU'S ANALYSIS OF THE CONFUCIAN WAY

Mou begins his short exposition of the uniqueness of Chinese philosophy by an unqualified affirmation that China has indeed produced philosophy even through its cognitive systems evolved differently from the classics of Continental and Anglo-European thought. He challenges any historian of Chinese philosophy to take an unbiased look at the history of that tradition (1974, 1–2). The problem is that many modern historians of Chinese philosophy have been hopelessly biased towards Western models, so much so that in their extreme forms they have distorted the shape of the history of Chinese philosophy. His favorite example here is Fung Yu-lan's *History of Chinese Philosophy*.[6] Mou charges that Fung's use of the New Realism, learned at Columbia University, caused Fung to misjudge various issues in the history of Chinese philosophy, such as his interpretation of Chu Hsi, and led Fung to misunderstand completely the proper periodization of Chinese philosophic history. To separate the history of Chinese philosophy into the two periods, the classical philosophers and their scholastic commentators, does a grave injustice to the creativity Mou (1974, 2–3) finds in all periods of the history of Chinese philosophy.

Having critiqued Fung's interpretation of the history of Chinese philosophy, Mou offers his own criteria for describing philosophic systems. Mou defines philosophy not as a reflection on questions of logic and epistemology, a form of discourse he believes characterizes modern Continental and Anglo-American philosophy, but on the more general meaning of life, the evocation of what it means to think about being human. If we accept that philosophy is the broadly conceived search for the explication of human life, then Mou (1974, 4–5) suggests that Chinese philosophy is qualified by two further criteria: intersubjectivity and morality. For the purposes of this essay, once we have understood what Mou means by intersubjectivity, the scope of his reflections on moral valuation as a profound axiology will become clear as a necessary corollary to the proper manifestation of mind and nature.

At this point Mou mentions (1974, 5–6), rather as an aside, that the mainline Confucian tradition is hardly a religious one if we restrict our understanding of religion to those traditions that have an overt theo-volitional principle. Without a god the Confucians cannot be considered theologians. What relates Confucianism to Western religious traditions is that it is concerned with the larger questions of life that have been traditionally the domain of theology in the West. Given that Confucianism is concerned with the total life of persons, it is the functional analogue of Western religion.[7] Therefore Mou's theory of Chinese philosophy could also be interpreted as the enunciation of a Confucian philosophy of religion. Even more than that, it is an affirmation of a New Confucian who believes that his tradition adequately serves the same religious and spiritual purposes that Christianity has served in the West.

Thus, according to Mou, mainline Confucianism is both a religious and a philosophical doctrine, and if we assume that religion is a more generic term than philosophy, then Mou's Confucianism is truly a religious faith. While Mou specifically denies the fact that he is a theologian, lacking as he does any self-conscious theory of personalized divinity, this does not hinder us from considering him more than an "objective" philosopher of religion who refuses to take a stand in any one religious tradition. Mou declares and defends its validity with all the vigor (and sometimes polemic) of a great theologian.

Prior to our examination of Mou's defense of the philosophic and religious dimensions of the Confucian tradition, it is useful to describe just what Mou takes to be the "mainline" of the orthodox Confucian way. In his discussion of the Neo-Confucian tradition in the *Nineteen Lectures* and in *The Uniqueness of Chinese Philosophy* Mou describes what he assumes to be normative Confucianism in those sections dealing with the classical and Sung-Ming Neo-Confucian schools. In many respects this revisionist interpretation of orthodox or mainline Confucianism is one of the most arresting aspects of Mou's ongoing examination of the sources of the Sung Neo-Confucian revival. I should note that this concern for the definition of orthodoxy and the proper understanding of the "transmission of the Way" is highly traditional. Nothing could be more Confucian than worrying about lineage and teachings.

For Mou, the normative tradition beginning with Mencius in the classical period is *the* mainline. So while Mou is impressed with Hsün Tzu's intellectual genius, he still does not consider Hsün Tzu on par with Confucius and Mencius in defining the essential contours of the classical tradition. It is clear from all his writings that he takes a traditional view of the transmission of the Confucian Way, with Confucius and Mencius as the great foundational figures of the pre-Han classical period. Certain other texts are also extremely important, such as selected appendices of the *I-Ching* and the *Chung-yung*. As we shall see repeatedly, Mou (1974, 12) argues that "the moral nature of Chinese philosophy is rooted in the concept of concern." Mou acknowledges his colleague and friend Hsü Fu-kuan for the modern thematization of the concept of concern. This concept of concern is linked to cosmic creativity in the effective unity of lived experience. Cosmic creativity finds its symbolic representation in Confucius' notion of *jen*. It was Confucius' insight into the fusion of intersubjective morality with cosmic creativity that made Confucius the founder of the Confucian Way, which, of course, was an expression of the primordial teachings of the pre-Chou sages and worthies. *Jen* as the essence of humanity is the fusion of human nature/*hsing* and the Way of Heaven/*t'ien-tao*. On one level *jen* means a moral code, the affection of loving the people. But there is also a deeper meaning, which is "the fundamental root of the nature of creativity," or creativity itself. This fundamental axiological notion is rooted in two basic life values. The first is what Mou calls the intuition of yielding or primordial balancing. The second is that of a committed perseverance to the task of seeking sagehood without ceasing or, as the Book of Poetry puts it, a perseverance "profound and unceasing," the presence of awakened steadfastness in search of the Way. According to Mou creativity itself is the Way of Heaven.

Mou argues, from the 1960s on, that the key texts for this mainline Confucian tradition are the *Analects, Mencius, I-Ching* and *Chung-yung*. As with most great reformers, Mou certainly has a canon within a canon. The conspicuous absence of the *Ta-hsüeh* is one key to understanding Mou's critique of Chu Hsi. The mainline Confucian tradition is a profound exploration of the fundamental issues of humane values, or as he puts it, "a question of life values." This is a "concerned" and persevering focus on what makes for humane life in terms of intersubjectivity and the search for human community, hence this is the locus of what, in the Western tradition, would be questions of spirituality, transcendence, cosmology and ontology. What Confucian spirituality seeks is a deepened intersubjectivity and an autonomous morality.

Mou Tsung-san always returns to four key elements of philosophic and spiritual analysis. All these themes are central to his articulation of Chinese philosophy in general and Confucianism in particular. In brief these four themes and their key texts are:

1. *T'ien-ming* as ~~creativity~~ itself expressed in the cosmological mode; thematized in *I-Ching* and *Chung-yung*.
2. *Jen* as creativity mediated by concern for others as the human response to *t'ien-ming*; thematized in the *Analects*.
3. *Hsin* as the human mind-and-heart disclosed as the ~~experiential unity~~ of the relational concern of being human in a community. For Mou *hsin* is also *pen-hsin* or fundamental mind-and-heart as creative or active reason; thematized in *Mencius*.
4. *Hsing* as human nature as the active creation of new values for life; also thematized in *Mencius*.

In Mou's estimation, a Confucian thinker is only orthodox or mainline insofar as he or she expresses these linked series of notions. As we shall see, Hsün Tzu, the *Ta-hsüeh* and Chu Hsi do not represent this Mencian mainline. Nonetheless, Mou has the highest respect for the philosophic genius of the wayward duo of Hsün Tzu and Chu Hsi; part of the problem is that they were brilliant and, at the same time, incorrect. This philosophic brilliance helped to seduce the less astute away from what Mou takes to be normative Mencian Confucianism, the true heart of the cumulative tradition.

Mou begins his exposition of the history of Sung Neo-Confucianism in the *Nineteen Lectures* by reminding us of a crucial if now minor figure, Hu Wu-feng (1106–62). Mou argues that Hu was actually the Sung thinker who best synthesizes the diverse depositions of Chou Tun-i, Chang Tsai and Ch'eng Ming-tao.[8] Although Hu is not considered a bellwether figure during the Sung, Mou stoutly and polemically maintains that it is really Hu and *not* Chu Hsi who best represents the mainline tradition of the Confucian Way flowing from the classical Chou sages and worthies to the Northern Sung masters.

In his novel, and some would say quixotic, nomination of Hu Wu-feng as the quintessinal Sung thinker, Mou contends that there are really three major schools in the Sung-Ming Neo-Confucian tradition:

1. Ch'eng I – Chu Hsi—which has always been considered, erroneously, the mainline tradition.
2. Lu Chiu-yuan – Wang Yang-ming—an interesting branch of Mencius thought, but not really the mainline either.
3. Chou Tun-i – Chang Tsai – Ch'eng Ming-tao – Hu Wu-feng (and in the late Ming, Liu Tsung-chou)—as the real mainline tradition, although this fact has been obscured by the dominance of Chu Hsi.

For Mou, it is the third transmission of the Way, beginning with Chou Tun-i and ending with Liu Tsung-chou (1578–1645), that is the proper, orthodox mainline as defined by Confucius and Mencius.

Mou (1983, 394) goes on to argue that Hu Wu-feng's synthesis contains the essential philosophic and cosmological mainline of the Confucian tradition as found in Mou's early shortlist of canonical Confucian texts: *Analects, Mencius, Chung-yung* and the appendices of the *I-Ching* as noted above. It is interesting to note that Mou includes the appendices of the *I-Ching* but not the *Ta-hsüeh*. The reason for this is Mou's belief that Chu Hsi chose the *Ta-hsüeh* for his own philosophic purposes and that, as an early text, it does not really reflect what Mou takes to be normative Confucianism. He makes the case (1983, 400–01) that Chu Hsi is really much closer to Hsün Tzu and the *Ta-hsüeh*, a text related to Hsün Tzu's school, than to Confucius and Mencius. However, in no way does Mou belittle Chu Hsi's accomplishment. It is hard to think of a modern scholar who pays a higher compliment to Chu Hsi than Mou Tsung-san. Mou often refers to Chu Hsi as Master Chu, a sign of true esteem. The problem is that Chu Hsi is a master of a different Confucian tradition than the one Mou takes to be normative.

Returning to the analysis of the Confucian tradition, Mou (1974, 9) begins his examination of intersubjectivity by noting that even when Anglo-European philosophers deal with subjectivity they do so from an objectivist and analytic point of view. To analyze seems synonymous with objectivity for Mou. There seems to be the bias in his work that a profound epistemologist can never penetrate deeply into the true nature of reality if narrowly restricted to the technical philosophic goals of the post-Enlightenment West. At this point Mou argues that even the seemingly sophisticated epistemological activities of the Ch'eng-Chu school did not represent the pure analysis preached in the post-Enlightenment West. By intention Ch'eng I and Chu Hsi were concerned with questions of subjectivity and morality (Mou 1974, 10) even if they were not as profound in their teachings as the real, if obscured, Sung-Ming mainline.

The life of the true sage is concerned first and foremost with moral questions. The source of good and evil for Mou is to be found in the purely natural life, and here Mou quotes from Lao-tzu, where he says that to have a body is to have the problems of *this* body. Mou does not want to deny the body and its functions, including consciousness and intellectual intuition. Rather, he wants to make sure that an isolated, separate individual, the premise that each person is *an* island, leads us astray and far from the intent and truth of the Confucian tradition (1974, 11). The defining characteristic of the Confucian moral life is the act of concern for others that is essentially relational in structure

(Mou 1974, 12–13). Here again, when he searches for analogous Western or Indian concepts to match Confucian ones, he singles out the Christian notion of love and the Buddhist sense of "great compassion." While the title of his book indicates his interest in philosophy, his comparative illustrations show the strongly religious import of his work.

Having suggested that the central qualifying word to describe early Confucian thought is concern, Mou goes on to show how this concept is then related to other important elements of Confucian symbolic vocabulary, such as *ching* or reverence, *ching-te* or morality, *ming-te* or illumined virtue and *t'ien-ming* or the Mandate of Heaven. Mou argues that the Confucian dialectic of concern is quite different from systems of thought that have a more conventional theistic heritage. Mou believes that the most pure religious feeling is that of nothingness or dread, the smallness of a human being in the huge universe. This feeling of nothingness leads to a religious conversion experience that is often interpreted as the total negation of the empirical self (Mou 1974, 14).

But this sense of dread is not what the Confucian tradition takes as its central religious motivation. On the contrary, even while the tradition does have the sense of religious mystery to which all people are subject, it is not the crucial element for the elaboration of the tradition. There is no final diremption of being, no breaking of the chain of organic solidarity that ties the world together. The Confucian may not understand some particular aspect of nature or mind, but this does not mean that on principle he or she could not understand it with further reflection and study. Everything belongs to one realm of discourse and the cosmos holds out the possibility for one general explanation—founded finally on the moral concern of the profound ethical agent.

Mou argues that the distinctive Confucian sense of transcendence is revealed in the notion of the Mandate of Heaven, a most qualified first principle when compared to the theologies of the major West Asian religions. The ultimate order of the world as a manifestation of *t'ien-ming* is moral, shot through and through with values. Interpretation, as an aspect of such a moral world, is not value free, so we can see why Mou (1974, 16) is highly dubious about philosophic systems that are based on the assumption that facts and values are somehow held in mutual and antagonistic tension. As a Confucian Mou does not believe that a nonaxiological system can penetrate into the core of ultimate values or structures of being. For Mou the cosmic axiological order is truly metaphysical and not merely psychological. The claim here is boldly rational, if you accept Mou's definition of fundamental rationality as axiology, for a tradition which is often held merely to appeal to convention or aesthetic intuition (Mou 1974, 18).   *axiological*

While the immanent and transcendent are often considered opposites in West Asian and South Asian traditions, Mou (1974, 20) sees the normative Confucian Way as joining the ethical and religious dimensions in an effective unity of lived experience that he claims is the real meaning of the Confucian concept of nature. And what, we may ask Mou, is the primal quality that this nature embodies, both in humanity and in the cosmos? In the first place, it is profound beyond the power of complete verbalization. Following the cosmological tradition of the *I-Ching*, Mou states that it penetrates all realms and levels of existence. It is "creativity itself" (Mou 1974, 21). Creativity is *the* ontological principle. The final appeal is to the ongoing power of creative transformation that never ceases and not to some self-sustaining theo-volitional force or agent. Heaven produces human beings and they manifest this ongoing creativity in a unique manner.

But this is not all that Mou wants to say about the primordial quality of nature. He goes on to quote the *Shih-ching* (The Book of Poetry) as proof of the assertion that nature, which is also human nature, is actively good. In saying that the primordial nature is good Mou does not want to imply that we can then simply follow our own natures without reflection. The moral nature must be properly cultivated and not allowed to lose its foundation in morality and subjectivity (Mou 1974, 23). Left in a subsistent and uncreative state, what we end up with is subjectivism and not intersubjectivity and inner morality (Mou 74, 23).

Having reviewed briefly the early canonical texts, Mou evaluates Confucius' contribution to the tradition that he finds in two areas. Even though Confucius does not talk at great length about nature and the Mandate of Heaven, Mou (1974, 25–27) thinks that these concepts are implied by everything in the deep structure of Confucius' teaching. What is unique to Confucius is the concept of *jen* (Mou 1974, 25; 1983, 52). Confucius' notion of *jen* fuses the perception of sorrowfulness or unease that a sensitive person has with the all too obvious imperfections of this world *and* the sense of concern that seeks to model itself in harmony with the creative pulse of the universe. *Jen* takes the unification of the sense of concern and sorrow as its own nature and the nurture of the moral mind as its proper role (Mou 1974, 31). It is the creative concern of the universe finding its proper instantiation in human nature.

Mou also gives an interpretation of Confucius' concept of heaven as an important aspect of the transcendent dimension of the received tradition (also 1983, 49–50). By preserving this sense of mystery, the Confucian tradition guarded the presence of the transcendent element in the emerging Chou-Han synthesis. In one sense the continuing presence of Heaven serves an analogous purpose equivalent to the Christian notion of the Holy Spirit. Therefore Mou suggests that while Confucius himself tacitly preserves the sense of transcendence by his doctrine of Heaven, it is the *Chung-yung* that provides the continuity of immanent being that is the other aspect of the fusion of inner morality and deepened subjectivity. In humanity there is the movement from Heaven's pure creativity to the extension of self-realization, the lure of the creative principle in fact and concrete reality (Mou 1974, 35; 1984, 74–77). Pure creativity is *t'ien* while humankind is a more limited instantiation of this creativity. While Heaven is agentless, humans must make an effort to know and to do the good. In fact, Mou (1974, 37) argues that *jen* as perfect humanity is equivalent to *ch'eng* or self-realization in the *Chung-yung*, where the sage is conceived as a paradigmatic example of the fusion of knowledge and action. According to Mou there is a natural movement in early Confucian thought from natural speculations on the moral order of the universe towards a process of subjectivization motivated by the lure of the sage acting in harmony with the creative forces of the universe. The sage becomes what a human being ought to be through an ongoing process of self-realization.

Having shown how the various elements of later Confucian thought are latent in Confucius himself, Mou then proceeds to a discussion of the principle of intersubjectivity and objectivity. While the subjective dimension is clear in Confucius' concept of *jen*, it is in the *Chung-yung* that Mou finds the distinctive Confucian concern for objectivity. What is recognized concretely is the total interdependence of nature, an objectivity that becomes manifest through human effort in the world. Here Mou quotes Hsün Tzu to the effect that even evil cannot destroy the good of the world when the sage acts in harmony with proper destiny. What is really false is "materialization," the end of true creativity, the failure of the creative advance into ever more complex self-realization. Mou wants to contrast this Confucian theory of self-realization with the Christian principle of universal love that is based, he claims, upon the will of God and not the effort of humankind. Therefore, Christian morality is condemned to be a rule-oriented morality and not an inner reflection of the cultivated self (Mou 1974, 44–45).

Mou now introduces what he thinks is one of the most important symbolic resources in the Confucian tradition, the concept of mind-and-heart. In their discussion of the mind, the Confucians have most cogently expressed the real unity, the creative function of life in all its full relationality. In this regard, Mou feels that the old scholastic distinction between the School of Mind and the School of Principle is a false one in Neo-Confucianism. Mind and principle are two necessary moments in the full complexity of the Confucian vision and it was one of the problems of traditional scholarship that the two schools were seen as antithetic and not complementary (Mou 1974, 50–51).

With the introduction of mind taken as creative reason, Mou again returns to his comparison of the two roads of early Confucian thought: the *Chung-yung* and *I-Ching* represent the cosmological side of the tradition whereas Mencius represents the more purely intentional aspect of the school with Confucius as the patron of both methods (see also 1983, 77–78). Even the *Chung-yung's* cosmological or ontological formulations have self-determining creativity as their final goal. Humanity can participate in the creativity of the universe as a cosmotheandric agent of the highest order.

It is at this point that Mou makes a crucial definitional statement. He says that there are two different and contrasting ways of defining human nature. One has to do with "class difference," which is ultimately a logical and structural way of marking off the difference between humankind and the rest of the animal world. For instance humankind, as a class of concrete beings, could be defined as that animal that can speak. But this, Mou argues, is not the proper Confucian definition of nature as manifested through the active mind. There is a natural order to things, such as the ability to speak, but if this were not conjoined with the creative urge to realize this natural capacity then we would not have humanity, but only some highly sophisticated kind of ape.

What distinguishes humanity from the animals is the creative use of reason, the power of choice between right and wrong. Only when the structure of the universe is creatively understood do we have a proper definition of human nature for Mou (1974, 56). Humanity's essence is thus the creation of new values. Nor is this creativity a blind, appetitive or valueless ordering of the world, and here Mou (1974, 58) quotes the *I-Ching* to the effect that the structure of the Way is the alternation of the yin and yang, while the continuation of this process is the good itself. Having moved from a theory of subjectivity back to the ontological speculations of the *Chung-yung*, Mou again returns to an invocation of ethical concerns and naturally turns his attention to the second moment of the Confucian tradition, Mencius and his theory of human nature. Given that Mou posits the necessity of the concrete manifestation of moral reason as the most important aspect of Chinese philosophy, the rather cosmological approach of the *Chung-yung* is taken to be an abstract and tacit representation of the more representative and ethically centered philosophy of Mencius.

The source of human good must be in human nature itself (Mou 1974, 61). Even the recognition of evil, which is part of Confucian theory, is predicated on the ability to talk about a state of being beyond finite good and evil grounded in the moral recognition of perfection that has the capacity of surpassing even itself in ever greater degrees of harmony and intensities of moral insight and action (Mou 1974, 63). The Mencian line of reasoning is taken to posit a concept of human nature that implies the real subjectivity of this nature and which, in turn, would rely on objectivity for part, though not all, of its content. In a slightly earlier section, Mou argues that while Chinese philosophy lacks any overt trinitarian theology, there is an implicit advocacy of the unity of what Hegel would call God-in-self and God-for-self in deepened intersubjectivity that is God-in-and-for-self in true freedom, namely, real creativity.

Having explained *hsing* in the *Chung-yung* and *I-Ching* in relation to Mencius' concept of mind as active reason, Mou returns to the concept of nature, but here understood in terms of the Neo-Confucian synthesis.[9] The Sung philosophers have a theory of nature that is based on the shared assumption that there is really one nature, which we should interpret as the instantiation of creative reason in the person of the sage, but which is often confused with one aspect of this nature, the material or common nature. Mou asserts that the true self can only be understood in terms of the effort that it takes to realize the lure for perfection that is self-transforming as it seeks to transcend whatever present state of possible perfection it might be tempted to materialize. Thus the meaning of reality is what the mind intends to be its ever-creative goal for perfection and not some subsistent and lifeless logical modal construct that can never be transformed or modified (Mou 1974, 71).

The moral mind is therefore more than an ethical structure; Mou believes, to use his favorite Western metaphor, that it implies a content to Kant's categories. Not only do we have the intuition of space-time, but also the sense of the creative possibility of the moral mind that seeks to relate itself in community with the rest of the world. Mou argues that the "cosmic order is moral order" (1983, 82), and is hence realized through the mind of the sage as a profound ethical agent. This world is only objective in the sense that objects are understood as providing the context in which moral relationships are established. The examination of things as objects is the prior step to self-realization in which these things are comprehended in their full relationships to the emerging self and are judged to be either good or evil as qualified by this relationship. Value and truth are functions of the creative self that orders the world emerging in the creative unity of the fiduciary community.

While Mou is well aware that Chinese philosophy since the end of the Ming has not been particularly creative, he suggests that the Chinese view of life is still one viable alternative for philosophical reconstruction and that the history of Chinese philosophy leads us to believe that we have not yet seen the end of its creative advance. His view of the history of Chinese philosophy is conditioned by his opinion of the cosmological creativity of human nature. *Hsing* (nature) can change and be creative and therefore is not a mere structured, logical construct which somehow undergoes all kinds of adventures that leave it unaffected. Just as the human mind can make moral effort to reform itself, Chinese philosophy can renew itself and probably will, given the new stimulus of contact with the various schools of Western philosophy (Mou 1974, 79–88).

MOU'S THEORY OF RELIGION
AND ITS RELATION TO CONFUCIANISM

Mou (1974, 89) appends a lecture he delivered at the Tainan Theological Seminary as the twelfth chapter of *The Uniqueness of Chinese Philosophy*. Mou asserts that every society has an essence that imparts its own special genius and creativity to all other aspects of the social system, and he believes that this element is religion. Religion must fulfill two roles. On the practical level, a religion must influence the daily lives of the members of that society and he notes that Confucianism certainly qualifies here as a religious system (Mou 1974, 90). But a religion must also be a spiritual path, and this is just the aspect of Confucianism that has been most suspect in previous comparative treatments. What confuses some writers is the fact that Confucian spirituality does not depart from the tao of constant, moral and ultimately social conduct.

Next Mou highlights two aspects in Confucian life that he feels most cogently symbolize this Confucian Way of the secular as sacred. These involve the disciplined use of ritual and music. He wants to stress the particularly communal aspects of these two kinds of self-culture. The human self cultivated in ritual and music is hardly a lonely self, rather it is one that finds appropriate ends in the emergence of a fiduciary community. With the use of ritual and music, taken to express the foundations of Confucian self-culture, Mou argues that there is no doctrine of the diremption of being in Confucian theory. No Confucian could have written the *City of God*, for the city of men and women would have sufficed even if tragedy is affirmed. Religion can therefore be said to have a twofold influence on a person in the context of his or her particular society. An individual can choose the particular system of belief he or she wishes to affirm and this choice carries over into wider areas of shared human life, that is, ritual, music and general social organization (Mou 1974, 92).

Mou returns once more to an analysis of Confucius' main teachings, which, as we have seen, he equates with the doctrine of *jen*, nature and the Mandate of Heaven. Superficially, *jen* is a certain group of moral qualities, the most important of which is love. But on a deeper level, this moral quality of *jen* is best understood as creativity itself. *Jen*, which is finally the category of creativity beyond which there is no appeal either in fact or theory, is the foundation of the universe, and hence a process of becoming and not some quasi-material entity as a social or epistemological convention (Mou 1974, 93). *Jen* is a special kind of awareness, a moral sense that Mou takes to be central to the character of humanity as a creative agent and not a mere physiological type or class of being.

What is the special characteristic of this moral awareness? It is a persistence, an emphasis on the ability and inclination to keep on trying, as when Confucius is defined as one who knows that something cannot be done but tries nonetheless to do it. This effort, this persistence in the face of the powers of privatized materialization is how Mou defines Confucian spirituality. This is what the *I-Ching* calls the unceasing effort of the profound person. Confucius' favorite disciple Yen Hui is crucial to Confucianism at this point just because he was one who persisted in his effort, and in fact becomes the patron saint of persistence for the Neo-Confucians (Mou 1974, 94).

The implications of *jen* for a Confucian doctrine of human nature should be obvious. Human nature can *change* and in fact is human nature because it is not structurally constrained as other animals seem to be bound by their natures. The soul of the Confucian is what the person seeking sagehood decides to become—you are what you will to be, and you become more fully human as you create your own world as moral community (Mou 1974, 95). As we shall see, Mou's notion of creativity provides a link to the process tradition of A. N. Whitehead and Charles Hartshorne. In fact, Hartshorne has been one of the most persistent defenders of axiology as a fundamental mode of interpreting reality.

Historically the Confucians lack a Jewish, Christian or Islamic notion of the 'person' of God as the ground of being. But Mou (1974, 96) suggests that the Confucians have a concept of prayer that he locates in the sense of wonder and awe produced universally in humankind when confronted with the problems of life and death, a cry for help that is common to all humankind. What is different in Confucianism is that this cry for help does not prompt the individual to turn to God for aid, but forces him or her to reflect again on what it means to be human. The Confucian religious stance is not prayer, but a questioning attitude that seeks to realize the Mandate of Heaven. Mou (1974, 96) contends that *if* the subjective and objective sides of reality are interrelated through moral practice and effort, then and only then will the true heart of Confucian religion become clear as a profound spirituality.

Humanity as an abstraction or static essence is not viewed as a final creation even in the lives and texts of the sages. Rather, the process, the how, the method of becoming human is the real informing characteristic of Mou's understanding of authentic Confucian religion. The process has no limits and is therefore called a transcendent one. Mou likens the whole effort to that of the bodhisattva's vow—the process is unending in its scope and completely moral in its intention. Mou counters the argument here that this is an entirely too optimistic view of human nature by saying that this is the wrong question to ask. The question is not whether the human personality is completely good from the beginning because the real Confucian viewpoint is concerned with how to deal creatively with what is at hand and not just to worry about what is there to begin with. The Confucian focus is on the results and how the person finally relates himself or herself to a common world (Mou 1974, 98).

MOU'S CRITIQUE OF CHU HSI

It is now useful to review how Mou applies his understanding of Mencian Confucianism as a critique of Chu Hsi as the major representative of the key, if distorted, "mainline" of the post-Sung tradition. This critique amply demonstrates Mou's desire to be a reformer of the Confucian way. Given the fact that Chu Hsi is certainly the major Confucian thinker of the last 700 years, any modern Confucian must come to terms with Chu Hsi's massive legacy, both in terms of Chu's own thought and its impact on generations of Confucians—many of whom were also critics of Chu's thought. I have provided my own interpretation of Chu's notion of transcendence in the preceding chapter as background for Mou's analysis.

One feature of Mou's religious interpretation of Confucianism is the result it has had for his historical studies of various members of the Confucian tradition. Mou's most surprising conclusion concerns the place of Chu Hsi in the history of Confucian thought (1983, 400–01). Far from accepting Chu Hsi as the paradigmatic Neo-Confucianism thinker, Mou asserts that Chu Hsi does not represent the mainline branch of orthodox Mencian Confucianism at all, but rather has an overtly intellectual approach that verges on becoming distinctly non-Confucian in some of its fundamental assumptions. Mou links Chu Hsi to Hsün Tzu, that brilliant though aberrant late Chou Confucian.

Mou (1968–69, 1:49) begins his critique of Chu Hsi by presenting what he takes to be the three seminal schools of Sung Neo-Confucianism. The true mainline of Sung Confucianism is represented by Ch'eng Ming-tao and Hu Wu-feng as the authentic followers of Mencian orthodoxy. Both of these thinkers correctly stress the holistic, active and creative functions of reason that unifies the normative or formal side of reality with the dynamic side of Confucian cosmology, all of which implicitly demands a theory of *ch'i* or matter-energy (Mou 1968–69, 1:44–46).

The second Sung school is that of Ch'eng I and Chu Hsi. This school really belongs to the tradition of the *Ta-hsüeh*, which Mou (1968–69, 1:45, 54–55) feels is separate from the Mencian mainline and in fact has important affinities to Hsün Tzu. It will be remembered that the *Ta-hsüeh* was conspicuous by its absence in Mou's earlier reflections on the uniqueness of Chinese philosophy and the religious nature of Confucianism in particular. The third school is that of Lu Chiu-yüan (and Wang Yang-ming) which, while being very close to Ch'eng Ming-tao's position, is sufficiently distinct in its unique emphasis on the identification of the mind with active reason to establish a third school of Sung Neo-Confucianism. However, Mou (1968–69, 1:48) concedes that Lu's intent is basically the same as Ch'eng Ming-tao's and therefore is another representative of the Mencian position.

Mou (1968–69, 1:49) then contrasts the positions of the three schools, exposing a vertical or transcendent system of philosophy contrasted with a horizontal or mundane one. The vertical system, as its name would imply, includes those Mencian elements of self-transcendence Mou believes are crucial for any holistic understanding of Neo-Confucianism as a religious tradition. This vertical system seeks to unify the subjective-objective realms—the normative and concrete are fused with the moral and subjective sides of human life, all the time emphasizing the creativity of the mind. The horizontal system, which is what Mou thinks Chu Hsi has developed, flattens out the world, as it were, and denies the creative and transcending aspects of the mind that should be essential for any Confucian thinker. What we have in Chu Hsi is a naturalism with a strongly rationalistic flavor.

For Mou, Chu Hsi makes two major errors in framing his system. The first is that he is so taken with epistemological questions that he confuses them for the ethical problems that should underlie all reflection in the Confucian tradition. Having muddied the waters of Confucian moral metaphysics, Chu Hsi mistakenly tries to base the intuition of the transcendental possibilities of creativity on empirical grounds, and hence develops a heteronomous ethical system instead of an autonomous ethical system as would be proper for a Confucian thinker (Mou 1968–69, 1:50–51). What Chu Hsi ends up with is an overly intellectual or technically rational philosophy that misses the living immediacy of the process of deepened intersubjectivity that should inform any distinctively Confucian philosophy.

Mou claims that Chu Hsi's horizontal system splits the unity of being that is fundamental to the Confucian tao. Being, change or activity imply each other in Confucianism and are not to be understood in mutual isolation, however slight the initial separation might seem. For Chu Hsi principle becomes merely subsistent and is separate from unified, creative reason (Mou 1968–69, 1:57–59). Invoking Heidegger at this point, Mou says that real (Mencian) Confucianism is a kind of vectored intending, a directional and meaning-oriented stance of being in the world, not a passive agency waiting to react to things that manifest themselves for an instrumental intellect (1968–69, 1:59). Chu Hsi's system essentializes the creative act of the process of *jen* and therefore "lags" behind the process. By dwelling on cognitive issues too much Chu Hsi leaves life one step behind and abandons the true meaning of the human ethical condition. Chu Hsi is thus seen as denying change or activity to what is properly transcendent and places the burden of active creativity on the phenomenal world that is below form. What we have here is merely material change and not sagely creativity and active concern for the world through the effort of achieving *jen* (Mou 1968–69, 1:68–69).

Mou argues that Chu Hsi really leans towards Hsün Tzu's theory of principle, conceiving *li* as the principle of formation of things and not the internal quest for self-determination or creative reason.[10] Mou (1968–69, 1:88–89) takes Hsün Tzu and Chu Hsi's position to be analogous to Leibniz's principle of sufficient reason. All of this intellectualized formalism is quite alien to what Mou understands to be the true vision of early Confucianism, except of course for Hsün Tzu. We have the very odd situation in the post-Chu Hsi world of an implicit Hsün-tzuean philosopher giving his unorthodox interpretation as if it were the correct Mencian concept of *pen-hsin* or fundamental mind. Thus Hsün Tzu has his final revenge on Mencius even though Mencius was declared the winner of their struggle by the very thinker, Chu Hsi, who betrays the Mencian tradition (Mou 1968–69, 1:100).[11]

In the third volume of *Mind and Nature*, which is devoted to a brilliant textual critique of Chu Hsi, Mou (1968–69, 3:243) hammers away at his main contention: Chu Hsi really does not have a Mencian theory of the morally transcendent mind at all, but merely one that relies on the cognitive powers of the natural mind. After defining Chu Hsi's usages in the crucial "Treatise on Humanity" (*Jen-shuo*), Mou (1968–69, 3:245ff.) goes on to prove that whereas Chu Hsi may use language similar to the Mencian mainline, he is promoting a whole new architectonic of meaning. Mou (1968–69, 3:277) asserts that *jen* is a static principle that Chu takes to be an abstraction and not a mode of creative being. Mou further (1968–69, 3:277) argues that Chu Hsi was, by implication, an epistemologist and not a moral metaphysician in the orthodox sense of Ch'eng Ming-tao and Hu Wu-feng. After using English to precisely define what he takes to be sound Confucian doctrine, he points out that Chu Hsi had an external view of reality that effectively blocked him from the ontological depths of intersubjectivity based on moral decision (1968–69, 3:279).

All kinds of evils spring from Chu Hsi's initial errors. Mou shows that Chu Hsi has a passive concept of knowledge and consciousness, befitting his reliance on the external world for the sources of his values (1968–69, 3:322, 352). The objective viewpoint is ontologically prior for Chu Hsi while the subjective mode is needlessly subjectivistic for him. Of course this passive mode of valuation makes for a definition of the Supreme Ultimate (*t'ai-chi*) which lacks any reference to active or creative reason. While this is not the end of Mou's critique of Chu Hsi, it suffices to show how his more general principles of interpretation can be applied to one important figure within the NeoConfucian tradition with rather surprising results.

Nor does Mou restrict his critique to just Neo-Confucian philosophers allied to Chu Hsi. In *Mind and Nature* and in three more recent books, *Intellectual Intuition and Chinese Philosophy, Phenomena and Thing-In Itself* and *Buddha Nature and Prajna*, he relates what he says about Chu Hsi to an ongoing comparison with certain major Western and Chinese Buddhist thinkers. Most important to Mou in the West are Kant, Heidegger and Husserl. Kant, for instance, goes wrong for just the same problems that plague Chu Hsi. Kant fixed his gaze too strictly on the "externality" of space and time, while the true Confucian, through the power of intellectual intuition or imagination, fixes his or her attention on something that is without purely spatial or temporal correlates, yet stands behind and supports these basic dimensions of human life. This intuition and its content can only be understood as the moral, creative mind that is the true nature of all human beings.

We have now come full circle. Mou's own position allows him to define religion and philosophy in such a way as to be able to not only deal with questions emerging from the Confucian tradition but with related questions embedded in any cultural system. The creative moral mind is not limited by the customs or habits of one culture but spreads itself over the whole range of human discourse. It is universal and yet never static, an ongoing process of deepened intersubjectivity through an intentional effort at self-definition and realization.

INTO A RELATIONAL WORLD OF SOCIAL CONCERN

Tu Wei-ming dedicates his study of the *Chung-yung* to Mou Tsung-san, acknowledging Mou as his teacher and as a guiding light of the New Confucian revival. Tu clearly recognizes the importance of Mou's contribution to modern Confucian thought. Most specifically, Tu notes that Mou has been instrumental in reformulating and commending what they both label in English, moral metaphysics. No doubt Tu would want to argue that this is Mou's most significant contribution to making the Confucian Way available to the modern global philosophic community. What Mou has done is to mount a defense of Confucian systematic philosophic and religious discourse in response to the analytic, epistemological and hermeneutic claims so characteristic of modern Western thought. Mou himself has repeatedly noted that it is just in the areas of philosophic analysis, epistemological precision and hermeneutic insight that the Confucian tradition seems lacking when compared to post-Enlightenment European philosophy. Mou accepts that this is the case when one applies Western criteria to Confucian thought. Furthermore, Mou believes that this criticism is partially justified, especially in the modern period. But Mou argues strongly that Confucianism has internal resources to provide a sophisticated and modern analytic, epistemological and hermeneutic reformulation of the Confucian Way. Stimulated by modern and contemporary European and North American philosophy, Mou seeks to frame just such a vigorous exposition of Confucian truth.

Tu Wei-ming deeply appreciates Mou Tsung-san's spirited defense of the Confucian Way as expressing something of permanent worth for all humanity. His own work, in terms of the Confucian metasystem, is predicated on Mou's achievement (with typically generous appreciation of the other New Confucians as well). But there is perhaps one problem with Mou's thought that Tu's own work corrects, or even better, supplements in a most traditional way. Even when we recognize the worth of Mou's philosophic project, some scholars have noted a curious lacuna in this most impressive edifice. The problem is this. Almost all previous reformers of the Confucian Way have focused not only on metasystematic questions of philosophic and spiritual analysis and practice but also on the social conditions necessary for the Confucian Way to flourish in their time and place. As almost everyone has noted about the cumulative Confucian tradition, it always embodies a social ethics and profound social critique aimed at reforming society in order to allow for decent human life. While no one doubts the passionate nature of Mou's defense of the Confucian

Way, he seems never quite to address the perennial Confucian concern for the proper and humane ordering of human society.

Of course, there are practical reasons for Mou Tsung-san's lack of sustained reflection on the reformation of society. Given the collapse of the Chinese empire in 1911, the disastrous interludes of early civil war, the tragedy of the Japanese invasion and the imposition of Communist rule in most of China, it is hard to see what purchase any Confucian of his generation could have made on the political scene.[12] But with a few notable exceptions such as Hsiung Shih-li and Liang Shu-ming, most of Mou's generation sought to distance themselves conceptually and practically from what they rightly saw as the last sorry gasp of a discredited state ideology—the disturbing spectacle of Confucian China as represented by the moribund Ch'ing state and the terrible and tragic-comic machinations of various "Confucian" warlords. Of course Mou agrees with a great deal of this specific assessment of the end of imperial Confucianism. No one can be more harsh on the failure of the decadent and exhausted imperial Confucianism of the Ch'ing state than Mou. And we need to remember that in terms of his own life, Mou was forced to flee to Hong Kong, a British colony, in order to survive with integrity as a Confucian scholar. It is a mark of his commitment to the Confucian Way that he did not become simply a reformer of the Taoist tradition of exile and withdrawal during those years! In the Hong Kong situation I rather suspect that he realized the futility of preaching reformed Confucianism to Her Majesty's civil service.

I do not want to give the impression that Mou Tsung-san was not concerned with the reform of Chinese society. We must remember that Mou was one of the signatories of the famous 1957 "A Manifesto for a Re-appraisal of Sinology and Reconstruction of Chinese Culture" along with Carsun Chang, T'ang Chün-i and Hsü Fu-kuan (Chang 1962, 455–83). Further, Mou and his colleagues devised a most Confucian undertaking in Hong Kong; they founded a college, New Asia College, now a constituent part of the Chinese University of Hong Kong, stands as a monument to the Confucian concern for learning in service to society that has always been a hallmark of Confucian social ethics. While it may be true that Mou has not devoted himself to a detailed reconstruction of the social basis for a modern Confucian society, he has certainly contributed to institutions that will help the coming generations carry out just this task. And in fact, the work of Tu Wei-ming, in many regards, marks just such a modern Confucian commitment to the formulation of Confucian social ethics. Nowhere is this more conspicuous in Tu's thought than in his reflections on fiduciary community as the basis for civilized human society.

Mou Tsung-san has recognized the need to revise, reformulate and reform the entire range of the Confucian tradition. He has also embraced a particular personal obligation in the process of reform: he has sought the systematic intellectual and analytic reform of the tradition. Nowhere has Mou ever claimed to be a sage or even a *chün-tzu*, a worthy person. What he has claimed is to be a committed Confucian seeking to get the Way for himself and his generation and to pass on an adequately formulated Confucian philosophy that can become the basis for an adequate social practice. That he has not personally devoted himself to this second task is hardly something that deserves harsh condemnation. We all labor in the vineyard of the Lord in our own ways. Tu Wei-ming has, to borrow an image for the irenic side of the classical Christian humanist tradition, stood upon the shoulders of a giant in order to continue the process of reform in the Confucian tradition.

As we shall see in our explorations of Hartshorne's process theology in chapter 5, one of the many perennial problems of religious discourse in the West has been how to balance the claims of divine transcendence and immanence. This is also one of the areas of ongoing debate for Christians and Confucians. Tu Wei-ming (1989a), himself profoundly influenced by Mou's analysis, is quite clear about this matter in his discussion of fiduciary community as a crucial aspect of Confucian moral metaphysics. It is also a concern of Mou's and he expresses it most cogently through an observation about Christian discipleship and Confucian sagehood. Mou notes that the best a Christian can do is to be a disciple of Christ; no follower of Jesus can properly make the claim to be another Christ or equal to Christ. But a Confucian can certainly seek to emulate the Confucian tao, to become a sage—although Mou is quite careful, as is Tu, to point out just how difficult the Confucian path is in both theory and practice. Mou's hypothesis is not just the contrast of Christian pessimism and Confucian meliorism, it touches on profoundly differing visions of transcendence and immanence.

I should be careful to indicate that I believe that both Mou and Tu have accurately read and understood what has been the mainline classical Christian tradition. There is very little doubt that Christians, along with Jews and Muslims, have been staunch defenders of the singular transcendence of God's divine nature. Anything less would seem to mock the religious experience of all the people of the book as the Islamic tradition expresses the interrelationships of Jews, Christians and Muslims. But there have always been nagging doubts about the theological formulation of these notions of transcendence. It is important to pause and consider just where the problem lies. It does not really reside in the notion of transcendence per se—at least this does not seem to be the case because Mou himself defends a Confucian sense of religious transcendence. Rather, the problem lies in what we make theologically and philosophically of the religious notion of transcendence.

Mou and Tu agree that the sharpest formulation of the transcendence question comes from the people of the book because the root religious metaphors of all the great Semitic traditions are developed from a sense of awe of the divine reality. This makes the question of transcendence a profound one for them. It also generates a feeling of separation, of a gulf between the cosmos and creator. The deep structure of this kind of discourse demands a certain kind of rhetoric, which gives these traditions their bite through doctrines of creation *ex nihilo*. Then there is always the question of how to understand these religious insights in terms of human reason, the proper function of theological exploration. Here things become much more problematic, at least in modern Western thought and most specifically in process theology.

Many early Confucian-Christian dialogues came to grief on the issue of the nature of divine transcendence. One can see this most dramatically, for instance, in the pioneering works of the great Matteo Ricci (1985). It was almost impossible for premodern Christian theologians to make any sense of all kinds of characteristic Confucian claims. For instance, most early missionary scholars had a great deal of trouble grasping what the Neo-Confucian masters meant by *li, t'ai-chi* or *ch'i*. And they all came up short when confronted with the passage in the *Chung-yung* where it is suggested that heaven, earth and humanity form a creative trinity. From the perspective of process theology, the theologies of the early missionaries did not allow them to enter into a fruitful dialogue with their Confucian friends. The last point should be stressed. Many of these early missionaries considered Confucians their friends, even if they could not appreciate Confucian religiosity.

CHUNG-YUNG AND MUTUALITY

On the other side of the debate, Tu Wei-ming (1989a) puts his finger on the problem that so many Confucians have had with the classical Christian notion of God. He first indicates that the *Chung-yung* is often difficult for a Western audience because of its "organismic" vision.

> The first chapter of the *Chung-yung* actually expounds the locus of all its major concerns: the human way. Originated in Heaven and rooted in the nature of every person, the human way is thought to have both metaphysical and psychological significance. (Tu 1989a, 9)

While the language is that of Confucian discourse, the organic vision of the *Chung-yung* makes quite a bit of sense for process theology as an organic Western cosmology. The *Chung-yung* affirms the essential unity of Heaven and humanity, which could be paraphrased as the God-world polarity as we shall see in the case of Charles Hartshorne. In this form of argument, with its special focus on the *Chung-yung*, Tu follows the spirit of Mou's reflections on similar matters as we have seen above.

Beyond the unity of Heaven and humanity, the *Chung-yung*, according to Tu (1989a, 9), also teaches that it is through self-realization "that Heaven's true intentions are manifested," thus affirming another ancient Chinese belief that "man can make the Way great," but that "the Way cannot make man great." While Tu wants to affirm the mutuality of Heaven and human nature, he also sounds the characteristic Confucian note of self-realization as essential in the spiritual quest of humanity. We must look to ourselves and not depend on some infusion of external grace to perfect our natures even though we can clearly recognize the unity of our natures with the wider Way of Heaven and Earth. As Tu (1989a, 10) notes, "professing the unity of man and Heaven, *Chung-yung* neither denies nor slights a transcendent reality."

However, the essential point that Tu wants to make is that the mutuality of Heaven and humanity lies at the heart of the teaching of this early Confucian classic. He also believes that this teaching is quite different from the Jewish and Christian traditions and no doubt he is correct as far as most of the classical Christian tradition goes. As Charles Hartshorne (1983; 1984b) has argued at such great length, the classical tradition has been increasingly challenged over the last few centuries in precisely the area that Tu finds problematic. For instance, Tu, who is a sympathetic observer of contemporary Christian thought, points out that in the Christian tradition "it is vitally important to recognize the ontological gap between Heaven and man" (1989a, 9). Yet Hartshorne, while agreeing that you can find a multitude of Christian theologians proclaiming the glories of this mysterious gap, argues that this is really a theological mistake, and one that Christian theology is now gradually beginning to replace with better doctrine.

Therefore, in contradistinction to the burden of the classical tradition of the notion of divine transcendence, at least one school of contemporary Christian theology does not recognize any "ontological" or metaphysical gap between humanity and God. There is surely a necessary distinction between the divine reality and humanity, but it is not the classical ontological gap between creator and creation. This is a point of potential convergence for the dialogue between process theology and the New Confucianism. Such an organic vision of the cosmos has profound implications for Confucian-Christian dialogue both on classical theological concerns and also a modern sensibility for social ethics appropriate to the modern world.

Tu Wei-ming further points out:

> To say that man, by self-effort, without a leap of faith, can become one with the Creator is novel, if not, blasphemous, in the Judeo-Christian framework. It is true that one can emphasize the divine nature inherent in each human being, as differentiated from placing more weight on the notion of original sin, but it remains extremely difficult to entertain the idea that self-knowledge is both the necessary and sufficient reason for knowing the Christian God. (1989a, 9)

Yet here, too, Hartshorne and other process theologians affirm a great deal of what Tu claims for the *Chung-yung*. Creativity is not merely the prerogative of the divine reality. God has created a universe of actual entities that, in their finite fashion, also increase the universe by one, adding their measure of creative advance and providing a world for God's redemptive activity (called the consequent nature of God by Whitehead). Although there needs to be a great deal of mutual clarification at this point, a process theologian affirms what we can know of God is always mediated by human nature and culture, properly interpreted as including a transcendent pole.

Therefore the doctrine of dual transcendence allows for more fruitful and comprehending discussion between Confucians and Christians than was possible using the classical notion of deity and human nature found in the classical Christian tradition and its modern variations.[13] However, I would not want to make the much stronger and different claim that it is the only theological option for promoting Confucian-Christian dialogue. Paul Knitter (1985), Alan Race (1983), David Lochhead (1988) and Carl Braaten (1992) have pointed out there are a number of viable models of fruitful dialogue being developed today in Orthodox, Roman Catholic, Lutheran, Anglican and Reformed circles.

As noted in the previous section on the proper interpretation of the religious nature of the Confucian tradition, Mou Tsung-san (1974; 1984) finds the distinctive Confucian form of 'objectivity' in the *Chung-yung*. The key term in the *Chung-yung* for this objective nature is *ch'eng* as self-realization or actualization. Mou believes that what is recognized in the Confucian tradition as objectivity is the total interdependence of nature, and therefore that the objectivity of the cosmos becomes manifest through human effort in the world. Mou (1974, 44–45) quotes Hsün Tzu, certainly not considered a mainline Confucian by him, to the effect that even evil cannot destroy the good when the profound person acts in harmony with proper destiny. What is evil, in Mou's eyes, is a false sense of "materialization," the end of creativity, the cessation of the creative advance into evermore complex forms of self realization and actualization.

Along with the concept of *ch'eng* as expressed in the *Chung-yung*, Mou (1974, 64ff.) introduces what he thinks is one of the most important symbolic terms in the Confucian tradition, the concept of *hsin*, or the mind-heart. For Mou, the mind-heart is creative reason as the moral mind, the capacity to transform self and relate in a meaningful and humane way to others. The essence of being human is hence the creation of new values.

The discussion of the moral mind leads Mou into his interpretation of the place of mind-and-heart in the philosophy of Mencius. He argues that the Mencian line of reasoning about the mind posits a concept of human nature that implies the real subjectivity of human nature that in turn relies on objectivity for part, though not all, of its content. For Mencius, the mind becomes active reason, the capacity to unite the immanent and transcendent aspects of reality. Mou (1974, 71) asserts that the true self can only be understood in terms of the effort that it makes to realize or actualize the lure for perfection that it finds immanent in itself as it seeks to transcend whatever present state of perfection it might be tempted to materialize, to make unchanging and dead. Thus the meaning of reality is what the mind intends to be its ever creative goal for perfection, and not some lifeless logical type that can never be increased or modified.

According to Mou, this moral mind is more than a mere subjective ethical agent relying on individual whim. It is the human dimension of creative possibility that seeks to relate self in community to the rest of the world. Value and truth are functions of the creative mind that orders the world in creative unity, the goal of fiduciary community as discussed in the *Chung-yung*. It is to this vision of a fiduciary community in the *Chung-yung*, which Tu Wei-ming shares with Mou, to which we now turn.

In Tu Wei-ming's concept of fiduciary community we find yet another possible point of contact for Confucians and Christians. In his monograph on the *Chung-yung*, Tu (1989a) is at pains to try to explain what Confucian fiduciary community is *not* prior to providing the proper definition. Tu thinks that this is necessary because of the misuse of Confucian symbols for authoritarian purposes throughout the long history of imperial China. All too often, he asserts, Confucian symbols such as filial piety were used to mask the aims of an authoritarian government. This need not be the deployment of these symbols in the modern period. As Tu puts it, "indeed, the Confucian concept of filial piety is only marginally connected with political control. It was not conceived as a basis for exercising autocratic powers" (Tu 1989a, 41).

The real axiological point of filial piety, and by extension the other Confucian social virtues, Tu (1989a, 41) asserts, lies in a recognition of the need for a "concern for social solidarity." The Confucian symbol system makes use of a vital biological bond to indicate the profound social nature of reality. We are not individuals in an atomistic sense at all, but are rather intersubjective creatures who create and are co-created by our relational environment. Tu feels that he must stress this point in order to fully explain the "primordial content" of the Confucian language of family ties. As he points out, the truly filial Confucian child is not necessarily a totally obedient child. Filial piety is an appeal to an ideal state of social relationships and not always a celebration of an imperfect status quo.

Beyond trying to explicate filial piety as a root metaphor for Confucian social solidarity and the foundation of philosophic axiology, Tu Wei-ming also attempts a reformulation of other key Confucian social relationships and virtues in his discussion of fiduciary community. He makes this ethical move by first showing how this reformed Confucian moral code, the *li* as ritual, rites, good custom, decorum, good form or even natural law, is interposed between *jen* as humanity and *i* as fitness or appropriateness. As Tu puts it, "*i* mediates between the universal principle of humanity and the particular situations in which the principle of humanity and the particular situations in which the principle is concretely manifested" (Tu 1989a, 52). In terms of concrete social ethics, there is, for Tu, the "problem of structure" in terms of just what common principles, social bonds or virtues need to be practiced in order for humanity to be properly manifested.

Tu continues by pointing out that after the *Chung-yung* discussed the ruler's role in political leadership (which we have already noted above), the text turns its attention to the five universal ways (*ta-tao*), the three universal virtues (*ta-te*) and the nine principles (*ching*) of government. The five universal relations are the famous five Confucian social bonds, namely the relationship of ruler and minister, father and son, husband and wife, elder and younger brother and friend to friend. Tu notes "although they are not meant to be comprehensive, they do represent, in the eyes of the Confucian at least, basic human relations" (1989a, 54–55). He further notes that each one of these relationships is thematized by one of the key Confucian moral principles of *ch'in* as affection, *i* as righteousness, *pieh* as separate functions, *hsü* as order and *hsin* as faithfulness.

It may not be farfetched to suggest that the five moral principles, as integral parts of Confucian ethical education, are intended to evolve a fiduciary community through five basic forms of human communication. A fiduciary community so evolved is a society of mutual trust instead of a mere aggregate of individuals. (1989a, 56)

In order to make manifest these moral principles, the true Confucian must practice the three universal virtues of wisdom, humanity and courage. Tu goes on to point out that it is *jen* that reigns supreme as the virtue of virtues in the Confucian ordering of the priority of virtues. All the principles, virtues and decent forms of social governance "can all be seen as a progressive articulation of the concept of humanity (*jen*)" (1989a, 57).

Continuing the argument for Confucian moral metaphysics as fiduciary community, Tu demonstrates how, since politics is a form of moral rectification, government "can be taken as an extension of moral education" (1989a, 58). Hence Tu closes the traditional circle of outer kingliness and inner sageliness through moral education for the creation of a Confucian fiduciary community. Tu then proceeds to show how moral suasion is the true way of Confucian governance as it relates to the role of authority in society. All social relationships, even the complicated ones of universal governance "are based on a holistic vision of human relationship" (1989a, 66). The root metaphor of organic familial solidarity eventuates in government and society as fiduciary community.

Tu Wei-ming (1989a, 48) interprets the ideal of social solidarity in the following fashion. "Society so conceived is not an adversary system consisting of pressure groups but a fiduciary community based on mutual trust." One of the main aims of such a society is to establish persuasion as a mode of social organization. "The goal of politics is not only to attain law and order in a society but also to establish a fiduciary community through moral persuasion" (Tu 1989a, 48). Tu continues his analysis of community in the *Chung-yung* by showing how these ideals are to be accomplished through a process of education and proper ritual action. In this fashion he shows how his interpretation of fiduciary community is based on the cumulative Confucian tradition.

It is clear that Tu Wei-ming's interpretation of fiduciary community has a great deal in common with Whitehead's (1933, 31) vision of a civilized society in the *Adventures of Ideas*. Certainly the specific virtues are different and the cultures vastly diverse, but there is a commonality in the dream of the victory of persuasion over force that infuses both visions. Here, too, we can find a ground for dialogue grounded in the divine-human reciprocity emphasized by

Hartshorne's doctrine of dual transcendence and a commitment to fiduciary community. Both Confucians and process theologians hold out a qualified hope for human excellence and morality.

In fact, it is in and through attempting to realize a global fiduciary community even in the midst of cultural diversity that dialogue is possible and appealing. Many people have noticed how similar the Confucian and Christian concerns for the world and society are. Mou Tsung-san, for instance, has repeatedly pointed out that the Confucian profound person has a deep concern for the world and all its creatures. He feels that classical Christianity has, perhaps, been too eager to flee the world for a better hope of heaven. However accurate this impression is of much of classical Christian thought, there has always been the orthodox Christian insistence that this is God's good world. Christians may not have always loved all the aspects of the world, but a sound sense of biblical realism has forced them to accept it and try to transform it.

One important recent restatement of this Christian concern for cosmic social solidarity has been made by George Birch and John Cobb, Jr. (1981) in *The Liberation of Life*. Based on process philosophy and theology, Birch and Cobb offer a vision of creation from the humble life of a cell to the liberation of human life and the creation of a just, participatory and sustainable global society. Father Thomas Berry (1988), from a Roman Catholic perspective, has also paid eloquent testimony to the growing Christian awareness of global ecology as a key topic of Christian theology in terms of human-cosmic interdependence. I think that the New Confucians might feel at home with this new organic Christian vision of our social world shared by a growing number of theologians. A sense of moral concern is fused with the recognition of the ultimately relational quality of existence. Coupled with an emphasis on cosmic, social and personal creativity, Birch, Cobb and Berry would, I think, equally appreciate the Confucian hope for fiduciary community, *an* analogue for the Christian symbol of the Kingdom of God. As faith traditions and communities deeply concerned with social ethics, there is much room for future discussion between Confucians and Christians. It is to this discussion with Charles Hartshorne that we now turn.

5

Process Theology and Dual Transcendence

THE QUESTION OF TRANSCENDENCE AND IMMANENCE

The next two chapters return to some theological questions broached in chapters 1 and 2. They seek to engage Confucian and Christian responses to the issues of transcendence and immanence as well as multiple religious participation. I do not pretend to speak for the whole of the Christian theological community or even my particular branch of the Western theological and philosophic lineage in any definitive way. This disclaimer is not given out of scholarly modesty. Rather, I wish to practice what I take to be a real fact, the irreducibly pluralistic, specific and historical dimension of all religious traditions and forms of philosophic inquiry. For any major religious tradition there are many lineages, many histories, many theologies and philosophies. From inside the pluralist vision of theology, the sooner that we learn to do theology honoring this pluralism, the better off we will be in terms of the emerging world of global thought. While this is not the only possible Christian response to the issues raised here, I believe that it conforms to the reality of the situation. Frankly, until and unless Christian theology takes religious pluralism into account, it risks forfeiting any claim to speak to a wider world. Of course, one of my other assumptions is that Christian theologians do want to speak to a wider world, a world including the other great communities of faith.

The discussion that follows chronicles the beginning of a serious theological encounter between Confucians and Christians. In the give and take about the notions of transcendence and immanence we can see the outlines emerging of some of the main themes of Confucian-Christian dialogue. From the Christian perspective, it is an exploration of the question of the nature of God. To some Christians such a point of departure is too theologically abstract. Where, they will ask, is the Christian confessions of Jesus as the Christ? Where is the scandal of the cross and the victory of the resurrection? In terms of a strictly confessional approach, these questions have merit. However, when Confucians and Christians begin dialogue with such radically different understandings of reality and history, the prior question of God or divine things cannot be avoided. For the Christian to confess the second person of the trinity makes little sense until the nature of God *a se* has been explained and examined in comparative analysis. Incarnation without a context is meaningless, especially to a tradition such as Confucianism, a tradition constituted as an axiological *ars contextualis* without any clear definition of divine things as deity. The method chosen to map the way between these two different religious is process theology.

The key question raised by modern Confucian-Christian dialogue, in terms of fundamental theology, is the relationship of divine transcendence and immanence. Just as during the era of Ricci, Leibniz and the first Jesuit sinologists, it is often stoutly maintained that Christianity is a religion of divine transcendence whereas Confucianism is a tradition of divine immanence—if there is anything divine about the Confucian tradition at all. But as with so many religious questions, things are not always quite as they seem in the first instance. For example, there is hardly any concept so immanent in its implications as the incarnation of Christ; nor does the Confucian reverence of High Heaven or the Supreme Ultimate lack a profound sense of the transcendent dimension. Hence Confucians and Christians almost always query each other about the relative balance between transcendence and immanence in their traditions. This is a question drawn from the actual practice of dialogue as it concerns the essential self-understandings of divine matters for both parties.

The question of balance of transcendence and immanence, although it is a technical issue in academic theology, points directly to the foundational question of all theology, what do we mean by God? Of course, the divine referent is defined differently in each religion, so much so that some traditions, such as Buddhism and some forms of Taoism, would not accept the notion of God as defining what they take to be the essence of the really real. There is always a root metaphor for the divine reality at the heart of any religious tradition. It may or may not bear much resemblance to West Asian notions of God, but it does serve as the living heart of the community of faith. Almost instinctively Confucians and Christians begin their discussion of the nature of the divine reality by asking the question of the relationship of divine transcendence and immanence.

The search for some kind of description adequate for an understanding of the question of transcendence and immanence is complicated by the fact that the debate relies on technical language defined and refined by centuries of Western theological debate. The one real point of agreement at the earliest stages of Confucian-Christian dialogue is that Christian theological language concerning divine transcendence and immanence does not always connect in helpful ways to the description and comprehension of what the Confucian are talking about when they refer to the religious elements of the tao. Hence this is a question complicated by the process of dialogue as conversation seeking conceptual cross-cultural clarity, of trying to get clear about what the two sides are actually talking about when they raise the question of transcendence and immanence.

One of the benefits of dialogue will be, over a period of time, the generation of a technical language in English more supple in dealing with the religious experience of Confucian East Asia. As we have noted before, it is still difficult to define the precise religious dimensions of the Confucian tradition using Western academic categories. In some respects, Western intellectuals are in a somewhat analogous position to the Chinese intellectuals of the Wei-Chin (220–420 C.E.) period. The Wei-Chin Chinese intellectuals were forced to come to grips with the arrival of South Asian and Central Asian Buddhism in China. It is now clear that the Chinese were not only able to understand the Buddhist dharma but were also able to creatively transform it into distinctive Chinese forms of Buddhism, replete with their own academic way of describing reality or emptiness. Much the same thing will, no doubt, happen as Confucian-Christian dialogue continues its negotiations of language, cosmology and religion. Confucians will learn how to define themselves in Western languages and Western Christian scholars will learn how to understand what their Confucian colleagues are trying to tell them about the rich symbolism of Asian language and religious life. At the present moment we are just at the beginning of the process of explaining Confucianism and Christianity to each other.

In the beginning of the dialogue process, how do we begin to converse with conceptual tools supple enough to encourage preliminary communication? We must begin somewhere, and I suggest that process philosophy and theology provide as good a set of tools as we are likely to find in the kit of Western intellectual life. As we will discover, the modern process tradition, beginning with A. N. Whitehead and continued by his students, has been keenly interested in comparative philosophy and theology. Given the openness of process thought to non-Western forms of thought, we can employ its concepts as bridging forms to reach out to Confucian colleagues. In this regard, process thought can play a role in Western thought much like the Neo-Taoism of the Wei-Chin period. Ultimately the Confucians, Taoists and Buddhists realized that they could not go on using the Neo-Taoist vocabulary of thinkers such as Wang Pi (226–249) and Kuo Hsiang (d. 312), but Wang and Kuo did provide a place to begin the conversation. Whitehead and Charles Hartshorne have already begun to play this role in the new Confucian-Christian dialogue. The shade of Leibniz must be smiling as Confucians and Christians again seriously try to understand each other.

As Whitehead once noted, the main enduring theological question is always, what do we mean by God? What we mean by God will entail the rest of the details of our religious thought, action, ritual, poetry, justice and passion. While it would be silly to say that religion is just a concept of God, there can be no religion that does not express in some fashion what it takes to be the divine ultimate even if it rejects a propositional approach to divine truth and piety. It strikes me that before we can answer this question in the context of Confucian-Christian dialogue, we must attend to the question of transcendence and immanence as this remains a key way these two traditions have begun to understand their radically alternative ways of comprehending and serving the divine ultimate.

The question of divine transcendence and immanence is also the question of how God and the world are related. While this is cast in resolutely theological language, language that derives from the Christian side of the dialogue, it is language about the ultimate meanings of human life. If God is the ultimate point of reference for Christians, then we cannot understand the world without understanding how God both transcends and resides in the world. If there is no world, then why would we mundane creatures even ask the question of relationship with the divine ultimate? The question of transcendence and immanence can, upon demand, be transposed into a secular key. The question then is, what does it mean for us to be true human beings in relationship with each other? I believe that Confucians as well as Christians give a religious answer to this question. Other secular answers can be given in terms of politics, art and personal development; but at least we should ask the question if we are at all interested in intercultural communication as well as the nature of truth. Confucians and Christians surely need to ask the question because there are few other traditions as interested in the relationship of a real divine and a real world made up of real people, seeking to be in tune with the divine reality.

OVERVIEW OF THE PROCESS TRADITION

Just as I have selected Chu Hsi, Mou Tsung-san and Tu Wei-ming for analysis from among the Confucians, I will also defend my own theological perspective as a tool for Confucian-Christian dialogue. I am convinced that every theologian operates from within a specific tradition, whether acknowledged or not, and in my case this is the process theology movement. One of the benefits of interfaith dialogue is the recognition that we are dealing with highly divergent traditions and schools within complicated cumulative religions communities of faith.[1] For instance, there is no single unified historical theological tradition called Christianity, although there is a family of churches and people who recognize each other as Christians and are so recognized by others. W. C. Smith (1981) and other historians of religion argue that there are almost as many different types of Christianities over the centuries and around the globe as there are faithful Christians. So rather than trying to present some kind of abstract or disembodied universal theological rationale, I begin my defense by framing my understanding of Confucian-Christian dialogue from within the perspective of modern process theism.

Although this is not the place for a historical review of the development of process philosophy and theology, a short historical explanation of the roots of the tradition is necessary.[2] While process theology is quite well known in North America, Europe and in some Asian circles, I have found it gratuitous to assume a global awareness of this relatively recent theological and philosophic school. After this short examination of some key features of the process movement, I will apply these insights to the emerging Confucian-Christian dialogue. The key topic selected for a more protracted examination later in this chapter is Hartshorne's doctrine of dual transcendence, offered here as a bridge between Christian and Confucian notions of the relationship of the divine reality and the world of finite creatures. The notion of dual transcendence is a way to begin to understand and question the role of divine-world relations in Confucianism and Christianity.

Process theology names a school of thinkers who find their inspiration in the work of Alfred North Whitehead (1865–1947).[3] Whitehead's work in philosophy and natural theology has been carried forward over the years since his death by a distinguished group of students and friends. Prominent among these scholars and theologians are Charles Hartshorne, Norman Pittenger, William Christian, Daniel Day Williams, Bernard Loomer, David R. Griffin, John B. Cobb, Jr., Henry James Young, David Tracy, Lewis Ford, Marjorie Hewitt Suchocki, Jorge Luis Nobo, Dorothy Emmet, A. H. Johnson and Jay McDaniel to mention just a few (and in no particular order).[4] There are other scholars, critically stimulated by Whithead's interest in the analysis of society and cosmology, who are also active in developing Whitehead's thought for intercultural discourse.

One of the most interesting examples of the intercultural use of Whitehead's mature thought is found in the work of Robert C. Neville (1978, 1980, 1982,

1987, 1991a, 1992), who has written several important studies informed by but still critical of process thought that focus on the question of understanding Buddhism, Taoism and Confucianism. Another important contributor is David Hall (1982a, 1982b, 1987), who is now seeking to elaborate a new philosophy of culture that is heavily indebted to Whitehead. Hall (1987) has also collaborated with Roger Ames in a joint study of Confucius. One of the main themes of the Hall-Ames study is that there was no early Confucian doctrine of transcendence analogous to such notions found commonly in Western philosophy and religion. Whatever notions of the Confucian Ultimate that may resemble Western transcendence are much later additions to the tradition and cannot be attributed to Confucius as the founder of the tradition. Hall and Ames agree that Neo-Taoism, Buddhism and Neo-Confucianism have notions of transcendence, but assert that these are additions to a distinctively nontranscendent classical Confucian tradition to be found in the *Analects.* Chapters 3 and 4 directly addressed the question of the Confucian understanding of transcendence by means of the examination of the thought of Chu Hsi, Mou Tsung-san and Tu Wei-ming. My conclusion is that Hall and Ames overstate their case.

While all these Western scholars, especially the theologians, have built on the work of Whitehead, none do so in a purely repetitive manner; all seek to expand and modify what they have found useful in Whitehead's work. In some cases, most specifically with Cobb, Tracy, Neville, McDaniel and Hall, their work takes into account interfaith dialogue. Cobb (1982), Neville (1982, 1987, 1991a, 1992) and Tracy (1987, 1990) have tried to write with an eye on the global nature of modern theology and philosophy in terms of engagement with Buddhist and Confucianism. However, no process scholar has yet attempted a study focused solely on the nature and prospects of Christian-Confucian dialogue, although Neville has been a participant in the new international Confucian-Christian dialogue.[5]

The interest shown by scholars such as Neville, Cobb, Tracy and Hall in interfaith dialogue is typical of the process tradition as a whole. While not all process theologians are concerned with interfaith relations in a sustained way, the whole orientation of the movement as such encourages such a research project. Whitehead, as demonstrated in all his later philosophic works (1926, 1933, 1978), was personally interested in the potential for interaction between the great religious traditions of humankind. For instance, the chapter on the need for a new reformation in Christianity in *Adventures of Ideas* (1933, 305) begins with the story of a successful and peaceful negotiation in India between the English Viceroy Lord Erwin and Gandhi. The relational, organic and pluralistic nature of Whitehead's philosophy encourages just such an interreligious approach to the study of different cultures. As David Hall (1973, 1982b, 1987) has noted in his thematization of a Whiteheadian philosophy of culture, any process thinker is committed in principle to a global intellectual vision, to the depth and breadth of what Whitehead called civilized human experience and culture. Therefore, process theologians have often been involved in interfaith dialogue, encouraged to do so both by the example of Whitehead's reflections and by their own creative elaborations of process thought.

Whitehead (1978, 8) had some awareness that his philosophy has a special affinity with certain strains of Indian and Chinese thought.

> In all philosophic theory there is an ultimate which is actual in virtue of its accidents. It is only then capable of characterization through its accidental embodiments, and apart from these accidents is devoid of actuality. In the philosophy of organism this ultimate is termed 'creativity'; and God is its primordial, non-temporal accident. In monistic philosophies, Spinoza's or absolute idealism, this ultimate is God, who is also equivalently termed 'The Absolute.' In such monistic schemes, the ultimate is illegitimately allowed a final, "eminent" reality, beyond that ascribed to any of its accidents. In this general position the philosophy of organism seems to approximate more to some strains of Indian, or Chinese, though, than to western Asiatic, or European, thought. One side makes process ultimate; the other side makes fact ultimate.

It would be fascinating to know precisely what strains of Asian thought Whitehead had in mind. We know from his biography and from various random quotes that he was interested in Buddhism, although he did not approach the study of Buddhism with any scholarly depth. Yet many Asian philosophers have found Whitehead's emphasis on the processive modalities of reality an invitation to dialogue[6] and the process movement as a whole has been well represented in the intercultural philosophic discussions of the last fifty years. John Cobb, Jr., has been the most prominent of the second generation of process theologians in this regard.

In this chapter I will demonstrate that process theology and philosophy provide a viable matrix for Confucian-Christian dialogue from the Christian side of the conversation. But process theologians must bear in mind that they have an obligation to try to explain to their Confucian and Christian colleagues the nature and structure of their approach and why it provides a way forward in interfaith dialogue. In any event, the clarification and rectification of terms us surely an honorable task for Confucians and Christians. Both Christian process thinkers and New Confucians are riding the sea in the same disturbing boat of modernity, which, in Tracy's terminology, makes fundamental theologians out of all of us because it denies any easy access to only one tradition as a warrant for faith and scholarship. Both New Confucians and process thinkers seek ways to appropriate a fiduciary commitment to their traditions and also to make use of the best modern thought. Both groups realize that such a dual commitment demands a modification of their traditional philosophic positions and a renewal of their religious faith in terms of a global vision. Neither philosophy nor religion can remain unmoved by the encounter between modernity and the impact of religious pluralism.

I should add one important caveat. Process theology is not the only viable or useful intellectual tool for undertaking interfaith dialogue. Nonetheless, as I will argue in chapter 6, I believe that process thought is a theology that deserves to be "received" in the full ecumenical sense of the term reception. There are other theologies of dialogue and religious pluralism that deserve to be received by the Christian churches as well. For instance, David Lochhead (1988) has written an important study based, in part, on the work of Karl Barth, which may surprise many. Paul Knitter (1985), in his influential *No Other Name?*, also demonstrates a keen interest in showing how dialogue relates to liberation and feminist theologies and be an ally to both of these important theological movements. George Lindbeck (1984) has written a postliberal interpretation of Christian doctrine in an ecumenical and pluralistic world that relies on modern language philosophy and linguistics. John Hick (1985, 1989) continues an examination of religious pluralism as part of his general philosophy of religion. Robert C. Neville proceeds to ramify his attempt to articulate a renewed Platonic and Christian view of religious pluralism in all his recent works. Even theologically literate sociologists such as Peter Berger (1992) have gotten into the act of analyzing religious pluralism. Christians are discovering the dialogical potential of many schools of thought, all of which is to be applauded by those of us who are pluralists. It would be ironic if a process thinker committed to pluralism argued for a monistic methodological approach to dialogue in the midst of such fecund diversity.

I am not unmindful that this embrace of pluralism and my attempt to live with modernity is not without its problems. It does not pretend to find some privileged viewpoint outside of the various contemporary systems of thought and belief, some hypothetical value-free perspective that provides a perfect comparative methodology. As Alasdair MacIntyre (*Three Rival Visions of Moral Inquiry*, 1990) has pointed out so eloquently, it is just this recognition of the radical nature of pluralism that is one of the problems of modern life. Without some common frame of reference, which is what pluralism makes so difficult to define, it becomes hard to see how we can have dialogue across cultural and religious boundaries. Pluralism, which seeks to be honest about these differences, can then easily degenerate into a relativistic indifferentism where no judgments of good or ill can be made. In responding to the challenge of relativism, MacIntyre makes a good argument for what would qualify as an adequate form of comparative philosophy in a pluralistic age. In terms of the classical Christian theological tradition, he notes that this is precisely what Aquinas did in order to create a comparative theology when he was confronted by the pluralism of the older Augustinian theology and new Aristotelian texts and sciences at the University of Paris in the twelfth and thirteenth centuries.

MacIntyre argues that any good philosophy of pluralism, that is to say, a philosophy that takes diversity seriously when confronted by it, must do three things. First, it must seek to understand the other tradition in terms of that tradition and not impose some other system or category of thought on it. This is both an ethical question of not defaming the dialogue partner as well as a mark of humane scholarship. Second, the comparative philosophy must seek to show, again using arguments from within the other tradition, what the main problems of the tradition are. Furthermore, the investigating philosopher also has the obligation to defend the other tradition in terms of the best possible arguments she can find to articulate the vision of the other tradition in its own terms. There is no room for producing anything less than the best the tradition can do to defend itself against or solve its own problems. Third, the comparative philosopher, in proposing a new vision, must express how the main problems of another tradition cannot be solved by means internal to the tradition itself. Having shown the impasse of the other tradition in its own terms, any solutions offered to the dialogue partner must be shown to arise because of the radical nature of the dialogue itself and be fitting for all truth-bearing aspects of the traditions in question. The new comparative philosophy or theology thus becomes a multilinguistic methodology for analysis and synthesis.

MacIntyre also hopes, in his case based on the model of Aquinas' achievement in the thirteenth century, that we will be able to demonstrate that the new theology or philosophy provides solutions to the problems of the other tradition both from its internal perspective and from the new vision generated from the dialogical interaction of conversation. The solutions offered have a unique twist for the dialogical partner. The other tradition must be able to recognize its previous position as expressed by the new theology and see the wisdom of the suggestion made by the dialogue partner. In MacIntyre's case, having gotten inside other modern North Atlantic ethical traditions, the renewed Thomistic theology will be able to help foster real dialogue that recognizes radical differences that exist between and among rival philosophic and theological positions. Such an adequate theology will not be able to make the differences disappear but will be able to assist in civil if sharp debate. This is as much as MacIntyre can hope for in a pluralistic age. It is not a bad hope. My hope is that process theology can provide such an expedient means for interreligious dialogue without becoming blind to the real differences between traditions.

AXIOMS OF PROCESS COSMOLOGY AND THEOLOGY

As has been previously noted, the process theology movement is a diverse one, with new subschools and interpretations emerging from the suggestive matrix of Whitehead's original cosmological vision. Notwithstanding this internal diversity, I maintain that there are a core of Whiteheadian axioms that are central to the categorial articulation of any process theology systematically related to Whitehead's philosophy. The core axioms of Whitehead's philosophy, when specified in theological language, provide a paradigm for process theology as a model for interfaith dialogue.

It is an interesting question whether there are any emerging process philosophies and theologies not systematically related to Whitehead's key axioms at least by strong direct influence if not actual emulation. Robert C. Neville is the best-known exemplar of this kind of post-Whiteheadian philosophic quest. Neville, although he would be the first to admit his debt to Whitehead and the process movement, now rejects any systematic affiliation with orthodox process theism. Neville (1974, and especially 1980, 1981, 1982, 1989, 1991a, 1991b, 1992) believes that he is developing a modern and more Platonic alternative to the Aristotelian mainline of the process movement based on his notion of creation *ex nihilo*. Neville's main displeasure with orthodox Whiteheadian process theology resides in what he takes to be an inadequate or inconsistent notion of God as creator. Neville argues that the Whiteheadian and Hartshornean concept of God (or social divine person for Hartshorne) does not do justice to the radical ontological demands of creativity in a pluralistic world or any world at all for that matter. Orthodox process thinkers may, Neville asserts, have a most adequate cosmology but lack an equally responsible ontological doctrine. Neville seeks to present just such an ontological counterpoint to process thought in his research project. We will return to Neville's critique in a later section. It is now time to return to Whitehead's axioms.

The list of the four key Whiteheadian axioms are neither totally arbitrary nor out of line with the burden of the received scholarly tradition. There are other lists that have been suggested (for instance, Hartshorne 1973, 100–03). But Whitehead thematizes these axioms over and over again in all his mature works, and as such they inform his presentation of process or organic philosophy. It must also be kept in mind that this is a minimum list that could be expanded by recourse to the work of Hartshorne (1973) or Gray (1982). It leaves in abeyance many more detailed and interpretive questions pertaining to Whitehead's work. All Whitehead scholars agree that there are many murky passages in Whitehead's often highly rhetorical and colorful prose.

Whitehead's fundamental axioms can be explained in terms of three basic principles and one hope—an expression of Whitehead's faith in the ultimate rational nature of the cosmos. As I have noted, there are other lists, but one cannot begin to understand Whitehead's mature philosophy without recourse to all of these key concepts.

THE ONTOLOGICAL PRINCIPLE

First, there is the ontological principle. This axiom states that to ask for any reason whatsoever is to ask for some definite actual entity. "The ontological principle can be summarized as: no actual entity, then no reason" (Whitehead 1978, 28). Another formulation is, "The ontological principle can be expressed as: All real togetherness is togetherness in the formal constitution of an actuality" (1978, 32). This axiom covers all that can possibly be or become in our or any world. It is the foundation for the incurably social, relational and pluralistic nature of Whitehead's cosmology. It is also one of his more contentious philosophic points. To many critics, such as Neville (1980), this hardly seems like an ontological principle at all. It can be the foundation, as Neville believes it is, of a rich cosmology. But because of its positing of the notion of actual entities as the ultimate elements of reality, it cannot express the plenitude of creation demanded by a proper secular or theistic ontology. Whitehead, however, is clear in his defense of the ontological principle as a principle of actual entities. "The ontological principle declares that every decision is referable to one or more actual entities, because in separation from actual entities there is nothing, merely nonentity—'The rest is silence' " (1978, 43). Whitehead was not very much in favor of news from nowhere, to borrow a metaphor from another school of the Anglo-American philosophic tradition.

THE PRINCIPLE OF RELATIVITY

The second axiom is the principle of relativity, often believed to be one of Whithead's more interesting philosophic notions (1978, 33). It is not, as we shall see, ~~a principle of relativism or indifferentism~~ nǫt, a charge often discussed in terms of the modern interfaith dialogue movement. Whitehead's definition of relativity is:

> That the potential for being an element in a real concrescence of many entities into one actuality, is the one general metaphysical character attaining to all entities, actual and nonactual: and that every item in its universe is involved in each concrescence. In other words, it belongs to the nature of a 'being' that it is a potential for ever 'becoming.' This is the 'principle of relativity.'

The universe for Whitehead is a becoming of one out of the many, and vice versa. It also points to the pluralistic nature of reality even as it demonstrates the relationality of the cosmos. Of course this solidarity, as exemplified by Hartshorne's notion of dual transcendence, has profound theological ramifications. There is no final disjunction of entity from entity, of creativity from created fact, of the divine reality from the mundane cosmos. Facts and values, forms and fantasies, God and the merest puff in the farthest reaches of empty space are all mutually conditioned and conditioning. In terms of actual interfaith dialogue the case can be made that what we have is an encounter of persons in dialogue. They know who they are relative to the partner; what is not relative nor indifferent is the fact that there is some kind of definite relationship.

THE PRINCIPLE OF CREATIVITY

The third axiom (1978, 31) is the principle of creativity. This is the axiom that is often cited in order to give the tradition its name as process philosophy or theology.

> 'Creativity' is the universal or universal characterizing ultimate matter of fact. It is that ultimate by which the many, which are the universe disjunctively, become the one actual occasion, which is the universe conjunctively. It lies in the nature of things that the many enter into complex unity.

This axiom points to the method by which the other two axioms find their concrete manifestations in the pluralistic world of common and uncommon experience. There are actual objects in the world and they are all related to each other, and the way they are so connected is through the creative advance into novelty that is the universal of universals, the creation of a new one out of the previous many.

Such a doctrine, for instance, differentiates Whitehead's version of pluralism from Neville's Christian doctrine of creation *ex nihilo*, which cannot be equated with creativity as the category of the ultimate for the actual entities because it is beyond cosmological specification. For Whitehead, God is the supreme exemplification of creativity and not an ontological exception to the cosmological categories that govern the finite lives of all the other creatures. For Whitehead, but not for Hartshorne, God is an actual entity in a determinate way even though profoundly different, richer and more worshipful than any other entity. Neville does not believe that such an ontologically constricted divine reality can be the creator of the heavens and earth. Neville is not alone in finding difficulties with Whitehead's notion of creativity. It is often alleged that creativity is really the divine agent of the cosmos, prior and superior to the finite God of process theism. Hence Whitehead's God, constrained by creativity as are all creatures great and small, is not a fit object of worship and not the God of wonder and awe found in the Christian scriptures.[7]

THE HOPE OF RATIONALISM

The fourth item cannot be called an axiom in Whitehead's thought in the same sense as the first three. It is the hope of rationalism, the point of faith in cosmic and religious solidarity that lies at the heart of the system. It is an intuition about the ultimate meaning of things. It is the hope that the world has a meaning, however obscure and dim it may appear to us because of human finitude, ignorance, perversity and error. As a hope for rationality it is also a point of connection with the Confucian tradition. De Bary (1991a, 137), in a study of the great Ming Neo-Confucian thinker, Wang Yang-ming, argues much the same point can be made for the whole Confucian tradition.

> He [Wang] retains a faith in the fundamental rationality of man; and for all his insistence on discovering right and wrong for oneself, it does not occur to him that there could be any essential conflict between subjective and objective morality, or that genuine introspection could lead to anything other than the affirmation of clear and common moral standards.

The same argument can be made for Chu Hsi as well. Given that this is such a clear statement of Confucian moral metaphysics, as defined by Mou Tsung-san, this faith in the rationality of the cosmos is likewise a faith in the rationality of the *t'ien-tao*, the Way of Heaven.

Whitehead (1978, 67) defines the hope for rationality:

That we fail to find in experience any elements intrinsically incapable of exhibition as examples of general theory, is the hope of rationalism. This hope is not a metaphysical premise. It is the faith that forms the motive for the pursuit of all sciences alike, including metaphysics.

Whitehead could have also added theology to metaphysics in terms of his faith in the ultimate coherence of reality given his theological position as articulated in part 5 of *Process and Reality* and in the *Adventures of Ideas*. Of all of Whitehead's core themes this rational hope alone is an intuitive appeal to the lure of truth, beauty and the good that informs the givenness of the seemingly disjunctive pluriverse of concrete facts. There are always some things in any philosophy or theology that you either see or do not see as expressing wisdom and reality.

What kind of philosophy are we talking about when we review process thought? For instance, do we discover in process thought a form of metaphysics, ontology, cosmology or axiology? It is important to remember that Whitehead called his work cosmology and was very circumspect in naming traditional metaphysical or ontological claims for his philosophy. The reason for this was that he was unsure whether human consciousness could penetrate to the depths of reality in order to uncover the real metaphysical or ontological principles that would obtain for any cosmic epoch.

But, putting aside the difficulties of language, deficiency in imaginative penetration forbids progress in any form other than that of any asymptotic approach to a scheme of principles, only definable in terms of the ideal which they should satisfy. (1978, 4)

In the introduction of *Process and Reality* (1978, xiv) he notes,

There remains the final reflection, how shallow, puny, and imperfect are efforts to sound the depths of the nature of things. In philosophic discussion, the merest hint of dogmatic certainty as to finality of statement is an exhibition of folly.

And Whitehead did not want to encourage folly in either philosophy or theology. Therefore it is something of misnomer to label process thought metaphysics if we take this to mean assertions about ultimate or final statements about reality. Perhaps the best we can hope for is a rigorous cosmology or axiology like the Neo-Confucian *ars contextualis*. Any such philosophic doctrine leaves ample room for religious commitment in terms of the specification of its doctrines. It has also been noted that Confucianism, at least, unfolds a cosmology and axiology. Here too the similarities between process thought and Confucianism are apparent.

However, from time to time, Whitehead (1978, 65–66) did speak about "metaphysical assumptions" that inform his philosophy. For instance, he argues "(i) That the actual world, in so far as it is a community of entities which are settled, actual, and already become, conditions and limits the potentiality for creativeness beyond itself." This speaks to the pluralistic and realistic side of Whitehead's thought.

> (ii) The second metaphysical assumption is that the real potentialities relative to all standpoints are coordinated as diverse determinations of one extensive continuum.... An extensive continuum is a complex of entities united by the various allied relationships of whole to part, and of overlapping so as to possess common parts, and of contact, and of other relationships derived from these primary relationships. (1978, 66)

Taken together, I have called these relationships those of form, dynamics and unification.[8] These are the terms that I use to explicate the concrescence of any creature, event or ritual action. As I have argued in chapter 3 in my discussion of Chu Hsi, I believe that we can find analogues for these three notions in Sung Neo-Confucian discourse. Form, dynamics and unification, taken as fundamental specifications of Whitehead's basic axioms, provide a heuristic set of categories to explore the conceptual side of the Confucian-Christian dialogue. I further believe that these three fundamental specifications make sense as methodological tools when applied to philosophic traditions wherein process, relationality and relativity are key thematic elements. I will argue that Whiteheadian theology as well as Neo-Confucian and New Confucian speculation are related in sharing these three elements of process, relationality and relativity—or form, dynamics and unification. I believe that it can be demonstrated that Chu Hsi's mature philosophy is governed by this triad of form, dynamics and unification as well. This is not all these traditions share, but it is a bridge for conversation between them.

Whitehead (1978, 136–37), in his discussion of Locke and Hume, frames the triadic nature of these fundamental specifications of the emergence of any creature. "These various aspects [of the elements of experience] can be summed up in the statement that *experience* involves a *becoming*, that *becoming* means that *something becomes*, and that *what becomes* involves *repetition* transformed into *novel immediacy*." Prior to this summary statement, he points out that this becoming of novel immediacy involves forms that are repeated, the dynamics of creativity and the final unification or harmony of values, such that something new has emerged in the cosmos, both for the divine reality and for the other creatures.

Two further questions need to be acknowledged. First, is this an adequate list of essential axioms when thematized in terms of form, dynamics and unification? Second, does this list remain faithful to the intent of Whitehead's thought? A completely satisfactory answer to both questions would involve us in a lengthy exegesis of Whitehead not really germane to our present task.[9] Nonetheless, our expectation is that this is sufficient to define Whiteheadian process thought as a distinctive type. The list, at least in theological circles, serves to differentiate process theology from much classical Christian theology and to suggest possible modes of conversation with the Confucian tradition. Nonetheless, there is always the chance that the list will need to be modified in terms of the future history of the process tradition as it continues in conversation with Eastern philosophies. As Whitehead noted, one of the real problems of philosophy is narrowness of vision when better, more expansive vision is possible. Still, I cannot conceive of Whitehead's philosophy without any of these key axioms. In that sense it is a minimalist list in line with Whitehead's own mature thought.

A DIALOGICAL GOD AND THE TAO OF PROCESS

As I have noted in chapters 1 and 2, the questions of transcendence and immanence were of persistent interest at the two international Confucian-Christian dialogues conducted in 1988 and 1991. If Hall and Ames (1987) are to be believed, the question of transcendence is a major concern for any Western thinker in trying to come to terms with the Confucian tradition. The relationship of the divine reality to the secular world was of interest to the New Confucians and the Christian theologians even before the two groups took it upon themselves to specify what they believed their traditions thought and taught about the transcendent dimension and its immanent manifestations. Neither the Confucians nor the Christians could appeal in a definitive fashion to the specifics of their traditions, but asked what both parties could understand in terms of the English notions of transcendence and immanence.

In terms of the question of transcendence, Hartshorne has argued at some length that his "neoclassical" concept of God, partially exemplified by the concept of dual transcendence, makes better sense of the divine reality than any other explanation of theism. For Hartshorne "neoclassical theism" designates what I have been calling the process movement as it pertains to theological categories. As Hartshorne explains it, the doctrine of dual transcendence has a number of implications for a reformulation of the classical notion of God. In the first place, it is a dialogical model for the essence of the divine reality.

> The model of creation is dialogue: X says. . . .Y responds by saying something more or less suitable, to which X in turn responds. It is a bad model of deity to liken it to those who wish to be heard but not to hear, to speak but to listen. (Hartshorne 1983, 174)

He further elucidates the notion by saying that

> The idea of dual transcendence of deity is uniquely excellent in two really distinguishable aspects, the one infinite, absolute, immutable, internal, and necessary as nothing else is, and other finite, relative, mutable, temporal, and contingent, also as nothing else is. The divine pre-eminence is not to be captured by asserting one side of these ultimate contrasts and negating the other. Rather there is a divine form of finitude, relativity, mutability, temporality, and contingency that in principle surpasses all other conceivable forms. (1983, 376)

Any Christian who takes the humanity of Jesus seriously should not be surprised by divine finitude and suffering, the very stuff of temporality as limitation. Nonetheless it is quite clear that the classical patristic debates about Christology took a decidedly different turn and tried to avoid the idea that Christ, as divine, could suffer. The notion that God could change through the contingency of suffering was felt to diminish the majesty of the divine perfection. Perfection was always to be unchanging.

As Whitehead put it in discussing the contributions of the Alexandrian and Antiochene theologians, "the theologians of Alexandria were greatly exercised over the immanence of God in the world. . . . It arises from the fact that the existents in nature are sharing in the nature of the immanent God" (1933, 166). Whitehead has the highest admiration of the theologians of Alexandria and Antioch, so much that he states that "these Christian theologians have the distinction of being the only thinkers who in a fundamental metaphysical doctrine have improved upon Plato" (1933, 214–15). The problem for the future of philosophy and theology was that these brilliant theologians limited themselves to thinking about the issue in a very special form, namely, as it relates to the doctrine of God as the second person of the Trinity. Whitehead believes that "Unfortunately, the theologians never made this advance into general metaphysics" (1933, 216). For Whitehead, the divine reality is the supreme exemplification of metaphysical principles, not an exception to them. Therefore, what could be said of Jesus as both divine and human must have a relationship to other human beings and not just as a predicate of the Christ as a divine being.

For Hartshorne, God is intimately related to the world and is not some distant, abstract, unconcerned or unmoved creator. Rather, "Divine actuality is the eminent form of creative process; and so it too involves an aspect of creaturehood, just as the creatures have aspects of creativity" (Hartshorne 1983, 314). Surely the idea of dual transcendence allows us to make sense of a great deal of the biblical witness about God, who for Jews, Christians and Muslims is not unconcerned and unmoved by what the creatures do, suffer and enjoy.[10]

Hartshorne's idea of dual transcendence draws heavily from Whitehead, although he would argue that it is not a mere repetition of Whitehead's thought. Whitehead inspired the whole process movement and yet not everyone within the tradition agrees on a proper Whiteheadian interpretation of God. In fact, this is considered one of the most problematic areas of Whitehead scholarship. The difficulty comes from the fact that Whitehead was not always as consistent as we might have liked in framing his theology. For instance, where is the quarrel between those who follow the literal text of Whitehead and affirm that God is an actual entity and those, following Hartshorne, who believe that Whitehead, in order to be coherent, must have meant that God is a society of occasions or a "social individual." A great deal of scholarly ink has been spilled over this distinction, although it is not always clear what bearing such a debate means in the world of living religion. It may well be the case that Hartshorne does for Whitehead what Hume did for Locke, namely to make coherent what was confused by the founder of the movement. Whether this is always an improvement remains to be seen.

What lies, at least partially, at the root of the argument is the oft-noted fact that Whitehead had a tendency to mix his technically precise discussion with much less precise and evocative rhetoric. I fear that most religious people have been more moved by Whitehead's visionary portrait of God than by his meditation on the exact relationship of God's primordial and consequent natures and on whether God is an actual entity or a "social individual." Of course the integrity of the popular vision of relational divinity relies for its consistency on the details of philosophic argument. Nevertheless, the religious appeal rests elsewhere than in technical cosmological debate. The appeal is to a God who is a fellow sufferer who understands, who cares and is steadfast in creating the best from what is not always the best for the emerging creatures.

In part 5 of *Process and Reality*, Whitehead unfolds his fundamental vision of God. Although Whitehead may not have been an orthodox Christian, this section could only have been written by someone deeply nurtured by the Christian imagination. For instance, the evocative and often melancholy picture of God is Whitehead's appropriation of the meaning of the life and death of

Jesus of Nazareth. In these six paragraphs Whitehead explains first where traditional Western religion has gone wrong; and second, where the possible corrective for these theological errors may be found. The whole discussion is bracketed by a mention of Buddhism, demonstrating that Whitehead was always aware that the discussion of divine reality need to be a global conversation if it was to be intelligible in the modern world.

The errors that Whitehead (1978, 342–43) rejects are: the notion of God as (1) an unmoved mover; (2) an imperial ruler; (3) and the personification of moral energy, a ruthless moralist. Whitehead (1978, 343) is quite clear and unequivocal in rejecting all three as mistakes. "Hume's *Dialogues* criticized unanswerably these modes of explaining the system of the world."

Let us for a moment look briefly at these three erroneous notions, starting with the most philosophic, the unmoved mover. Whitehead states that we have inherited this idea from Aristotle, whom he also calls the last disinterested Western theologian. In specifically Christian terms, the unmoved mover as God becomes identified with the doctrine of the "eminently real" nature of God. "The combination of the two into the doctrine of an aboriginal, eminently real, transcendent creator, at whose fiat the world came to being, and whose imposed will it obeys, is the fallacy which has infused tragedy in the histories of Christianity and Mohametanism [*sic*]" (Whitehead 1978, 342). The fallacy Whitehead rejects is the fact that this notion of God's nature denies the ultimately social, interrelated nature of the cosmos, including even God. For Whitehead everything, including God in divinity's most supremely worshipful aspects, is connected to everything else. The notion of an eminently real and unmoved mover violates the organic and relational essence of reality, both mundane and divine. This is a crucial point for any process or organic theology.

The second error has to do with the fashioning of the image of God in the manner of an imperial ruler of the ancient Middle East. Not all idolatry need be physical, made out of gold or stone. A much deeper idolatry, according to Whitehead, lurks in our minds when we try to attach to God the political attributes of a tyrant, however benign the tyrant may be. "The Church gave unto God the attributes which belonged exclusively to Caesar" (Whitehead 1978, 342). A very important corollary is the question of authority in a faith tradition. If we do without the image of the "divine Caesar," how can we retain a sense of urgency or moral commitment, the willingness to act in a responsible and even sometimes heroic fashion?

However, before we move on to the third fallacy, let us deal with the question of authority. Basically, the process tradition argues that we need to deal with the notion of a God who persuades or lures rather than dominates through command or revelatory fiat. Whitehead calls this the victory of persuasion over force, which was expressed intellectually by Plato and was acted out in the life and death of Jesus of Nazareth. Of course, the note of victory for the Christian comes with the account of the risen Lord. Yet the basic point is clear to Whitehead: Jesus comes to persuade rather than command or overwhelm us as a tyrant. In fact, Jesus persistently rejects the temptation of secular imperial power to rule this world. From a process perspective this is not a simplistic rejection of the political process. Far from it, for the point is much more profound. It is an affirmation of persuasion and ideal aims rather than absolute power and control. The metaphor is more of a seed planted than a forest destroyed. Process theologians argue that this view is justified by the biblical sources that stress the concern and sorrow of God for all creation. Although one must be very cautious about theologizing about mundane political movements, there is a religious command for participation in the divine love of creation and persuasion rather than destruction wherever possible. We are commanded to choose life rather than death if we are commanded at all.

The third fallacy is that of the image of God as the personification of moral energy, a "ruthless moralist." In counterpoint to the ruthless moralists, Whitehead defended the tender elements in the divine reality. "It dwells upon the tender elements in the world, which slowly and in quietness operate by love; and it finds its purpose in the present immediacy of a kingdom not of this world. Love neither rules, nor is it unmoved; also it is a little oblivious to morals" (1978, 343). We too, need to sound the note of caution. Whitehead is far from being a simplistic meliorist. The world is not all sweetness and life for him. He realizes that the incarnate career of the young preacher Jesus ends with the agony of the cross, the pain of death and the suffering of the final rejection, however momentary. "Philosophy may not neglect the multifariousness of the world—fairies dance, and Christ is nailed to the cross" (1978, 338).

Whitehead's vision of God is not some form of nineteenth- or twentieth-century gospel of happiness. Happiness, adventure and peace play a role, but so too do suffering and the cross. For the Western mind a steadfast vision of the cross is central to the Christian tradition. It is a stumbling block, but not in the sense that much of the tradition has understood it because there is nothing mysterious about the fact that God can suffer for and with the world. Having dealt with the question of meliorism we can deal with the positive side of the image.

One of the key notions for Whitehead is that religion as a spiritual path ought to embody the quality he called "peace," most profoundly explained in the chapter by the same name in *Adventures of Ideas* (1933, 366–81). In a sense Whitehead is entering a plea against the idea of the world as created and ruled by a ruthless moralist, where every action would have its predetermined outcome. I suggest, in more orthodox or classical Christian vocabulary, that we here find the process notion of grace, of the freedom of God to forgive and redeem less than perfect creatures. Quite clearly this is not, in context, a call to antinomian life-styles. Rather it expresses Whitehead's own interpretation of the notion that God is cosmic love and that we can see this divine love in action in the life, death and resurrection of Jesus (1978, 344).

This is not the only viable notion of God, but it does take seriously the "Galilean origin of Christianity." In terms of explaining his own understanding of what he was trying to do by exposing these three traditional fallacies of Western theology, Whitehead said he was trying to "add another speaker to the masterpiece, Hume's *Dialogues Concerning Natural Religion*" (1978, 343). Just because Hume has refuted the concept of God predicated on these three fallacies does not mean that a process theologian cannot explicate a concept of God based on alternative philosophic principles that will satisfy Hume's critique. To refute a bad notion of God is not the same as refuting an adequate notion of God, and the process notion is adequate in two important ways. It is adequate for general human experience of the divine reality as concerned with the world, and faithful to the specific story of the Christian tradition.[11]

When I have the opportunity to read modern critics of Western philosophy and religion, such as Robert Neville (1987) in *The Puritan Smile*, I always have a great deal of sympathy for the Confucians of the Wei-Chin period. The Wei-Chin Confucians knew that they were caught between two eras, right in the middle of what we now call a paradigm shift. The classical world as defined by the late Chou and early Han thinkers was rapidly fading, disappearing right before their eyes. One gets much the same sense in reading a great deal of contemporary Christian scholarship. Similarly, there were strange new gods before the Wei-Chin Confucians—the wise and compassionate Buddha from the West. No one was sure that the dharma would mean for the Chinese tao. Surely the situation of Western intellectuals is now tantalizingly the same. For the first time since the end of Western antiquity and the rise of Islam, we have really new gods before us, plus several distinguished ghosts lurking behind us, as Neville reminds us by evoking our Puritan heritage in order to challenge the reigning liberal post-Enlightenment philosophies of the North Atlantic world. To more and more thoughtful persons, the purely Anglo-American and European resources of our civilization seem to be exhausted, moribund—or at least in need of the infusion of fresh ideas. Or on a more positive note, North Atlantic Christians are equally aware that we are being enriched by teachings from the East, including Confucianism in its own way. Another feature of the present paradigm shift is that Western intellectuals are not overly equipped for such happenings, nurtured as they have been on the political and cultural success of the West since the sixteenth century in almost all fields of human endeavor. The West has not faced such a grand and pervasive intellectual challenge since the end of the Greco-Roman world and the rise of Islam. At least since the Renaissance, and certainly since the European Enlightenment, we have assumed that Western civilization was where the action was, is and will be for all time. All other cultures were either rapidly disappearing or modelling themselves eagerly on us. No other civilization posed any kind of intellectual or material threat to the West, and were not even considered as equal cultural units. Nonetheless, especially after the end of the colonial period, these easy cultural, religious and political convictions have been eroded.

In most contemporary Christian theology this challenge finds expression in two differing set of reflections. One of these has to do with a growing sense of the relational nature of our world. I have already discussed this in some detail in terms of the question of dual transcendence and the basic Whiteheadian axioms. We now live in a world of relationship, ecology, holistic thinking and so forth. Somehow Christians are struggling to find theological expression for this new sense of cosmic and human solidarity. The old world of comfortable and reductionistic substance metaphysics simply will not do, nor can we any longer affirm a classical notion of God's utter and simple transcendence.

The other dimension of the paradigm shift is that, along with our new notions of solidarity, we inhabit a radically pluralistic world. This sense of pluralism pushes us in the opposite direction, or so it seems, from our affirmations of cosmic and social solidarity. Somewhat paradoxically, we affirm that we live in a relational world, in solidarity with all creatures and yet this world of holistic relationships is manifestly and incurably pluralistic at all levels of analysis and praxis.

Striking the right harmony between these two balanced yet discordant sensibilities is difficult and often leads to some rather strange results. One way culture critics try to deal with the issue is to predicate what we can label "civilizational paradigms" as manifested in specific claims about such entities as the Chinese, Indian, Islamic or Western mind. These civilizational paradigms imply that there is something unique about the way the Chinese mind goes about thinking in contradistinction to the typical Anglo-European philosopher. Of course, there is an element of truth to these claims. The great cultural traditions of humankind really are different and they have gone about their intellectual tasks in divergent ways, yet, with a bit of careful investigation, we discover that all the great cultures are capable of many intellectual modalities and harmonies.

One recent example of this comparative civilizational analysis is Hall and Ames' (1987) *Thinking Through Confucius*. The two authors claim that Confucius, and by extension a great deal of early Chinese culture, simply had no notion of what would be considered the idea of transcendence in the classical West. Hall and Ames go so far as to dismiss modern Confucians who see in early Confucianism analogues to the Western sense of transcendence, refuting Mou Tsung-san and Tu Wei-ming as both too Neo-Confucian and too Westernized in their concerns to properly explicate the thought of Confucius. The point that Hall and Ames want to make is not that one cannot find notions of transcendence in the history of the Chinese tradition, but that transcendence in any Western sense of the term is philosophically a late arrival on the Chinese scene. If the Sung Neo-Confucians have a strong transcendent edge to their thought, as Mou and Tu argue, then this is derived from the Neo-Confucian confrontation with and appropriation of T'ang Buddhist systematic thought. Hall and Ames vociferously argue that it is anachronistic to read this Neo-Confucian transcendent worldview back into Confucius' own way of person-making and the pursuit of the wisdom of the sages.

Whatever the philosophic, philological or scholarly merits of Hall and Ames' argument, they are largely irrelevant for contemporary religious dialogue. Dialogue begins, as noted before, when people meet to talk. The assumption is that they are living partners capable of changing their minds, and that their cumulative traditions are what they say they are for them. Self-definition is one key element in any dialogue. If Mou and Tu say that there is a form of Confucian transcendence it is neither profitable nor fitting for the Christian or secular partner in dialogue to try to persuade them that they are in error— at least as part of the dialogue per se.

If the discussion takes a scholastic turn, it is appropriate, however, to point out what a careful reading of the other tradition proves. If that reading is radically different from what is believed within the tradition then it may prove to be a stimulus to further internal reflection, but that will be up to the those within the hermeneutic circle of any tradition. The task in dialogue for modern Confucians and Christians is to come together in order to understand what transcendence might mean in light of the dialogue itself. My view is that Confucians and Christians are probably much closer in their understanding of transcendence than at any other time in the history of the two traditions.

On the Christian side something like Whitehead's process and relational axioms underlie much of the modern imperative for dialogue, albeit unexpressed or inarticulate in form. Of course, other schools of theology will formulate the task of dialogue in a different fashion. David Lochhead (1988), through a careful exegesis of Barth, announces his version of the dialogical imperative in terms more reserved than Cobb, Knitter, Hick, Tracy or Neville. In terms of our method of audience analysis, Lochhead has provided dialogue theory with an internal Barthian systematic theology with proper attention to the fundamental questions even though the accent of Lochhead's work is on the systematic tradition of theology. Yet there is the pressing sense that there is an emerging global agenda that we must confront together for the common survival of humankind. For instance, the grave problems of the deepening ecological crisis cannot be resolved through the resources or efforts of any one national, ideological, regional or religious family (McDaniel 1989). The reversal of the destruction of the ozone layer needs the attention of Confucians and Christians, as well as everyone else.

Common sense decrees modesty; one of the lessons of the dialogue movement so far is that we are just beginning, just commencing the joint exploration of meaning across cultures. It is only the first step to study the history of a tradition or to read its texts, and another matter entirely to meet living representatives of that tradition. We must not be premature in closing any kind of conversation, even those that seem nonsensical. New and old topics need to be examined. The examples of fiduciary community and dual transcendence discussed in chapters 4 and 5 are just two possible topics and it should be noted that a number of other subjects such as comparative social ethics were part of the agenda of the international dialogues in 1988 and 1991.

As Neville (1987) has reminded us in *The Puritan Smile*, we now also have to learn to live with the ghosts of our early modern past. For those coming from modern liberal protestant traditions this means that we have to reexamine our Puritan and neo-orthodox heritage, whereas the Confucians must look back to the great Sung-Yüan-Ming-Ch'ing achievements and especially have to come to terms with its painful and sad demise in the mid-nineteeth century. Both of these aspects of our traditions are dead yet live again in dialogue. The ideal of an ethically motivated scholar-official is something that should be resurrected in the modern world. The lack of ethical backbone in much of modern culture is frightening. Mere technique takes over and the sense of civilized, humane values means precious little in the money markets of Toronto, New York, London, Bonn or Tokyo. Together we can perhaps relearn seriousness without becoming grim in defense of special or parochial interests.

One of the real benefits of dialogue is that it can stimulate the development of a moral imagination for global community. This sense of global morality must have room enough to imagine cultural diversity and pluralism; it must temper its seriousness of purpose with the modern awareness that we live in a complex world and need to develop a tolerant interreligious ethic without betraying the search for truth. Confucianism and Christianity, as major religious traditions, have an important role to play in the promotion of such an ecumenical vision.

Both Confucianism and Christianity have a keen sense of the limits and excellences of human nature and now share a set of chastened expectations. These old ghosts need to become friends to help exchange ideas and share visions of the future. Perhaps in doing so they will discover new life; at the very least they will cultivate serious and friendly conversation, which in and of itself is not a bad model for civilized life in a pluralistic world.

DUAL TRANSCENDENCE AND THEOLOGICAL METHODOLOGY

I have emphasized Hartshorne's doctrine of dual transcendence because it allows a Christian discussion of the Confucian sense of divine things to flourish in terms not available to previous generations of missiologists and theologians. He is convinced that only a doctrine as radical as dual transcendence will make theological sense of our modern relational sensibilities. For Hartshorne the notion of dual transcendence is a link between classical Christian culture and the modern world. Anything less, Hartshorne asserts, will lead to incoherence and the death of critical religious thinking.

In terms of Confucian-Christian dialogue, the doctrine of dual transcendence allows a Christian theologian to make sense of the famous Confucian dictum "humanity makes the *tao* great, not that *tao* makes humanity great" (*Analects* 15:28). The relational nature of the divine-human reality can be affirmed and discussed as an insight into reality and not as an error. Hartshorne clearly wants to express the deep conviction that the life and actions of human beings do matter to God. There are real relations between the mundane world and the divine reality and not just among the three members of the Holy Trinity itself.

The crux of the theological problem for making sense of God-world relations in process theology centers on what Hartshorne has labelled the doctrine of dual transcendence. As he explains,

> God is exalted above the other realities not as cause surpasses effect, or unity, plurality, or being, becoming; but rather as eminent cause surpasses ordinary causes, and eminent effect, ordinary effects; similarly, as eminent

being *and* becoming surpass ordinary being or becoming, or eminent unity *and* plurality surpass ordinary unity and plurality. (1983, 314–15)

Hartshorne is here building on the insights of Whitehead found in part 5 of *Process and Reality*.

What Whitehead means here, as he does when he says that the world transcends God, is that each worldly actuality has its own self-determination and that deity, by prehending these actualities, has its (hers, his) own actuality enriched. Our free acts, and all creaturely acts, add new content to God's awareness. (1983, 315)

One of the main points that Hartshorne wants to make is that Whitehead was *really* breaking with a great deal of classical Christian theological tradition. This break with tradition is not just rhetorical for Whitehead and Hartshorne. "When Whitehead wrote 'there is a reaction of the world on God,' he is breaking with an immense tradition, according to which there is not genuine *interaction* between God and his creatures" (Hartshorne 1983, 315). Transcendence, for Hartshorne, does not mean some kind of static perfection, timeless and unaffected by the world. "Rather, God and what God knows are endlessly added to by the cosmic creative advance" (Hartshorne 1983, 166). But, because he sees himself as a theist, Hartshorne makes a clear distinction between the divine form of creativity and the limited creativity of the created creatures. Although both forms of creativity illustrate creativity as a virtue of freedom and determinate, the divine reality is unsurpassable in form and act.

Deity is the unsurpassable form (surpassable only by this very form in a subsequent phase) of creativity; the creatures are instances of surpassable forms of creativity. Every actuality, divine or otherwise, is both creature and creator in relation to others. *The* creator is the eminent or unsurpassable form of creative-created actuality. (1983, 78)

Hartshorne wants to contrast Whitehead's and his novel doctrine of dual transcendence with what he takes to be the classical notion of one-way transcendence, best represented by Aristotle.

Aristotle's God enshrines this bias: Totally uninfluenced by the course of events, in solitary immutable splendor, he influences the world that cannot influence him. But Aristotle, to his lasting credit, saw that this meant that God does not know the world. (1983, 25)

With Whitehead (1978, 342), Hartshorne believes that this grafting of the notion of an unmoved mover onto Christian theology was a great tragedy, both for common piety and for theological articulation.

This notion of dual transcendence, of course, is not the only modal possibility for thinking about God found in the long history of Western theological reflection. Hartshorne lists the major forms as the following:

> We have the unmoved mover not knowing the moving world (Aristotle); the unmoved mover (inconsistently) knowing the moving world (most theologians until recently); the unmoved mover knowing an ultimately unmoving (or at least noncontingent) world (Stoics, Spinoza); and the not wholly unmoved mover knowing a moving world (Socinus and many others, often unaware of their predecessor). (1983, 366)

For those who might now be tempted to think that the notion of dual transcendence fails to do justice to the theological testimony concerning the divine majesty of the unchanging aspects of God's nature, Hartshorne has an answer. If for so long so many thinkers of philosophic genius held a doctrine of God at variance with the doctrine of dual transcendence, there must be a reason.[12] Hartshorne frames his explanation this way.

> The impassable and immutable God can be retained, though only as an aspect of the divine life in its fullness. Some version of what Whitehead calls the primordial divine nature is needed in any theism; but it cannot be the concrete divine actuality, it cannot be God knowing you or me or the movement of the atoms in the present universe. (1983, 77)

He suggests that the positive qualities of God's primordial nature are crucial to a religious understanding of God.

> However, the eternal principle of good is God's eternal essence and is in no sense arbitrary or contingent. It is what God could not chose not to will and what we can fail to approve only by failing to understand it ourselves. It is the beauty of holiness, or incorruptible all-embracing love. (1984a, 203)

Actually, Hartshorne really prefers to the notion of eminence to transcendence for the most profound aspects of religious piety.

> The transcendent is exalted above all other things, actual or conceivable; but the exact formula for this is not unsurpassability, but "unsurpassability *by another*." Any complexity can be surpassed, but the being already transcendent. God is surpassable only by himself. This I take to be the religious meaning of "eminence," which is word less abused historically than transcendence. (1970, 236)

He prefers to talk about eminence because of his rejection of the classic notion of omnipotence, which he finds to be both illogical and ethically repugnant

(1984b, 1–49). Hartshorne argues that along with a better notion of transcendence, we also need a better ethical or moral notion of God's power in the world. In terms of Christology, Tom Driver (1981) has made much the same argument in pointing out that Christian notions of the person of Christ have had dramatic and often harmful ethical and social implications down the centuries and across cultures.

This concept of dual transcendence does have dramatic implications for a new understanding of the relationship of God and humanity. The contributions of men and women really and ultimately matter to God; human beings enrich and expand the life of God. This kind of understanding necessitates the revision of a number of traditional Christian themes such as creation, freedom and destiny, sin, redemption and so forth. Dual transcendence helps highlight certain aspects of Christian theistic humanism that are analogous to Confucian concepts such as human nature, the Will of Heaven, the Way of Heaven and the creation of civilized human values by the sages.

THE TRIPARTITE CREATION

How does dual transcendence and the other allied notions in process theology relate to the notions of form, dynamic and unification? My argument is that these three traits, which inform Chu Hsi's mature metasystem, are analogous to the three fundamental Whiteheadian axioms and to Hartshorne's notion of dual transcendence (Berthrong 1980b; 1987a). If that is indeed the case, then this affinity between the basic themes of the Chu Hsi school and the two major proponents of process thought is a basis for the claim that process theology provides a useful Western comparative tool for dialogue with Confucianism.

My textual inspiration for the tripartite formulation that was explicated in the earlier sections of this chapter as well as in chapters 2 and 3 is drawn from two Whiteheadian texts. It is useful to repeat these key texts at this point. The first text states that

> these various aspects can be summed up in the statement that *experience* involved a *becoming*, that *becoming* means that *something becomes*, and that *what becomes* involves *repetition* transformed into *novel immediacy*. (1978, 136–37)

The second way at getting at the issue is through Whitehead's insight into the nature of the extensive continuum (1978, 66).

An extensive continuum is a complex of entities united by the various allied relationships of whole to part, and of overlapping so as to possess common parts, and of contact, and other relationships derived from these primary relationships.

As I have already argued, these are only two of many statements that indicate that there are, in the coming into being and perishing of any creature, elements that can be identified as form, dynamic and unification. In the Indian context I could add Brahma, Vishnu and Siva for comparison and contrast.

I hope to be responsibly reticent about the claims I make for these seeming similarities of the great Southern Sung Neo-Confucian master and the modern Anglo-American philosopher. Whitehead was never more insightful when he warned about grandiose claims when he said that "the merest hint of dogmatic certainty as to finality of statement is an exhibition of folly" (1978, xiv). This cautionary note must be struck again and again when entering the murky waters of comparative philosophy and theology. As Wilhelm Halbfass (1988) has so admirably documented in his study of the impact of India on European thought, the ability to misunderstand and misinterpret the philosophic and theological system of another culture is almost endless. Yet process thinkers, Neo-Confucians and New Confucians are all rationalists who believe that, in principle, the world is amenable to rational interpretation if not complete clarity of exposition.

Amid all the fascinating similarities of process thought and Neo-Confucianism, I believe that there are three key points of contact. First, there is the organic nature of both systems. It is always important to remember that Whitehead did not call his philosophy "process philosophy." Rather, Whitehead (1978, xi) called his system a philosophy of organism. I believe that there is little doubt that Sung Neo-Confucianism can be defined as a form of organic philosophy predicated on its insistence on the unity of principle and nature, Tao and world, and what is above form with what is within form. As Chu Hsi and his followers never hesitated to proclaim, principle is one but its manifestations are many (*li-i fen-shu*). However complicated the cosmos is for the Neo-Confucians, it is fundamentally and formally an organic unity.

The second key point of contact is the irreducibly relational cosmology affirmed by process theology and Neo-Confucianism. This notion of relationality is closely allied to the organic nature of reality as defined in the first point of compatibility. Nonetheless, relationality needs to be explicated from within the process and Neo-Confucian traditions. For Whitehead, this is expressed in terms of the mutual entailment of God and the world that he so eloquently outlined in part 5 of *Process and Reality*. For Chu Hsi and his school, the relational affirmation comes with the insistent affirmation that *li* and *ch'i* can never be separated even for conceptual purposes.

Third, Whitehead posits the ultimate and creative aspect of this cosmic epoch in the following fashion.

> God and the World stand over against each other, expressing the final metaphysical truth that appetitive vision and physical enjoyment have equal claim to priority in creation. . . .Opposed elements stand to each other in mutual requirement. . . .Neither God, nor the World, reaches static completion. Both are in the grip of the ultimate metaphysical ground, the creative advance into novelty. Either of them, God and the World, is the instrument of novelty for the other. (1978, 348–49)

This expression of the "grip of ultimate metaphysical ground" of creativity is precisely the sort of Whiteheadian doctrine that offends orthodox Christian theologians. From the early and influential critique of Stephen Lee Ely (Ford and Kline 1983) about the lack of the religious availability of Whitehead's God to Neville's sophisticated ontological challenge (1980), this affirmation of the central role of creativity in God's primordial and consequent nature has been a major reason for the rejection of process theology by many theologians. These theologians may marvel at Whitehead's ability to speak about God in a modern voice—few deny the fascination engendered in many modern intellectuals by Whitehead's insistence in speaking about God. The problem is that they believe that Whitehead's notion of God is not the God of the Christian church.

The notion of creativity is also a key feature of the Sung Neo-Confucian and New Confucian movements. The creative advance into novelty, so central to process thought, would hardly have seemed novel to Chu Hsi, Mou Tsung-san or Tu Wei-ming. The notion of creativity as *sheng-sheng pu-hsi* (ceaseless creativity) is key to understanding Neo-Confucian cosmology. The whole Neo-Confucian tradition shares with process thought a commitment to a cosmology grounded in creativity with an outcome of a pluralistic cosmos. New Confucians such as Mou and Tu agree with this aspect of Chu Hsi's School of Principle. Further, if David Dilworth (1989, 173) is correct in his application of the method of archic comparative analysis, both Confucianism and Christianity share a creative principle as their "motivating and integrating intention."

However important the notion of creativity is for the Neo-Confucians and process theologians, I believe the main element of contention for both of these traditions with orthodox Christian thinking comes from their affirmation of the relational quality of the world. This is defined by Whitehead in terms of the principle of relativity that is crucial to the whole structure of his thought. In the Neo-Confucian synthesis all we need to do is remember a crucial text such as Chang Tsai's famous "Western Inscription" (Chan 1963, 497–98), a text so often read as a Neo-Confucian hymn to the organic and correlative nature of the cosmos. While Chang Tsai does not enunciate a cosmological schema in the "Western Inscription," no one can miss Chang's point about the absolute relativity and organic solidarity of all the creatures under Heaven.[13] For Chang Tsai, we are all brothers and sisters in the Way; Whitehead would certainly have agreed with Chang's sentiment.

Such a relational understanding of reality will be highly problematic for both Confucians and Christians in a modern world characterized by economic and political disunity, lack of community and the destruction of all tradition and stability except for a very secularized modern, Westernized version of technical rationalism. The problem is probably even better understood by the New Confucians because Chinese culture has been under attack by the forces of the modern West since the Opium Wars began in 1839. Even if they had wanted to remain indifferent to the changes, Confucians have been forced to understand this strange, violent, aggressive and expansive "barbarian" presence of the West. For instance, Mou Tsung-san, the most philosophically alert of the New Confucians, began his career as a logician and has ended it with a continued fascination with Kant's philosophy, going so far as to translate some of Kant's most important works into Chinese. What major Western philosopher or theologian can claim such a familiarity with the Neo-Confucian tradition? Or any Asian tradition? Actually, theologians may be ahead of the professional philosophers because they cannot escape an interest these days in comparative religion if they want to remain current with the thinking of many of their lay people. Lay Christians are often practicing Buddhist meditation and want to know, quite nervously, what their priests and pastors thing about such activity. The problem becomes acute in the area of what I will call "truthful encounter."

This truthful encounter between religions, of course, has been going on for a long, long time; it is hard to think of any historic period when religions did not interact with each other. One point often mentioned is that the unique feature of the modern encounter is the growing self-consciousness of the interaction. One wonders if this is really entirely accurate.[14] People have always been self-conscious about the interactions of the great religions of the Axial Age; that is why they are forever trying to convert each other, or at least convince the other part to leave them alone with their soteriologically sufficient truth. Perhaps what is really different is the scope of present religious encounters conjoined with the explosion of information technology that provides a historical recorder of what is going on. We can no longer hide the encounter from ourselves.

It is precisely this growing historical record that demands a place for truth in the record of the encounter. Both sides of any dialogue will have their say and it is increasing difficult to suppress the weaker party because of a common recognition of certain human rights as international civil liberties. Hence, we must be more honest about what is going on because nothing is hidden anymore. For instance, there have always been syncretists, those often brave or naive souls who have ventured beyond their natal religious traditions in search of a new or reformed truth. Or they may find that Buddhist insight meditation throws more light on their Christian prayer life than Barthian sermonic discourse. These kinds of religious explorers are likely to demand an increasingly honest chronicle of their adventures in search of truth. False information about other tradition, for instance, is being challenged as Christians try to understand Confucians and Confucians experiment with modern Christian articulations of theistic doctrine.

Whatever the outcome of this truthful encounter, we will have to pay attention and we have to acknowledge what was probably always the case: most religious traditions borrow good ideas from each other unless the ideas are bolted down. Few religious ideas are embedded in concrete. They are, in the end, really meant to be shared. The observation of copyright has never been a strong point for a living religion, nor would organic, relational and processive thinkers have it otherwise. As the Muslim theologians have long ago pointed out, reason is God's finger on the earth. Whatever truth the finger indicates should be appropriate for a person of faith. As Chuang Tzu so long ago argued, what need do we have to worry about a finger pointing at the moon if it helps us see the moon? Chapter 6 directly addresses the question of truthful encounter in terms of the difficult question of multiple religious participation as an outcome of interreligious dialogue.

6

Dual Citizenship

SYNCRETISM REVISITED

PROLOGUE: INVITING THE QUESTION

As briefly explained in chapter 1, the question of dual citizenship qua multiple religious participation arose during the First International Confucian-Christian Dialogue (8–14 June 1988, Chinese University of Hong Kong).[1] The topic was considered important enough to warrant being put on the proposed agenda of the Second International Confucian-Christian Dialogue. The issue of multiple religious participation did indeed become an important focus of this conference held at Berkeley in July 1991. As Confucians and Christians renew their historic conversations, the questions of influence, impact, modification, borrowing and transformation—there is no simple way to describe the complicated patterns of interaction that emerge when Confucians and Christians speak and listen to each other—are recognized as significant issues to be addressed and pondered from the perspectives of both traditions.[2]

Over the last two decades the ecumenical Christian churches, guided by the Vatican's Pontifical Council for Interreligious Dialogue and the World Council of Churches' Sub-Unit on Dialogue with People of Living Faiths, have initiated a number of bilateral and multilateral dialogues with representatives of the various faith traditions of humankind. While there had been a vigorous Confucian-Christian encounter from the sixteenth to the nineteenth century in China initiated by the learned Catholic and Protestant missionaries, this dialogue was much less in evidence until the 1988 Hong Kong meeting.[3] Many of the participants in the First International Confucian-Christian Dialogue realized the historical significance of the event. They perceived that they were symbolically renewing a long-interrupted conversation between Confucians and Christians, a conversation now global in scope due to the East Asian diaspora.

Still, there is resistance to the notion of Confucian-Christian dialogue. Often this opposition comes from Christians who wonder if the New Confucianism of people like Mou Tsung-san and Tu Wei-ming that has emerged from the political and social wreckage of "late imperial" Confucianism is a fit dialogue partner. On the one hand, many Christians question whether there is an authentic and living Confucian religious tradition these days outside of the fond Proustean daydreams of a few Chinese, Korean, Vietnamese, Japanese, North American and European scholars. At least for the participants in the two conferences, the spirited interaction at the June 1988 and July 1991 conferences put an end to the question of Confucian morbidity. For those at Hong Kong and again at Berkeley, it is the case that Confucianism is most definitely a living tradition with profound religious dimensions. On the other hand, there are those, often Asian (Confucian and Christian) women, who believe that Confucianism is all too alive, at least in the patriarchal constraints of the traditional Confucian understanding of the subservient role of women. In both cases there is resistance to dialogue with either the dead or living Confucianism. And then there are some Confucians who reject the notion that their tradition is a religion in need to dialogue with Christians at all.

Adding a third partner to the dialogue, many social scientists on both sides of the Pacific have become fascinated with the "Confucian" legacy of East Asia in response to the economic transformation of the region.[4] These social scientists ponder what role traditional Confucian values have played and will continue to play in the present global economic restructuring with its profound tilt towards the Pacific Rim and its many large and small dragons— all of whom have a Confucian past and perhaps a Confucian future. If Confucianism is a ghost in modern Asia, it is a lively ghost refusing to be buried in the museum of antiquities. While primarily interested in the economic, political and social dimensions of Confucianism, the social scientists recognize that religion is also an important and persistent part of the worldviews of East Asians and shapes the values of any cultural system.

Recent political events in China, such as the 1989 summer drama in Tiananmen Square, also raise profound questions about the survival of Confucian discourse and symbols. The old notions of scholarly remonstrance against a government that has lost the Mandate of Heaven played themselves out nightly during the international television coverage of the May–June 1989 drama in Tiananmen Square. If Heaven, and the aging Chinese leadership, do not hear as the people speak, then the rest of the world does. What more Confucian gesture is there than demonstrating students who see themselves as the conscience of the nation? Confucians from Mencius to the brave Ming scholars of the

Tung-lin Academy would have understood something of what the students and their supporters were about even if they would have been perplexed by the large statue dedicated, appealing to French and American sensibilities, to the spirit of democracy. And on the other side, the old quasi-Marxist leadership appealed to the Confucian sense of order and respect for authority, the persistent glue of the ancient imperial Confucian social order.[5]

THE QUESTION OF DUAL CITIZENSHIP

A number of theological issues were raised at the 1988 and 1991 international conferences in Hong Kong and Berkeley, but none was more provocative than the question of multiple religious allegiances and participation. For better or worse, this was called the question of dual citizenship. This was a particularly worrisome challenge for the Christian participants and probably an equally difficult concept for many Confucians as well. Whatever their natal tradition, very few people are happy being labelled eclectic in religious matters. Most people prefer to see religion as a focus of integrity in their lives. Anything that threatens this primary focus of integrity is seen as disruptive of personal and social integration. While many Christian theologians argue for the ultimately disruptive nature of the Christian gospel qua revelation and proclamation, they are less than enthusiastic about the disruption coming from more than one religious tradition.

In many ways, the question of multiple religious commitments, allegiances and participation (dual citizenship) is an extreme example of a related series of questions at the forefront of Christian missiological reflection for the last few decades. In general, these questions are thematized as the debate over the relationship of the Christian gospel to all local cultures. The common assumption of the modern gospel-culture debate is that even the so-called Christian religious cultures of Western, Eastern Europe and the Middle East are only partial expressions of the Christian faith. The modern conventional wisdom on these matters is that no culture, nation or people can claim to have captured the gospel entirely in any specific cultural form. All cultures are challenged by the gospel and transformed uniquely by it, giving rise to the church in its local environment. No creature or society can know all the ways of the Lord.

Notwithstanding human finitude in appropriating divine matters, there have always been certain limits to this reappropriation of traditional cultures within the Christian family of churches. For instance, human sacrifice has never been considered compatible in any cultural setting with the Christian gospel. Further, it was assumed that once a person became a Christian, she or he gave up any other religious commitments. One crucial part of the equation is the assumption that a person *has some form of religion* prior to conversion to the Christian faith. In the modern period this can be a dubious assumption for some people. What does this assumption of monoreligious faithfulness mean in post-Christian North America where a person may become converted to the Christian faith, or Judaism, Buddhism, or Islam for that matter, from no readily discernible form of historic faith other than a commitment to the "North American way of life?" The answer to the question is not obvious. For many people living in traditional Christendom there is so little left of the historic Christian tradition that they are not giving anything up when they join the church. Many may not even consider themselves to be "cultural" Christians. As Peter Berger (1992) has shown, the way out of traditional religion has not been a movement into another religion but away from any religion at all.

The question of dual citizenship arose when some of the Confucian participants in the 1988 and 1991 consultations asked whether they could be Christian-Confucians. This was often done with considerable humor since the Confucians realized that this was not the typical question to be addressed in such formal dialogue situations where it was assumed that a person represented either one tradition or another, but not both. By this question the Confucians meant a number of different things. One point turned out to be the fact that they were seriously considering the theistic claims of Christianity and saw these theistic claims as supplementing and enriching, but not replacing, their Confucian identity. Another point had to do with the East Asian willingness to consider formal participation and membership in many religious communities.

In one sense this was a New Confucian version of "supercessionist" theology, but with a very radical twist. What superseded the old Neo-Confucian identity was something that was both Confucian and Christian. The argument was tentatively extended that there was nothing in the core of Confucian teachings that could not incorporate Christian theism, given that the Confucian tradition, especially from the Sung, was agnostic or indifferent about theistic claims; perhaps in Confucianism's encounters with the early modern Christian missionaries it was even more than agnostic. Confucianism was simply indifferent to the perennial charms of classical Western theism. So the question of theism, it was suggested, did not touch the core of the Confucian or Neo-Confucian traditions. Hence a modern Confucian, stimulated by Christian claims, could adopt or modify a Christian model of God in order to clarify Confucian claims about the religious dimension of their own tradition. It was clear that there was not enough time at the Hong Kong or Berkeley meetings to do more than introduce this idea. What did emerge from the conversation at both conferences was the recognition that it is a *very* important question and that it should be placed on the agenda for future meetings.[6]

No one at the Hong Kong or Berkeley conferences was sure just what to do with the question of multiple religious participation. Part of the uneasiness stemmed from the fact that such a notion gave credence to one of the most frequently heard condemnations of the dialogue movement, namely that it will all end in a kind of syncretism. Syncretism, as the Christian participants explained, is perceived in official ecumenical Christian circles as something to be studiously and devoutly avoided. Whatever else dialogue may be, the World Council of Churches, for instance, has made it abundantly clear that syncretism is not one of the legitimate goals of dialogue. Reflecting the experience of many of the European churches during the Nazi era, the WCC in fact rejects the notion of syncretism in its major policy statement, *Guidelines on Dialogue with People of Living Faiths and Ideologies* (1979), on the theory and practice of dialogue.

The *Guidelines* put it this way. "Despite attempts to rescue the word 'syncretism' it now conveys, after its previous uses in Christian debate, a negative evaluation" (1979, 14). The authors of the *Guidelines* have two very specific problems in mind. The first is that Christians in dialogue will "go too far and compromise the authenticity of the Christian faith and life." For instance, the degradations of many German Christians during the Nazi period is never far from the thought of ecumenical Christians after the horror of the Holocaust. The second danger has to do with "interpreting a living faith not in its own terms but in terms of another faith or ideology" (*Guidelines*, 1979, 15). This tendency is rejected on the basis of sound scholarship and actual dialogue practice that seeks to let each tradition speak for itself and not project the thought world of one tradition holus bolus onto the other. There is an insistence in the *Guidelines* on seeing religious traditions as genuinely distinct from each other and not just more vague localized approaches to God *pro nobis*.

This rejection of a positive interpretation of religious syncretism is a very commonly shared assumption of Christians involved in officially sponsored dialogue. Even John Hick, hardly a conservative in these matters, expresses distaste for multiple allegiances in religious matters. In his Gifford lectures he states,

> we have to ask concerning these primary affirmations whether they conflict with one another. They conflict in the sense that they are different and one can only centre one's religious life wholeheartedly and unambiguously upon one of them . . . but not more than one at once. (1989, 373)

Not even the most radical of the pluralist Christian theologians seems to have anything good to say about the possibilities for dual citizenship as a way to transform the deluded ego into the realized/saved self centered on reality as it is! Yet as both clergy and lay people engage in dialogue, they are influenced and transformed by the encounter. Some Christian dialogue participants have been so radically transformed and enriched that they ask the question of multiple participation in fear and trembling.

THE CONFUCIAN RESPONSE OF MOU TSUNG-SAN

For these reasons, the question of multiple religious participation was regarded as the most challenging theological question raised at the Hong Kong and Berkeley conferences. Could a Confucian adopt a Christian-influenced understanding of the divine reality without sacrificing the distinctive essence of the Confucian tradition? Could a Christian accept the Confucian notion of fiduciary community as an expression of the Kingdom of God? From the Confucian perspective, the reason given for this question was that Confucianism is basically, in its defining cumulative tradition, agnostic about the question of theism. Hence, a Confucian could accept a theistic element into her/his worldview and still remain a Confucian, albeit now a Christian-Confucian if the theism adopted were Christian-influenced.

What would a question like this mean when mediated through the thought of Mou Tsung-san? While not at the conferences, Mou's spirit and teachings certainly influenced much of the conversation, and a number of the Confucian scholars present are his colleagues and students. As I demonstrated in previous chapters, there is a consensus that Mou represents one of the most philosophically and religiously articulate, subtle and modern expressions of the living Confucian tradition of East Asia. This does not mean that all Confucians or students of the Confucian tradition are in agreement with Mou's moral metaphysics; they merely recognize its philosophic importance within modern Confucian discourse. The major criticism of Mou is that he has not offered an equally impressive agenda for social change, an agenda that has characterized the mainline of the Confucian tradition at least since the Sung. Without both the philosophic and social elements, not even Mou Tsung-san can claim to have truly reformed the Confucian tradition in light of its modern needs.

One of the distinctive features of Mou's thought is that he identifies a religious dimension in Confucianism. He is clear that Confucianism is different from the great theistic traditions of West Asia, namely, Judaism, Christianity and Islam. Of course, not all Confucians accept Mou's version of the Confucian way as including a strong religious dimension, but there is general respect for his intellectual achievement. The crux of the problem is that Confucianism has never been an "organized religion" in the same sense as Judaism, Christianity or Islam. A similar argument has also been make concerning the comparison of Confucianism with Buddhism and Hinduism. Confucianism is held not to resemble very much either the West or South Asian families of religions. As Tu Wei-ming comments about the religious dimension of the Confucian Way, "yet it has exerted profound influence on East Asian political culture as well as East Asian spiritual life" (1990, 112). On the basis of his published works, Mou agrees with his student's judgment.

I contend that it makes sense, from within Mou Tsung-san's realm of modern Confucian discourse, to ask the question of the possibility of dual citizenship precisely because Confucianism is a tradition with spiritual and religious dimensions. Unfortunately, Mou has published little in English and almost nothing of his huge Chinese corpus has been translated into English. Therefore, I will outline the basic structure of Mou's definition of the Confucian path (tao) and in what manner it is a spiritual and religious way. My citations will again be taken from *The Uniqueness of Chinese Philosophy* [*Chung-kuo che-hsüeh te t'e-chih*]. This small book, based on lectures given in the 1960s in Taiwan, represents an outline of Mou's understanding of the main trajectories of Chinese philosophy and the religious dimension of Confucianism. It is useful for our purposes because Mou devotes the twelfth lecture entirely to the question of the religious dimension of the Confucian tradition.

According to Mou, Confucianism is "an ultimate concern for life values" (1974, 89). This is Mou's core definition of the ultimate religious and philosophic values of Confucianism. He goes on to make it clear that the foundations of these life values can only be understood in terms of a spiritual tradition. "The foundational force of the life values of a culture are found in religion." The Confucian quest for self-transformation is played out in the arena of the world as human community. This is a theme that Tu Wei-ming adopts and makes central to his reflections on Confucian religiosity (1989, 93–121). Indeed, Tu argues that this understanding of life values and religious intent has always been a driving force in the Confucian tradition even if organized and thematized entirely differently from the West Asian and European experiences.

For Mou Tsung-san there are two key notions that are essential to understanding this Confucian vision. The first is what he calls concern as the basis for what I have labeled 'intersubjectivity' (1974, 12). Because Chinese philosophy is rooted in a profound sense of concern as relationality, it must, perforce, always be "inter" subjectivity and cannot be reduced to solipsistic subjectivism. Or as Mou says, "the moral nature (essence) of Chinese philosophy is rooted in the concept of *concern*" (1974, 13). Mou notes that he has borrowed and slightly modified the formulation of the key concept of concern as the key to the Confucian tradition from his good friend Hsü Fu-kuan (1974, 13). What Mou is driving at is the axiological nature of human conduct, the persistent focus of responsible life values of the person as embedded in the social nexus of community. One needs to get "it" (the tao) for personal, social and cosmic transformation. Nor can this profound concern for self and others be imposed from outside the person. The second defining notion of the Confucian tradition, according to Mou, is that the true Confucian manifests and realizes an autonomous inner morality of concern for self and others (1974, 4). To merely memorize and even follow a code of ethics is not enough to be in harmony with the Confucian tao.[7]

Within the cumulative Confucian tradition, Mou sees four main elements of analysis which support his two key axiological notions of concern consciousness and inner morality (1974, 15ff.). Although we have already introduced this material in chapter 3, a short review is in order in terms of Mou's interest in the religious dimension of the Confucian tradition. The first element is the concept of *t'ien-ming* as the creative cosmological Will of Heaven. Mou argues that *t'ien-ming*, as expressed in the *I-Ching* and the *Chung-yung*, is really creativity itself realizing an ordered creation (1974, 55ff.). The second concept is the classical Confucian virtue of *jen*, understood as creativity mediated by concern for the other as the proper human response and discernment of *t'ien-ming*. *Jen* serves to make concrete, for each person individually and as a responsible member of society within the fiduciary community of humankind, the cosmological creativity expressed by the Will of Heaven.

The third concept is *hsin*, the mind and heart of humanity. It is impossible, as we have seen in previous chapters, to give a precise or elegant translation of all the intellectual freight *hsin* carries in the Confucian tradition, and especially Mou's rendition of it. Suffice it to say, for Mou, *hsin* is the experiential unity of the self's concern for others as the active and creative reason of the person in community (1974, 64ff.). And fourth, Mou turns to the concept of *hsing* as human life lived through profound intersubjectivity and autonomous inner morality (1974, chapters 8 and 9). For Mou, *hsing* is human life as the creation of new personal and social values generating the particularity of human history and society.

As we have already seen in chapter 4, Mou Tsung-san also has a definition of religion, again with two major elements (1974, chapter 12). First, true religion aims to perfect the way of everyday life. For instance, for the Confucian this would be done through the five primary social relationships (perfecting the five key virtues) and their attendant rituals. Within the Confucian world, Mou believes that proper ritual action is the key for the perfection of the way of everyday life.[8] This is always one of the most problematic points for a modern Westerner to comprehend about the Confucian tradition. One can almost say that other's rituals are strange whereas our own rituals are taken simply to be the way the world is.

Second, the true Confucian needs to stimulate the incipient seeds of spirituality that define the Confucian understanding of transcendence. This can be done through the mature power of ritual action, concern consciousness and inner morality which combine to transform the egotistic self from self-centeredness to reality-centeredness. Through proper ritual action a person seeks to become a sage or at least a moral worthy. Mou always emphasizes that this spiritual quest is a process and never some static state of achieved perfection. Achieved values are to be critically tested against present experience in terms of concern and inner morality.

Mou also has some reflections on the proper way to nurture Confucian spirituality. The first is to cultivate an awareness/intuition of the notion of "yielding" as a modality of cosmic creativity as process. For Mou there is no gridlock for the cosmos as long as creativity is embodied in humane social action. Along with this awareness of "yielding" the profound person also needs to be steadfast, to persevere in seeking sageliness without ceasing.[9] The Confucian spiritual path is characterized by the persistent, profound and unceasing attempt to become a sage/worthy. In conclusion, Mou returns to the notion of intersubjectivity and quotes from the Ming Confucian, Lo Chin-hsi: "The great person is one who can link together the family, the country, and the world to form one body" (1974, 97). As always, the persistent question of Confucian spirituality is "how" to get the Way for one's self in relation to other persons and even the whole created order.[10]

Although Mou Tsung-san has never addressed the question of multiple religious participation per se, he has offered some reflections on Confucianism and theism. He points out in the twelfth lecture in *The Uniqueness of Chinese Philosophy* that Confucianism never conjoined its characteristic awareness of the transcendence and immanence of the Way of Heaven with a consistent concept of "God." Mou recognizes that there is an aboriginal notion of God in some of the earliest Confucian writings, but these were never developed into a coherent Confucian theism. Rather, the genius of the Confucian tradition moved in other directions for reasons internal to its own history. Nonetheless, Mou is aware that modern religious and intellectual history is the history of global transformation and self-conscious reflection on our intercivilizational and pluralistic world of discovery and encounter. What might not have been part of one tradition in the past could become an element of renewal in the present. Although Mou does not speculate on the development of a theistic element in the Confucian tradition, there is nothing in his understanding of the religious dimensions of Confucianism that would debar such a development in the future.

From my perspective as a Christian theologian, I suspect that Mou Tsung-san might well agree that a modern Confucian could indeed incorporate a refined theism into her/his quest for sageliness, at least as an interesting hypothetical question. It seems that there is nothing in the foundational elements of Confucian discourse, at least according to Mou, which would be violated by a theistic interpretation of *t'ien-ming* as *t'ien-tao*. In fact, Nicolas Standaert (1988) has made this suggestion in his recent study of the thought of the late Ming scholar Yang Tingyun, who Standaert believes came to just this conclusion during the first period of active dialogue between Confucians and Christians.

This concern for the religious dimension within the Confucian cumulative East Asian tradition is not unique to Mou Tsung-san. Mary Evelyn Tucker's study (1989) of the life and thought of the great Tokugawa Confucian Kaibara Ekken (1630–1714) demonstrates a similar pattern. Tucker believes that we cannot understand the Japanese Neo-Confucian tradition without analyzing its religious dimension. Just because East Asian Neo-Confucianism is not organized like the great Western theistic traditions does not mean that there was not a profound religious dimension to the Confucian tao. Tucker draws the distinction between the "spiritual" and "religious" in the following fashion: " 'Spirituality' refers that which includes intense personal experience of the sacred as well as the cultivation of that experience in a discipline aimed at self-transformation" (1989, 8). She goes on to define the "religious," which "is taken to mean individual or communal expression of spiritual experience as found in scripture, creed, practice, and institution." Therefore Tucker argues that "Neo-Confucianism can be regarded as having a religious dimension in the sense that the primary activity of Neo-Confucianism is the practice of moral and spiritual cultivation leading to self-transcendence and ultimate self-transformation for the benefit of the larger society" (1989, 9). As de Bary, Tucker's teacher, is so fond of pointing out, the Neo-Confucians sought to get the Way for themselves in order to be of service to others (1983, chapter 2).

Tucker's definition of the transforming vision of sagehood is worth quoting in its entirety.

In summary, this effort at self-transformation is one that involves:

1. Religious orientation leading to
2. moral and spiritual self-cultivation
3. resulting in action in the socio-political order and
4. union with heaven and earth.

All of these aim toward the realization of sagehood that is seen as the ultimate goal of Neo-Confucian study and practice. (1989, 10)

Tucker's summary definition and Mou Tsung-san's reflections on the religious dimension of the Confucian tao are of a piece. Tu Wei-ming calls this vision of transforming sagehood a profound humanism, an " 'anthropocosmic' creativity" (1990, 129). As always, even the New Confucians most interested in religious dialogue do not want to limit their understanding of the Confucian Way to its religious elements. Although Tu defines this as the Confucian way of being religious, he always places this Confucian religious dimension within his more generic definition of Confucianism as a profound humanism (1985, 131–48). Even Tu, perhaps the most "theological" of the New Confucians, does not want to label this "religion" because it does not conform to the model of the great West Asian religious traditions. Nonetheless, all three scholars of the East Asian Confucian tradition agree with W. C. Smith that there is indeed a Confucian faith commitment to something more divine than the merely secular outcome of human society.

THE CHALLENGE TO CHRISTIAN THEOLOGY

As I have repeatedly stressed, even this preliminary call for reflection on multiple religious participation is a very difficult challenge for most Christians. It is a subversive question even for a liberal pluralist theologian such as John Hick in *An Interpretation of Religion* (1989). The question has arisen in the context of the ferment of Asian and African intellectual and religious life as well as with the traditional elders of the aboriginal spiritual traditions of North and South America and the Pacific. It is also more and more on the minds of many North Americans who experiment with religions beyond their own. This question will not go away, even if classical North Atlantic theology has few tools to deal adequately with it, because until now the common assumption of the North Atlantic churches was that the world was going to become Christian, if not in the twentieth century then surely in the twenty-first. With the revival of the great religious traditions of humankind, liberal Christians are no longer convinced of their ultimate supremacy. One of the reasons for the rise of the ecumenical dialogue movement is to provide Christians with an adequate theology of divine plenitude.

As Peter Berger (1992) has perceptively pointed out in terms of the sociology of knowledge, this heightened sense of religious pluralism is a challenge with promise and curse. The curse has to do with the fact that religious pluralism adds another element leading to the demise of any solid sense of self within North Atlantic culture. As with one of Berger's favorite novelists, Robert Musil, the solid Cartesian self has become a hole into which all kinds of new roles and religious beliefs can find at least a temporary home. In many respects Berger believes the modern age is remarkably like the late Greco-Roman world of the early church. The curse of freedom to choose is also a blessing to create something new, even if the new self will be open to greater religious possibilities than were even dreamed of in late Greco-Roman antiquity. Real freedom to choose, as Berger notes, is never a very pleasant option. In terms of personal satisfaction, most people are much happier in ages when they do not have to invent themselves in a constant process of changing roles every decade of their lives.

Multiple religious participation is an urgent question in North America as more people become aware of the richness of traditional Asian and Native American paths of spiritual transformation. As the national Interfaith Dialogue Secretary of the United Church of Canada for nine years in the 1980s, I was often approached by people whose spiritual life had been profoundly altered and enriched through, for example, Buddhist meditation or contact with native elders. Some of these people asked very quietly what I thought of their involvement with other faiths and the fact that some even perceived themselves as Buddhist-Christians; the key issue they were probing was whether I thought that they were still Christians. This was never an easy question for any of them, for they knew that it would shock their ministers because of the commandment to have no other gods before them. My answer was never a simple one either. To generalize my typical response, I would ask them if they still considered themselves primarily or essentially Christians even if they were profoundly moved and transformed by their Buddhist practice. If they said they still held allegiance to Christ and the Christian movement, I told them that I thought of them as fellow Christians. The self-conscious renunciation of a faith is a formal act, a difficult act, an intentional act, and in my view, quite probably an unnecessary act.

The theological response to the challenge of multiple religious participation depends on how religion is defined in terms of institutional affiliation, propositional assertion or spiritual praxis. Is it a search for ultimate truth (whatever that might be)? Is it the quest for weaning the self from false illusions to the vision of the truth? Or is it assent to a particular set of rites, propositions, dogmas, teachings or dispositions within a particular cumulative historic tradition? Or is it formal membership in some sacred congregation of follow believers? For the most part, I agree with John Hick's most recent formulation of the religious quest: "religion (or a particular religious tradition) centres upon an awareness of and response to a reality that transcends ourselves and our world, whether the 'direction' of transcendence be beyond or within or both" (1989, 3).

By means of this definition of the religious quest, Hick wants us to focus our attention on the soteriological question of the marks of liberation/salvation as embodied in the lives of religious persons in order to assess the fruits of a religious tradition. A religion is a true religion when it produces religious people who move from self-centeredness to reality-centeredness. Or as Hick himself states, "the function of religion in each case is to provide contexts for salvation/liberation, which consists in various forms of the transformation of human existence from self-centredness to Reality-centredness" (1989, 14). Yet it is also clear as Hick continues his study that the question of the function and definition of religion shades off into the question of religious truth claims in light of soteriological practice.

Nonetheless, there is an emerging consensus of theologians involved in interfaith dialogue that Christians must not avoid the question of truth claims. However profound the soteriological test of a tradition may be, however noble its ethical teachings, that is not a sufficient basis for a Christian judgment in such an important ecumenical concern. The key question, as with the definition of religion, is what the search for truth through dialogue entails. For instance, do we see dialogue as a common search for truth, in whatever novel paths that search may take us, or as something else? If it is a clear and present truth we seek then we will need to be prepared for some novel theological transformations and permutations of religious self-identity in the new global city. Changing demography, the mass media, economic interdependence and much more all conspire to engender an enlarged or transformed vision of the truth. The question of dual citizenship is before us with a vengeance.

THE STABILITY OF SYNCRETISM

There is yet another key question we need to address, namely the stability of syncretism. As I have pondered the question, I have come to wonder if the notion of syncretism actually denotes something stable in the religious life of humankind beyond the general human proclivity to borrow a good idea or technique from our neighbors whenever and wherever we can. An example from intercultural life in the United States may be helpful. When I was attending the University of Chicago, the neighborhood of Hyde Park was often called, with a great deal of pride, the only "integrated neighborhood in the U.S.A." The point was made that there were many "changing" neighborhoods, locales in transition from one ethnic community to another, but few examples of neighborhoods where African Americans and Euro-Americans lived together for an extended period of time.[11] I wonder if syncretism might name a similar religious phenomena? Are there any more stable syncretisms than there are stable neighborhoods?[12]

In one answer to this question, China is often cited as a civilization where syncretism flourishes. What is meant by this is that the notion of religious identity is not as exclusive or rigid as it is when defined by modern Western religious professionals. A person can be a Taoist, Confucian and Buddhist more or less at the same time. But this is a question slightly different from that of syncretism per se. It is more properly the question of dual or multiple membership. Syncretism would point to something else, namely the creation of something that is not Taoist, Confucian or Buddhist. When I read some of the Chinese examples of syncretism I find that the thinkers involved, even if they have an interest in a number of different religious traditions, are still identified more with one tradition than the others. For instance, Lin Chao-en (Berling 1980) really remains a Confucian in terms of the deep archic variables of his thought just as the Venerable Chu-hung remains a Buddhist.[13] The supposed Chinese case of syncretism may point more to the digestion of materials from another tradition than to any stable outcome for the individual or for any of the traditions involved. In fact, the religious situation in the post-Axial Age has remained remarkably stable when compared to the proliferation of new religions in the Axial Age. At least this appears to be the case for the great Eurasian landmass from Tokyo to London. One wonders, however, whether this will continue to hold true for Boston or San Francisco. Any reading of a community bulletin board in the East Bay in Berkeley or Cambridge gives added insight into the syncretist mentality of this age.

What about stable counterexamples? Could Christianity itself be called a successful syncretism? What about Manichaeism? The Babylonian prophet Mani (216–77 C.E.) was one of the most successful syncretists in recorded history, but even his initially successful religion failed to survive as a historical force in an organized fashion beyond the thirteenth century. There is evidence that Manichaeism was imported to China, although there is nothing to suggest that Mani's syncretistic religion had a major or lasting impact on the Chinese religious scene![14] And while one could argue that Christianity itself is a syncretistic movement combining elements of early Judaism with other aspects of Greco-Roman religiosity, it is clear that the Christian movement is different enough from Judaism so that it makes little sense to call the daughter and the mother "the same" religion even a century or so after its emergence. There can be family resemblances, but that should not count in terms of considering syncretism as a stable phenomenon.

What seems more likely, following Edward Shils' (1981) analysis of the elements and transformations of tradition, is that traditions expand or contract over time. They absorb and reject foreign material, yet retain a sense of identity that prevails. Traditions can die according to Shils, but that also would not be syncretism. Hence, syncretism may point to a process rather than a result. Successful syncretism may be a shibboleth engendered by a fear of change or a dislike of another person's incorporation of new or novel elements of some other tradition into the hallowed tradition of tradition. In reality there seem to be very few successful syncretisms. What is denounced early on as syncretism often becomes a hallowed orthodoxy over time. Just remember the fate of the Christmas tree in the English-speaking world; it took decades for the more conservative clergy and lay people to accept this innovation from Germany. And if that is not enough, one can ask what Easter eggs have to do with the crucifixion of Jesus of Nazareth as recorded in the New Testament.

We would do well to remember Gadamer's discussion of what constitutes a genuine living tradition.

> Even the most genuine and solid tradition does not persist by nature because of the inertia of what once existed. It needs to be affirmed, embraced, cultivated. It is, essentially, preservation, such as is active in all historical change. But preservation is an act of reason, though an inconspicuous one. (1975, 250)

Further, we need to be alert to the processes of borrowing from neighboring religions, a practice of all living traditions even if they are unlikely to dwell on this aspect of the growth of tradition. One of the more embarrassing outcomes of the modern global media network is that religions will now have to be more honest about their borrowings, and must find some theological rationale for such activities.

Edward Shils suggests that the transformation of traditions comes about from endogenous and exogenous factors. The first and internally driving factor is that traditions have seeds for change in themselves as great creative texts of

Dual Citizenship

divine and human action (Shils 1981, 213). "The creative power of the human mind in confrontation with the potentialities resident in traditions produces change." Another way a tradition changes in terms of endogenous factors is because "traditions of belief also undergo change as a result of being subjected to the test of the claims their proponents make for them" (1981, 222). For religions this manifests itself in the soteriological claims made by believers. John Hick has argued (1989), at great length, that we need to apply the soteriological test to religious traditions. Do they reorient their proponents from the unreal to the real, from the egotistic to the divine? Do religious traditions, in spite of being all too human creations, provide the means for salvation? As proponents ask these questions in different times and cultures, they test their claims in ways that have never been done before. They seek coherence of what they preach and teach in terms of the production of saints and sages.

Shils also argues that traditions change because of exogenous factors. "Traditions change when their adherents are brought or enter into the presence of other traditions" (1981, 240). There is often an element of cultural change involved here, the transformation of migration, conquest and even colonialization. "Power exercises a charismatic force on its own and draws in the wake of its cultural traditions those who have overcome by it" (1981, 250). Once new traditions come into contact Shils postulates at least four possible transformations of the tradition in question (1981, 275–79).[15] These are: (1) addition, (2) amalgamation, (3) absorption and (4) fusion.

Shils' notion of "fusion" comes closest to the traditional understanding of syncretism. "A new syncretic synthesis in which several traditions have contributed to the emergence of a unitary pattern with a new and distinctive central, pervasive theme is one of the major features of the formation and growth of traditions" (1981, 279). For example, Shils believes that Christianity is an example of the fusion of Judaism with elements of the Greco-Roman world, the creation of a tradition with a new and pervasive theme. Traditions (1981, 279) can even articulate new root themes or soteriological trajectories through encountering each other.[16] Nothing in Shils' four categories of transformation mandates an easy or harmonious process for the traditions in contact. Traditions can, of course, also pass away through contact with other traditions. But Shils also maintains that there can be resurgences of even drastically attenuated traditions that have been given up for dead. This often seems to be the case these days for Confucianism, which was rather recently considered a dead or terminally ill tradition.[17] Religion and its strength over human beings exists in the minds and hearts of its adherents: if the faithful do not keep the faith, who would? Notwithstanding the modern revival of Confucianism in East Asia, it will clearly be a much transformed tradition in the twenty-first century.

The prognostication of the future of the Confucian tradition in modern Chinese culture is a highly complex undertaking. For instance, an entire issue of *Daedalus* (Spring 1991) has been devoted to the question of what it means to be Chinese today; a subtheme of many of the essays focused on the question of Confucianism in the modern world as a mark of Chinese culture. Some of the contributors to the volume, such as Mark Elvin, believe that "scriptural Confucianism" is dead although parts of it do live on in modern China. Other authors, such as Tu Wei-ming and Ambrose Yeo-chi King, are much more sanguine about the survival value of core Confucian values and modes of discourse. Yet even Tu and King are mindful of the fact that the revived Confucianism of the People's Republic of China will be radically different from the other epochs of Confucianism within the ongoing transformation of Chinese intellectual history. There is also the fascinating role in the reformation of the Confucian Way being played by Chinese intellectuals living in North America and Europe, as well as the contributions of scholars in Taiwan, Hong Kong and Singapore.

As a process theologian I find nothing startling about such an assessment about change, even profound change, in tradition. For process theology change is the order of the cosmos and the evocation of new values and renewed configurations of traditions has always been key to any living tradition. Shils simply has clarified many of the paradigmatic moves that a tradition performs in its constant dance with the new dawns of self-transformations. What will remain is a recognition over time that these are genuine transformations and that the religion as a coherent tradition remains, even if these transformations are true paradigm shifts in style, form and content. Clearly some things will remain as constants. It would be hard to conceive of Christianity without a profound concern for the New Testament as part of the canon and the confession of Jesus as the Christ at the center of personal piety.

The key question is the continuing self-recognition of the transformed tradition as part of the historic community of faith. In the end people define themselves even if they are labelled by others with this or that name. This recognition makes use of two interlocking methods. First, the adherents of the transformed tradition must see themselves as continuing the older tradition, albeit in a modified or reformed manner. This is crucial, for only people can name their faith, give voice to the sacred as revealed to them. If a group no longer sees itself as belonging to a tradition, then it is fairly safe to say that they are no longer a part of their parent tradition. The emergence of the Baha'i movement from within Islam is a case in point. The rise of the separate Christian community is also an example of this process. Second, and more pragmatically, the rest of the community of faith must be willing to assent to the continued participation of the renewed or reformed group within the broadest possible latitude of the family of the particular faith tradition. That does not mean that other constituent groups of the family of faith may be happy about recognizing the new group, for in point of fact, the older majority may be very unhappy and try to ignore or even suppress the transformed group. I take this to be what a great deal of what the search for heresy is all about. Or the older and more orthodox groups may give only the most grudging recognition of the other groups, always praying that its adherents will see the error of their ways and return to the true and orthodox way of the elders.

In the end, however, my conviction is that there will not be a dramatic or immediate change in either the Confucian or Christian traditions because of dialogue. Certainly neither tradition is going to absorb the other tradition into itself. Nor will there be anything like the creation of a syncretistic new religion, some strange melding of Christianity and Confucianism. This does not mean that Confucians and Christians will not learn from each other and be transformed. As I pointed out earlier, Confucian-Christian interaction has been a comparatively happy encounter. There is no reason intrinsic to either tradition that this should not continue. Nonetheless, historical events could overtake Confucian-Christian dialogue. Economic competition, hostility and chauvinism might emerge again to muddy the waters of peaceful dialogue as the great Asian countries become more and more successful on the model of Japan. North American and European racism is hardly a thing of the past as far as feelings about Asians go.

Further, I also believe that whatever is learned from each other, Confucians will remain Confucians and Christians will remain Christians. Even in the Chinese case, which is held to be more syncretistic than other great civilizations, it is still easy to see that thinkers remain identified with a particular tradition. It is true that Chinese intellectuals enjoyed dialogue with each other and were not averse to borrowing useful things, but one can always detect the true deep structure of their tradition, the archic variables that Watson and Dilworth posited by each great religion and expressed by each thinker as a member of that tradition. Conversion does happen and individual thinkers can have variant archic profiles, but most thinkers still remain true to one metaphor of life, one revelation, one manifestation of the divine reality, one body of texts which expresses this common vision.

Perhaps John Hick is correct when he maintains that a person can only have a real membership in only one tradition at a time at the deepest levels of the human soul. If it is the case, then the notion of dual citizenship is not really a happy metaphor even when disguised by the bland term 'multiple religious participation'. Such terminological innovations hardly capture the excitement people feel as they experience the richness of a new religious community by means of its living teachers, practices and community. Nonetheless, more and more people are experimenting with crossing over from one tradition to another and then returning with new insights from their spiritual journeys. There is more and more a sense that religion is as complex a phenomenon as any other in the modern world.

STILL THE QUESTION OF TRUTH CLAIMS

But even when all this is said and done, what is to be done about the different truth claims made by the Confucian and Christian traditions? This is one of the key issues for any such renewed dialogue and cannot simply be ignored in the name of good taste or fear of disagreement. Furthermore, one wonders why anyone would take part in a dialogue when it is somehow preordained that there would be total agreement about all the issues on the agenda. Dialogue is an adventure, not merely a checklist of items for ecumenical agreement. One of the most interesting things about dialogue is when something new is learned, when some new insight is achieved about what were taken to be old visions of the truth. At present there are no clear answers to this question, although I believe there are some clues about how the conversation will go.

First, Confucians and Christians are going to discover that they have a great deal in common in terms of modern worldviews. This will, no doubt, come as something of a surprise to both sets of participants because their traditions have been developed in comparative isolation from each other. For instance, both Confucians and Christians will probably realize that they disagree with almost all Buddhists, some Taoists and many Hindus on the metaphysical status and worth of the world. Both Confucians and Christians believe that the world is actual and what happens in the world really matters. As we have seen from our examination of process theology, many modern Christians believe that what happens in this cosmologically real and pluralistic world really matters to God. From the Christian side, the area of discussion about differences will focus on the Christian understanding of God, the role of Jesus as the Christ and the guidance of the Holy Spirit rather than on an argument about the nature of mundane reality. For both traditions pluralistic reality opens a window onto divine matters and this mutual recognition may come as something of shock because these two traditions have developed, at least until very recently in religious terms, in isolation from each other.

Second, both Confucians and Christians are still trying to find ways to come to grips with Western imperial expansionism and modernity, twin forces that have gone hand in hand to transform the entire globe since the sixteenth century. This is a struggle they share with all other religions. The problem here is precisely what modern people believe or know and how that relates to their inherited religious tradition. Often this leads to a differentiation between what one believes in terms of a modern worldview as cosmology and the inherited vision of one's religious tradition. While human beings are perfectly capable of believing different things, it is the case that most of us would prefer to have our secular worldview and religious map of the cosmos in some kind of harmony. Cognitive dissonance does not make for the music of the spheres.

Third, the issue of the relationship between religious traditions and their supporting philosophic visions needs to be carefully considered. This is an extremely complicated issue for it is never easy to separate the confession of faith from the dominant worldview (if there is one) of any given era. Sometimes the fit is so tight that there seems to be the possibility of something like the Christian philosophy of the High Middle Ages or the great Neo-Confucian synthesis of the Sung-Ming periods. But in times of dramatic world transformation such as our own, this unselfconscious identification of a religion with a particular philosophy is not so easy, nor is it clear whether religion or worldview dominates the truth-claim question. Most religious persons would argue that it is their faith than dominates their sense of truth. But what happens in those periods of history when precisely what is in question for the religious community is the notion of what the truth claims *are?* Where then does the adjudication of truth claims reside?

I think that we are living through a paradigm shift in Christian consciousness generated by the church's relationship to other religions. That has been much of the burden of this essay. There is a general lack of clarity in the North Atlantic Christian world as to what now constitutes the core metaphors, symbols, texts or dogmas of the tradition—and that is why the question of truth is so hard to fathom. How can one talk about the truth when the symbolic resources of the religion are in flux? Yet there are other ways that a religious person can get at truth claims, and these ways are often linked to the operational philosophy that the person embraces in quotidian life. Even in times of transition there are usually some ontologies and cosmologies operating

which control the means of which a person constructs the question of truth
claims even if these factors have never been strictly formulated.

David Tracy's tripartite division of the theological disciplines is useful again
at this juncture. The present dilemma of truth claims can be divided using the
notion of fundamental, systematic and practical theology. As I have noted in
previous chapters, the driving force behind interfaith dialogue and the question
of truth in dialogue comes from the practical side of theology, the day-to-day
engagement of lay and clergy with representatives from all the living faiths of
humankind. But in and of itself this kind of practical challenge to inherited
positions (such as *extra ecclesiam nulla salus*) does not resolve the question of
truth claims. All it does is to make these kinds of extreme and exclusive claims
sound hollow, the expression of ignorance based on nothing but error or
misunderstanding of the other community of faith. The question of truth still
remains even if the older views of the other traditions now appear unchristian
in terms of spiritual charity and intellectual accuracy.

Systematic theology is really little better off at this point, often being
reduced to making purely pragmatic appeals to a new dialogical practice with
few modern roots in North Atlantic theological tradition. As I noted above,
it is difficult now to uncover any pan-Christian consensus about what the
controlling root metaphors, symbols and teachings of the faith are; of course,
this has never been an easy task in any era, but the problem is compounded
with the emergence of the new churches of Asia and Africa who challenge
some of the long-held systematic theological views of European Christendom.
What we now increasingly discover is different lists of what counts for the
essential deposit of the Christian faith. These individual traditions and dogmas
are often proclaimed with a great deal of vigor, but as Peter Berger recently
noted (1992), if these folk are so certain about the truths of the faith, then
why do they always seem so nervous? The main problem facing systematic
theologians is that they have not yet formulated adequate new theologies for
the Christian ecumenical world, much less expanding their systematic theologies
to include the new reality of interfaith dialogue.

The arena of fundamental theology is, as one would expect, also in the
midst of a paradigm shift caused by the awareness of religious pluralism. Many
dominant forms of philosophy offer little comfort for a theologian in search
of a worldview helpful in integrating the religious pluralistic practice of daily
life with some kind of correlation of the systematic reflections of the historic
church. It is cold comfort to be told by the deconstructionists that all of this
is an illusion anyway and that there is no point to pursuing some kind of
logocentric presence behind or above the buzzing pluralism of the modern

airport. On the other hand, process theology does hold out the hope of some kind of rational discourse, even if the warrants and evidence for what counts for rational discourse will have to be expanded in terms of the emergence of truly global comparative philosophies.

In contradistinction to the disarray found in systematic theology these days, the fundamental theologian does have one minor advantage. The fundamental theologian qua philosopher is aware that he or she is working with a human philosophic instrument that ought not be confused with the living truth of the faith tradition. The philosopher is free to change his or her mind if necessary without a profound sense of guilt towards the philosophy as an heuristic tool. Until the philosopher decides to change schools or methods, at least she or he can pursue the truth questions raised by interfaith dialogue consistently from the perspective of that philosophy. This rootedness in one tradition as a heuristic device gives a certain coherence to the attempt not often found these days in systematic or practical theology—both of which are rootless traditions these days. The unity of philosophic vision may prove transitory, but at least it invites dialogue. It is precisely at this point that interfaith dialogue may prove illuminating as the chosen philosophic system, such as process theology, is challenged by the results of dialogue. Does it work? If so, why? And if not, then why not?

The way out of the present dilemma will not be easy. It will take three different kinds of dialogue. First, there will be the actual engagement of interfaith dialogue in terms of daily life and practice and in terms of its theoretical elaboration. This is now often called the dialogue of life. When the discussion of truth claims is added, then it is called the dialogue of meaning. Dialogue will cause people to change their minds and seek out new ways of talking together to explore ultimate life values, which is what Mou Tsung-san has argued is basic to all philosophy and theology. Second, there will then need to be a three-way conversation among fundamental, systematic and practical theologians about what can be received from these explorations beyond the tradition worlds of Christian life and thought. This will be as complicated an inner discussion as the external interfaith dialogue will be. Some critical correlation will need to go on between the etic and emic dialogues if there is to be any success. The churches cannot live by the findings of the fundamental theologians without recourse to some kind of translation into the languages of systematic theology. Nor can either fundamental or systematic theology progress without the spirit-filled correction and creativity of practical theology as it moves at will in our ever-changing world.

The last arena of dialogue, along with those of life and meaning, is that of the heart. While cooperation in terms of community life and explorations of meaning and truth are noble experiments, no religious dialogue is complete until the participants respond to the callings of the meditative heart. Surely the contemplatives of each tradition must be included in the dialogue for it to reach some manner of even tentative fruition. But, as in so many other dialogues, the dialogue of the heart can only come at the end of the process. The ability to speak from the heart to the heart relies on trust, understanding and the translation of the hopes and aspirations from one culture to another. The Confucian notion of the mind-and-heart must find its own links to the Holy Spirit that blows where it will. The Confucian-Christian dialogue is well begun. Its outcome is known only to High Heaven.

Appendix

Trends in the Interpretation of Confucian Religiosity

INTRODUCTION

Before examining current trends in Confucian studies,[1] it is necessary to provide concise definitions of key terms. This is important because even the question of the definition of terms is often contested in the study of the Confucian Way. For instance, the whole discussion of the religious dimension of the tradition is controversial in that some scholars accept the religious nature of the tradition while others reject it. There are also keen debates about the internal and external definition of the Sung Confucian schools as Neo-Confucianism (Bol 1992; Tillman 1992a). These are important questions because those who have the power to define the vocabulary used to describe a tradition often have the power to define the tradition as it is understood both within and without the Confucian world of discourse.

At least part of the problem arises from the fact that the English terms used to define the Confucian tradition are recent Western-influenced neologisms that need to be matched with more tradition Chinese terms used to define and interpret traditions, schools and lineages.[2] Hence I must briefly define what I mean by Confucian, for this is not historically self-evident for the simple reason that the term Confucian has defined different things in disparate times, places and cultures in East Asia. The experience of what it meant to be a Confucian was and is different for Confucius in Lu, Mencius in Warring States China, for Chu Hsi in the Southern Sung, for Yi Yulgok in Korea, for a Japanese bureaucrat in the seventeenth century, for an Osaka merchant banker in the Tokugawa era, for a modern Korean woman trying to understand her culture or for a modern Chinese intellectual teaching in the West. Nonetheless, all of these persons help define the Confucian Way.

Following modern ecumenical Christian dialogue theory, I argue that Confucianism is defined by what self-aware Confucians have themselves said it to be throughout its long historical development. While scholars outside the tradition have every right to say where the modern definitions depart from those of the past, I believe that it is the privilege of those within the tradition to define its present contours. Therefore, I will adopt the working definition of Confucianism as a religio-philosophic tradition, a definition influenced by the understanding of the tradition found in the works of Mou Tsung-san, one of the leaders of what is called the New Confucian movement.[3] In short, Mou defines the Confucian tradition as a combination of a personal and social ethics guiding daily human life along with a religious or spiritual teaching designed to provide for ultimate self-transformation in terms of the transcendent referent of the tradition. Mou's definition of these teachings are discussed in detail in chapter 4. These two elements, the ethical disciplines of daily life and a path of ultimate self-transformation, serve to define the totality of the Confucian Way. As an intellectual historian of Western, Buddhist and Chinese cultures, Mou believes that these two features define all of the great religious traditions of humankind. As we have also seen, Tu Wei-ming follows his teacher in defining the basic contours of the Confucian Way. Other New Confucians such as Liu Shu-hsien and Cheng Chung-ying likewise agree with Mou's assessment of the tradition.

While it is the case that each of the great traditions of Jasper's Axial Age have distinctive root-metaphors or cultural orientations, it is equally true that they have all demonstrated an exuberant diversity, an ability to transform themselves in novel circumstances while remaining faithful to the founding insights of their respective sages, saints and saviors. While the Axial Age defines a period of human history roughly from the first millennium B.C.E. to the rise of Islam, its intellectual, moral, aesthetic, religious, political, economic and scientific accomplishments are still with humankind today. Mou's formulation is another instance of a Confucian intellectual trying to describe, understand and commend the Confucian Way for himself and to transmit this way to others—always a key feature of any Confucian intellectual.

Many scholars will, no doubt, want to quarrel with Mou Tsung-san's identification of the Confucian Way with religion. Mou is aware that this is not a typical definition of Confucianism. In the past, when pressed, most Confucians argued for a definition of the tradition in terms of its ethical, philosophic and humanistic qualities—most commonly Confucianism was defined as a species of enlightened philosophic humanistic wisdom. The reasons for this Confucian choice of disciplinary self-definition are varied. The most obvious is that Confucianism has never resembled the three great monotheistic religions of West Asia (Judaism, Christianity and Islam).

Mou's argument rests on his observation that each of the world's great civilizations was founded on a bedrock of religious or spiritual conviction from which the philosophy and ethics of the cultures grow. While Mou notes that Confucianism was never at all like the religions of West and South Asia, he argues that it does embody the religious dimension of East Asian culture. In that regard, Mou affirms the Confucianism is the Chinese equivalent of the other great world religions. If one accepts the notion of religion as the basis of civilization, then Mou believes that one must allow for the religious nature of the Confucian Way in all its various forms. For Mou and his students, not all religion must be monotheistic or organized along the pattern of Judaism, Christianity or Islam.

Scholars holding the contrary position argue that Mou Tsung-san is playing the part of the Red Queen—defining terms to suit his own purposes. But then, what great religious reformer or philosopher has not done the same thing? One of the refreshing things about Mou is that he is so open about what he is doing. He seeks to describe, understand and commend the Confucian tradition. Mou clearly realizes that this means making choices about what part of the cumulative tradition he appropriates. His writings are always partisan. For instance, he suggests a new canon within a canon based on his revisionist reading of the Sung masters. In something of an intellectual tour de force, he argues that Chu Hsi's School of Principle, however brilliant, is only a secondary branch of the true tree of Confucian learning. Forgotten rivals to Chu Hsi, such as Hu Hung, are recommended as providing the real essence of the transmission of the Way. Just as with his Northern Sung masters, Mou redefines what counts for culture and learning. Part of this redefinition is the honest recognition of the profound religious significance of the Confucian Way, albeit different from West and South Asian religious norms.

THE SIX PERIODS OF THE CONFUCIAN WAY

As already outlined in the introduction to chapter 3, I suggest that the Confucian tradition is a drama with six distinct periods. The first period is the beginning of the self-referencing tradition commencing with Confucius, redefined and defended by Mencius, and ending with Hsün Tzu, the last, if most unorthodox, of the great early Confucians. We will call this the classic period. Second come the various Confucian intellectuals of the Han, such as Tung Chung-shu and Yang Hsiung, constituting a distinctive and pivotal period in the development of the Confucian Way and its relationship to the imperial Chinese state. Then there is a long middle or third period, roughly from the fall of the Han through the T'ang. This is probably the least known and least studied of all the segments of the Confucian Way except for some interest in such figures as Han Yü, Li Ao and Liu Tsung-yüan who are seen as precursors of the Sung Neo-Confucians.[4]

The fourth era beings with the great revival and renaissance of the Confucian way in the Sung, Yüan, Ming and Ch'ing dynasties, often called Neo-Confucianism.[5] In almost all respects, this long and fruitful period deserves to be internally differentiated beyond the general and bland designation Neo-Confucianism. While all its schools are clearly Confucian, there is an incredible internal diversity among the various schools and periods of its development. For instance, in the Ch'ing dynasty there is a submovement within Neo-Confucianism so unique that it deserves to be distinguished as the fifth period of the Confucian Way. This is the tradition known as Han Learning or the Evidential Research Movement. And sixth, we arrive at the modern era and what has been called the "New Confucianism," a movement of renewal that opens out to modernity and dialogue with the other great faith communities and ideologies of humankind.

Scholars, both Eastern and Western, have not been interested in all of these periods in an equal manner. The bulk of contemporary scholarship has paid attention to the classical and Neo-Confucian phases of the Confucian cumulative tradition in East Asia. Without belaboring the point needlessly, this is because those within and without the Confucian Way are of the opinion that these are the two most important and creative periods of the tradition, eras in which the tradition was given its basic direction by scholars of true genius. For the most part, scholars believe that the Confucian Way was given its definitive form by Confucius and his early classical followers and then revised and reconstituted by the great T'ang, Sung, Yüan, Ming, Yi, Ch'ing and Tokugawa masters.

So, for instance, most scholars have only been interested in T'ang figures such as Han Yü, Liu Tsung-yüan and Li Ao as proto-Neo-Confucians and not as fascinating representatives of the vitality of Confucianism during the late T'ang. However, with the recent work of Hartman (1986) on Han Yü, Barrett (1992) on Li Ao, Chen (1992) on Liu Tsung-yüan and McMullen (1988) on the relationship of Confucian scholars to the late T'ang state, there is a greatly revived interest in T'ang Confucianism. Of even wider scope, Bol (1992) has just completed a major study linking late T'ang intellectual history to the renewal of Confucian studies in the Northern Sung. We are increasingly realizing the profound continuity between aspects of T'ang and Northern Sung intellectual discourse.

One aspect of my exploration of the tradition is an examination of what is now called the New Confucianism, the most recent and least defined of the phases of the Confucian way. Because the New Confucianism, as an intellectual tradition that seeks to define a specific form of Confucian religiosity as part and parcel of the *ju-tao*, is not particularly well known in the West, I will dwell on its importance in the emerging global multifaith dialogue movement. The New Confucians seek nothing less than a total revitalization of the Confucian Way. Some members of the New Confucian movement, such as Mou Tsung-san, Tu Wei-ming, Liu Shu-hsien and Cheng Chung-ying, recognize that at least one important cultural orientation of the tradition is its much neglected religious dimension. Having shown interest in that aspect of the tradition, a number of the New Confucians have demonstrated a willingness to become partners with ecumenical Christians in the global interfaith dialogue movement.

Modern Confucians are called New Confucians precisely because they represent what is going on now in Confucian intellectual circles in terms of reviving and renewing the tradition as a way of life to be commended to the entire world. Far from being a dead tradition, a relic that can only be stored in a museum of intellectual history (Levenson 1968), the New Confucians argue that Confucianism is alive and showing signs of distinctive vitality.[6] This has been made clear through present scholarship all around the Pacific Rim. There is also growing interest in the incorporation of living Confucian values in national life as witnessed by recent developments in Singapore. For instance, the Harvard Confucian scholar Tu Wei-ming was recently asked by the government of Singapore to undertake the task of providing guidance for the modern teaching of Confucian values. Further, Taylor (1988), in his interviews with Okada Takehiko, has demonstrated how a contemporary Japanese Confucian is trying to apply Confucian insights to modern ethical and social problems. Similar movements are also taking place in Hong Kong, Taiwan and Korea and whenever the political climate thaws even a bit, there is renewed interest in the Confucian Way in the Peoples Republic of China.

As with all contemporary intellectual and spiritual movements, it is impossible to chart or predict its permutations. The reasons for this are broadly intellectual, political, religious and social. For instance, although there has been a dramatic growth in Confucian scholarship in the People's Republic of China, there is still a great deal of ambivalence concerning the role of the Confucian tradition, especially given its connections to the now discredited imperial Chinese state. However, at least the whole question of the role of Confucianism in modern China is now being discussed and debated.

Furthermore, first-rate scholarship is being published in the PRC about the Confucian tradition, often focusing on neglected areas such as the social and economic bases of the Confucian elite (Chang 1981). PRC scholars are analyzing what was going on in the concrete detail of daily life and political struggle during China's Confucian past. This is also not a totally neglected area of research in the Western scholarly tradition of Confucian studies either. For instance, Dennerline (1981) has provided us with a rich study of the local elite of the area around Chia-ting, including details of their daily life and family histories. Hymes (1986) has researched the family connections of the scholarly elite of certain local areas in the Northern and Southern Sung. Also, work on Chinese marriage patterns by Watson, Ebrey (1991b) and their collaborators is beginning to explore some of the familial aspects of Chinese life in terms of modern feminist issues of gender relations. Our understanding of the Confucian way will be deeply enriched by the examination of these neglected aspects of the social dimensions of the Confucian Way.

THE SCHOLARLY REVOLUTION IN CONFUCIAN STUDIES

Over the last four decades there has been a real ecumenical revolution in Confucian studies in the East Asian and the North Atlantic sinological worlds both in terms of quantity and quality. A great deal of the impetus for this renewal of Confucian scholarship comes from the research of a small group of famous Chinese scholars now called the New Confucians. In fact, a small group of the New Confucians even issued a manifesto in 1957 outlining their understanding of what is necessary for such a renewal of Chinese culture (Chang 1957–62, 455–83). The larger group of important and innovative thinkers who can be understood as part of the New Confucian movement includes such luminaries as Hsiung Shih-li, T'ang Chün-i, Ch'ien Mu, Mou Tsung-san, Hsü Fu-kuan, Thomé Fang and Wing-tsit Chan. Except for Chan and Fang, these scholars have published almost exclusively in Chinese and are not well known by the Western scholarly community although most serious and informed modern Western Confucian scholarship stands on the shoulders of these giants. Chan is an important bridge between this generation of Chinese scholars and their Western interpreters. He has rendered a tremendous service to the Western scholarly community by making known the highest standards of contemporary Chinese scholarship through his own exemplary translations, commentaries and monographic studies.

There is also a revival of interest in the Korean and Japanese Confucian traditions. In many respects, the work of scholars such as Masao Maruyama (1974), Tetsuo Najita (1987), Harry Harootunian (1970), Herman Ooms (1985) and Mary Evelyn Tucker (1989) have redefined our understanding of the permutations of the Confucian way in Tokugawa Japan. Wm. Theodore de Bary and JaHyun Kim Haboush (1985), Sung-Hae Kim (1985), Michael Kalton (1988), Young-Chan Ro (1989) and Martina Deuchler (1992) have achieved the same kind of results in presenting the creative advances of generations of Korean Confucian scholars.

A very important group of younger Chinese scholars, trained in Western scholarly methodologies and teaching Confucian studies in East Asia and the West includes scholars such as Tu Wei-ming, Liu Shu-hsien, Ts'ai Jen-hou, Cheng Chung-ying, Yü Ying-shih, Antonio Cua, Edward Ch'ien and Julia Ching. These thinkers and others have provided the bridge between the work of the earlier generation of the New Confucians and Western intellectual circles. In a very concrete sense, these two generations of Chinese intellectuals define the present state of the Chinese Confucian Tao.

It should also be clearly noted again that Confucianism is a living tradition in Korea, Vietnam and Japan. I leave the discussion of trends in Korean and Japanese to those more well-informed in the field and will focus my remarks on my own concentration, the New Confucianism of the Chinese tradition and its Asian and Western interpreters. The history of the East Asian renewal of Confucianism will provide scholarly projects for the twenty-first century.

These two generations of Chinese, Korean and Japanese scholars are not alone in their impact on Western Confucian studies. Many notable contributions have been made by non-East Asian authors; in North America the sustained effort of Wm. Theodore de Bary of Columbia University stands out as a model. De Bary has nurtured, stimulated and organized research projects that have transformed the whole field of Confucian studies. One of his most important contributions has been to articulate the humane and dialogical dimensions of the Confucian tradition. As a mentor de Bary has also been instrumental in educating a whole generation of younger scholars of the Confucian tradition who will carry on the work that he, Wing-tsit Chan and others have initiated through the work of the Columbia University Neo-Confucian Seminar.

GENRES OF SCHOLARSHIPS

Within the complex matrix of contemporary Confucian scholarship, three distinct genres have emerged. As with all such typologies, one must keep in mind that they are ideals and that many individual works tend to overlap each genre. Most contemporary works in Confucian studies, focussing on typical literature in English, can be broken down into roughly three major categories— institutional studies, life-and-times studies and ethico-religious studies.

Although hardly new, institutional studies come first because of their continuing importance in Confucian studies. The genre of institutional studies is exemplified in the series of books on Confucian and Chinese thought published in the 1950s and 1960s such as *Confucianism in Action, The Confucian Persuasion* and *Confucian Personalities*. More recently, this category is illustrated by such titles as Metzger's *Escape from Predicament*; Handlin's *Action in Late Ming Thought*; Dennerline's *The Chia-ting Loyalists* or Elman's *From Philosophy to Philology* and *Classicism, Politics, and Kinship: The Ch'ang-chou School of Next Text Confucianism in Late Imperial China*. A fascinating Japanese contribution to this genre is Najita's *Visions of Virtue in Tokugawa Japan: The Kaitokodo— Merchant Academy of Osaka*.

All of these studies try to show, in diverse ways, how the Confucian tradition interacted with the larger East Asian social reality. This can, of course, be done in differing ways. One can focus on formal institutional history or on the broader development of whole schools of thought such as Elman has done in his two brilliant studies of Ch'ing scholarship. Also, as I mentioned above, this seems to be a very important area for scholarship being done in the People's Republic of China. Wing-tsit Chan's *Chu Hsi: New Studies* is also a significant contribution to aspects of the interweaving of personal, intellectual and social history.

The next type is what I call rather irreverently the "life-and-times" genre. In many respects this has been one of the more enduring trends in Western scholarship, and one of the most important. The works in this area usually focus on the intellectual biography of a thinker, trying to provide insight into the thought, action and life of the person in question. Good examples of this genre are Hartman's *Han Yü*, Lo's *The Life and Thought of Yeh Shih*, Peterson's *Bitter Gourd*, Birdwhistell's *Transition to Neo-Confucianism: Shao Yung on Knowledge and Symbols of Reality*, Black's *Man and Nature in the Philosophy of Wang Fu-chih*, Tillman's *Utilitarian Confucianism: Ch'en Liang's Challenge to Chu Hsi*, Munro's *Images of Human Nature: A Sung Portrait* and Tucker's *Moral and Spiritual Cultivation in Japanese Neo-Confucianism: The Life and Thought of Kaibara Ekken (1630–1714)*. In many respects this genre provides the backbone for the other types, building up a corpus of studies on individual thinkers that is absolutely necessary for the study of a cumulative tradition such as Confucianism.

There is also a new and important sub-genre of the life-and-times group that has emerged in the last few years. While most of the studies mentioned above deal with only one thinker, scholars such as Peter Bol in *"This Culture of Ours"* and Hoyt Tillman in *Confucian Discourse and Chu Hsi's Ascendancy* have now attempted to present us with more synthetic studies of the intellectual history of the rise of the renewed Confucianism of the Late T'ang and Northern and Southern Sung. Building on the work of the Asian and Western scholars mentioned above, Bol and Tillman are in a position to provide a sweeping reevaluation of the history of the T'ang and Sung Confucian traditions. They demonstrate the diversity and internal richness of this great phase of the Confucian Way. It is also interesting to note that Bol and Tillman recognize the spiritual and religious dimensions of the T'ang and Sung schools of thought. In this regard they contribute to the next genre as well as to general intellectual history.

The third genre is the study of the religious, ethical or spiritual dimension of the Confucian Way. There is simply no easy way to define this broad category for one cannot simply use the term religion or religious as defined in a Western institutional sense to encompass the Confucian spiritual trajectories. But it is the case that a number of scholars have probed these important dimensions of the Confucian Way in the last few years. Some have done so from the inside as Confucians and some in a sympathetic mode from the outside. Examples of this genre are de Bary's *The Liberal Tradition in China, East Asian Civilizations: A Dialogue in Five States*, and *Learning for One's Self*; Tu's *Centrality and Commonality: An Essay on Chung-yung*; Cua's Dimensions of Moral Creativity: Paradigms, Principles and Ideas; Fingarette's *Confucius, The Secular as Sacred*; Cheng's *New Dimensions of Confucian and Neo-Confucian Philosophy*; Neville's *Tao and Daimon*; Hall and Ames' *Thinking Through Confucius*; or Taylor's *The Religious Dimensions of Confucianism*. Other examples will be discussed later. All the works in this genre have a very interesting feature—not only do they seek to describe the Confucian tradition and its development, they also defend its global human relevance for contemporary thought. They are, in the positive sense of the term, apologies for the Confucian Way. They intend both to transmit, reform and renovate classical Confucian teachings.

It is also useful to divide the ethico-religious genre into two subsections. In addition to those works that deal specifically with the ethical and religious content of the tradition described above I am concerned with a number of new studies which deal with the comparison of the Confucian tradition in terms of its interaction with Christianity. As scholars move toward intentional and formal Confucian-Christian dialogue, it is extremely important to understand the previous history of this encounter.

Interesting examples of this genre are such works as Ching's *Confucianism and Christianity: A Comparative Study*, Gernet's *China and The Christian Impact*, Spence's *The Memory Palace of Matteo Ricci*, Mungello's *Curious Land: Jesuit*

Accommodation and the Origins of Sinology and Young's *Confucianism and Christianity: The First Encounter.* Although not focused exclusively on the Confucian tradition, Schwartz's *The World of Thought in Ancient China* devotes considerable attention to the issue of the religious dimension of the Chinese tradition. I consider these works to be a subset of the larger ethico-religious genre because they investigate the religious or spiritual dimensions of Confucianism most seriously and they are not part of a separate genre of the history of the development of the Christian Church in China. These texts are not mission studies, but rather comparative analyses of the interaction of Confucianism and Christianity as diverse cultural modes of religious expression.

HUMANE LEARNING, RELIGIOUS SPIRITUALITY AND MORAL METAPHYSICS

While important intellectual breakthroughs have been made over the last three decades in all three of these genres, I will concentrate on the third area, namely those works focusing on the religious dimension of Confucian thought. In some respects this is the most problematic area of the three because for a long time many Western scholars, under the influence of religious taxonomies developed in the West, did not even recognize the religious nature of Confucianism. Confucianism was and is considered a profound humanism harboring a depth dimension analogous in some ways to the religious traditions of Europe, West Asia and India.

Western scholars were not alone in this evaluation. Many Chinese scholars preferred to define Confucian tradition as a species of philosophic humanism, rejecting the notion of Confucianism as a religious tradition. However, this evaluation of Confucianism as simply a form of nonreligious humanism is dated in terms of the discipline of the history of religion, a scholarly tradition now more ecumenical in its understanding of religious traditions outside of its initial West Asian models. For example, Schwartz (1985) has a nuanced and religiously sensitive discussion of the issues at stake in trying to define the religious dimension of the early Confucian tradition.

Because of limited space, I will confine my comments to the works of one Western and one Chinese scholar—both of whom have initiated paradigmatic discussions of the religious dimensions of the Confucian traditions. The North American scholar in question is Wm. Theodore de Bary, one of the founders of the great Columbia University tradition in Confucian studies. I will review *The Liberal Tradition in China, East Asian Civilizations: A Dialogue in Five Stages, Learning for One's Self* and, to a more limited extent, *The Trouble with*

Confucianism. As a representative modern Chinese scholar I have chosen Tu Wei-ming, with a focus on his two most recent books, *Confucian Thought: Selfhood as Creative Transformation* and *Way, Learning, and Politics: Essays on the Confucian Intellectual.*[7] Actually, these six works nicely complement each other, demonstrating the humane tradition of liberal learning in classical Confucian thought and the profound religious dimension of the Confucian tradition.

Tu Wei-ming has been actively involved in Confucian-Christian dialogue. He himself is fully aware of the long debate about whether Confucianism, and especially Neo-Confucianism, is to be considered a religion or even a species of religious thought. He rather neatly deals with the issue by paraphrasing W. C. Smith on the fundamental quality of the Confucian spiritual quest. Tu notes the following:

> Wilfrid Cantwell Smith, in his seminal study on the meaning and end of religion, makes a helpful distinction between 'a religion' as an institution characterized by a set of objectifiable dogmas and 'being religious' as spiritual self-identification of the living members of a faith community. Accordingly, the problem of whether Neo-Confucianism is a religion should not be confused with the more significant question: "What does it mean to be religious in the Neo-Confucian community?" (1985, 132)

The problem that Tu is dealing with here is the definitional difficulty that most Western scholars have because classical Confucianism and its Han, T'ang, Sung, Yüan, Ming, and Ch'ing decendents do not resemble the institutional religions of Western Asia and Europe. In a parallel situation in South Asia, Halbfass (1988) demonstrates that this was as much a problem for the definitions of the Indian intellectual tradition during the same period of early Western study of Indian religions. There were simply no simple equivalents to the Western notions of religion or philosophy in the classical Indian traditions. In the Chinese case, neither classical Confucianism, Neo-Confucianism nor New Confucianism, resemble classical Greek philosophy or Western Christianity. Be this as it may, Tu continues by making the very strong claim that Neo-Confucian religious style can be defined: "for the sake of expediency, being religious in the Neo-Confucian sense can be understood as being engaged in ultimate self-transformation as a communal act" (1985, 140).

One of the really refreshing characteristics of Tu's *Confucian Thought* is that he is so forthright in his willingness to discuss the religious dimension of Confucianism. Tu functions as a Confucian theologian because he seeks to describe, understand and commend the tradition. By this I mean he is not merely concerned with being an objective scholar, accurately describing the Confucian tradition in value-neutral terms. Tu points out that the essays in his book, besides offering basic information about the Confucian tradition, are also "self-consciously Confucian" responses to perennial human concerns. He summarizes his own self-understanding as a modern Confucian in the following manner:

> In the modern pluralistic cultural context, the Confucian "faith" in the intrinsic meaningfulness of humanity may appear to be finite, historical, secular and culturally specific. However, to the living Confucian, this faith is an articulation of truth, an expression of reality, and indeed a view of life so commonly accepted in East Asia for centuries, so obviously rational that it is singularly self evident. In this essay, I intend to demonstrate, based upon my own understanding of the Confucian project, that this humanistic claim about faith is of profound significance to the study of religion as an involving and developing discipline which may, in the long run, establish a unity of understanding and appreciation of ultimate concerns despite the seductiveness of sophisticated relativism currently espoused by some of our most brilliant and open-minded colleagues in social sciences and the humanities. (1985, 51)

This is a ringing defence of the proposition that Confucianism is a profound religious faith, a living one at that, and a tradition that has a great deal to offer the contemporary religiously pluralistic situation.

Tu (1989) has continued to explore and defend this understanding of the religious dimension of the Confucian tradition in his *Way, Learning, and Politics: Essays on the Confucian Intellectual*. He defines the three main problems of the classical tradition as the Way, learning and politics. For Tu, the notion of the Way points towards the distinctive Confucian understanding of the transcendent or the divine. He argues that this unique form of Confucian discourse "represents yet another type of symbolic thinking of the Axial Age different from either Judaic religion or Greek philosophy." (1989, 5). He goes on to analogize this primal Confucian religious insight in the following fashion: "If we take the Confucian reflection on the Way as analogous to fundamental theology, Confucian learning (*hsüeh*), the second area of concern mentioned above, addresses issues comparable to those addressed in systemic theology" (1989, 5).

Tu argues that "to realize humanity as the ultimate value of human existence eventually became the spiritual self-definition of a Confucian" (1989, 3). Interestingly, Tu even includes Hsün Tzu along with Mencius as an exponent of this distinctive form of Confucian religiosity.

> Even Hsün Tzu (fl. 298–238 B.C.), who criticized Mencius' theory of human nature, acknowledged that the cognitive function of the mind

is capable of recognizing and thus controlling human desires. Hsün Tzu thus insists that self-cultivation is necessary and desirable and that the highest manifestation of humanity is the form of sagehood that can be attained. He thus fully subscribed to the Confucian faith on the perfectibility of human nature through self-effort. In theological terms, the Confucian idea of learning to be human suggests a possibility for human beings to become "divine" through personal endeavor. (1989, 4)

According to Tu, if both Mencius and Hsün Tzu agree on the religious dimension of the tradition, this must surely indicate the core of what the Confucian faith means. While many scholars have shied away from discussing the spiritual aspects of the Confucian tradition, Tu, within the carefully crafted parameters of analogy, is willing to say that there is most definitely such a religious dimension to the classical tradition. Therefore, the later Neo-Confucian interests in these "ethico-religious" aspects of the tradition are not incomprehensible or incompatible in terms of the internal development of Confucian discourse.[8]

We now turn to the seminal work of William Theodore de Bary, a Roman Catholic, who, although he does not write from within the Confucian circle, acknowledges the spiritual dimension of Confucian thought. In fact, he even chooses to call one strain of Confucian thought prophetic, a descriptive term not usually employed in the discussion of the tradition. In defining the prophetic element of the Confucian tradition he says,

> By this I mean to indicate an extraordinary access to truth not vouchsafed to everyone which by some process of inner inspiration or solitary perception affords an insight beyond what is received in Scripture and by appeal to some higher order of truth gives new meaning, significance and urgency to certain cultural values of scriptural text. (1983, 14–15)

De Bary indicates that he believes that this prophetic dimension of the Neo-Confucian moral vision is an extremely important element of the liberal humane tradition of Chinese thought. De Bary also returns to this theme of prophet and covenant in his most recent critique of the problematic elements of the tradition (1991b). The very choice of analogy, of prophet and covenant, demonstrates the deeply religious elements of the Confucian tradition.

Another of de Bary's contributions to contemporary Confucian scholarship is his defence of Chu Hsi's distinctive form of religiosity. Chu Hsi and his school have fallen on hard times with the demise of the imperial state, though many New Confucians argue that this is a good thing, for it will allow the real Chu Hsi to emerge after his long imperial Babylonian captivity. We only need remind ourselves that the most vibrant recent forms of Confucian thought in the Ming and Ch'ing were not often affiliated with Chu's philosophy. Nonetheless, no one would deny the continuing importance of Chu's philosophy defining the general parameters of Confucian discourse from the thirteenth century on. People may have disagreed with Chu and even have rejected his philosophy, but his synthesis was simply the benchmark against which all other Confucian thinkers sought to establish their own form for the reclamation of the way. De Bary's (1991) *Learning for One's Self* is yet another in his series of illuminating reexaminations of the history of the impact of Chu Hsi's thought, this time in terms of the philosophic formation of the Chinese intellectual self from the Sung masters to Lü Liu-liang (1629–83).

One of the marks of de Bary's scholarship is his consistent appreciation of Chu Hsi's project and its creative ramifications in Chinese intellectual history down to the present. This does not mean that de Bary is in any way a partisan of Chu's philosophy in the traditional Chinese sense of lineage affiliations. Just because he appreciates the work of Chu Hsi does not mean, as it so often seems to mean for other scholars, that he must reject Wang Yang-ming and his followers. I think that this is one of the more important trends in de Bary's thought and one which I hope will be copied by many other scholars working in the field.

It is not very profitable to observe modern Western and Asian scholars continually refining the great intellectual battles of the past between the schools of principle and mind. In fact, one of the real strengths of the scholarship of such thinkers as Mou Tsung-san and Ch'ien Mu is to demonstrate the sterility of these traditional debates between the adherents of Chu and Wang. This is not to discount the fact that there are grave differences between these two great Neo-Confucian thinkers, but to continue the almost stylized debate between the proponents Chu Hsi and Wang Yang-ming is to overlook some of the most important aspects of the Confucian tradition. The fruitfulness of de Bary's program is that he refuses to be drawn into these debates and therefore helps us look beyond those old quarrels towards new possibilities for interpretation and reaffirmation.

I should note in passing that de Bary is not alone in this endeavor. Cua (1985) and Knoblock (1988) have been restoring the tarnished reputation of Hsün Tzu, who was often considered the bête noire of the Confucian tradition. Nonetheless, no one, not even his later detractors, ever underestimated Hsün Tzu's scholarly and intellectual brilliance. He was, no doubt, the most intellectually articulate of the classical Confucians. Cua reappropriates Hsün Tzu, arguing quite convincingly, I think, that any contemporary reconstruction of the Confucian way must pay attention to Hsün Tzu, for he offers one of the most sophisticated forms of Confucian discourse. Not to appreciate Hsün Tzu is to neglect valuable material for a new Confucian synthesis. For instance, Mou Tsung-san has argued that the development of a rigorous analytic method for the Confucian tradition is essential for its modern renovation. While Mou himself believes Hsün Tzu does not represent the Confucian mainstream, it is precisely Hsün Tzu's underappreciated systematic gifts that are now necessary for Confucianism to enter into progressive conversation with other philosophic and religious traditions.

De Bary is aware that he is going against a number of scholarly grains even by the choice the title of his book, *The Liberal Tradition in China*. He accepts the fact that his language may sound strange for a number of reasons. The first is that the reader, aware of the differences between the Chinese and Western traditions, might question the very use of the Western concept of 'liberal' in any Chinese guise. Part of this hesitation comes from the fact that liberalism itself is under grave attack in the West from both the right and the left. To be a self-proclaimed liberal these days is not an easy task.

The second point that de Bary defends is actually closely related to the first, namely whether there is anything vaguely resembling the Western 'liberal' tradition in China. His defence of the use of the term liberal is linked to many of his other scholarly themes and in fact depends heavily upon his interpretation of the philosophy and teachings of Chu Hsi. De Bary argues in this and other works that Chu Hsi's philosophy, interpreted in its broadest sense, is a liberal teaching par excellence. According to de Bary, Chu's thought demonstrates a breadth of insight, depth and intellectual openness and integrity that make it a paradigm for a comparative understanding of the liberal tradition in China. In fact, de Bary argues that any comparative and historical study of what we in the West call the liberal tradition must now take into account the work of Chu Hsi and many other members of the Confucian tradition.

De Bary highlights two aspects of the Neo-Confucian liberal tradition that he feels help contribute to the vitality of that tradition in the Sung revival. By extension he considers that these two characteristics need to inform any new creative synthesis in the Confucian tradition. He argues,

> first I should like to characterize the intellectual climate of the Sung period as one in which a new emphasis on the vitality and creativity of the Way, as well as a new critical temper, abetted each other in the reappropriation of the past and amplifying a tradition to make them serve contemporary needs. (1983, 9)

Creativity and faithfulness are both keys to the renewal of the Confucian Way in the modern world. According to de Bary, Confucianism will need to find ways to be faithful to the fundamental trajectories of the tradition as well as to modify creatively its root-metaphors and cultural orientations where necessary.

In one respect the New Confucians function as theologians for their tradition. Tradition is important for them and provides a standard to measure their own activities, thus they continue the project of the Neo-Confucians of the Sung, Yüan, Ming and Ch'ing. None of these thinkers could avoid being interested in tradition, or would want to do so. De Bary indicates the profound Confucian concern for just these matters in the first chapter of *The Liberal Tradition in China*, "Human Renewal and the Repossession of the Way." The discussion of the repossession of the Confucian way brings out one of de Bary's most important points. He emphasizes repeatedly the necessity within the Confucian tradition to "get" the tradition for oneself.

Although de Bary argues strenuously that the Confucian tradition is not one of 'individualism' in the Western sense, he asserts that it places a heavy burden on the person as a responsible social agent. The Confucian, for de Bary, is a person implicated in a much larger social and cosmic reality than the personal concerns of any one individual. In many respects, de Bary's interpretation of the Confucian sense of self resembles the idea of person adumbrated by W. C. Smith in *Towards a World Theology*.

Over and over again de Bary (1983, 21; 1991) points out that the proper goal of Confucian study is "learning for the sake of oneself." The Confucian scholar, at least according to Chu Hsi, was not merely a passive spectator in the drama of human life. Nor was the Confucian scholar, according to de Bary's reading of Chu, paralyzed by old social conventions or mores; rather, the true Confucian scholar was a person set free by this appropriation of the tradition for the heroic task of renovating Chinese society. As de Bary puts it, "thus the concept of the orthodox tradition or repossessing the way expressed a certain ideal of the heroic individual as the reactivator of traditional values and as the agent of social reform and human renewal" (1983, 20).

Here de Bary is trying to overcome both the Western and Chinese stereotype of the Confucian scholar as reactionary pedant. He argues that the true Confucian scholar, at least as Chu Hsi sees it, is a renovator of the age and not merely a reactionary defender of the social conventions of the times. Although the Confucian is profoundly committed to tradition, he or she realizes that this tradition must be infused with the personal sense of sagely integrity. Furthermore, this sagely achievement is one of renewal and self critical awareness and action. De Bary makes the point this way:

we may be entitled to speak of a kind of individualism expressing itself in the cultural activities of the Neo-Confucian scholar, and we may observe certain values associated with the autonomous mind—self-consciousness, critical awareness, creative thought, independent effort and judgment— finding their way into the basic text of the school. (1983, 65)

And of course, de Bary is as aware as anyone else that although this creative spirit is expressed in many of the foundational Neo-Confucian texts, this does not mean that it is embodied in the lives of all Confucian scholars.

It is at precisely this point that many scholars in the Peoples Republic of China object to much of the contemporary Western interest in Confucianism. They often point out that Western scholars are fascinated by the tremendous creativity they see in the Neo-Confucian texts, but that these Western scholars did not have to live through the last corrupt phases of the institutional use of Confucianism by the Chinese imperial authorities. While some PRC scholars may applaud this Western interest in the creative aspect of the Neo-Confucian tradition, they want to keep its more negative social results firmly fixed in our sight. They believe that only in this way will all scholars of the Confucian tradition finally come to a better understanding of the role and function of the Confucian tradition within Chinese culture in anything like an adequate sense of historical and social reality.

Nonetheless, de Bary has mounted a defense of the classical Neo-Confucian tradition at its best. He has pointed out its comprehensive features in terms of scholarly enquiry embodying a sense of social reform and commitment. He has also demonstrated that the Confucian project does allow for a prophetic (if not covenantal, 1991b) critique of the society that it helped to create. While very few Confucians will be happy with the image of a revolutionary tradition, they are often quite capable of acting in revolutionary ways. De Bary's interpretation of Chu Hsi demonstrates how, through repossessing the Confucian tradition, the Confucian of any age can help in the renewal of his or her society, and by extension, how these ideals of reform and renewal within the Chinese liberal tradition provide inspiration for the creation of a global humane consciousness in our modern world.

In *East Asian Civilizations*, de Bary (1988) expands his reflections on the Confucian tradition in ways that are extremely important for Christian-Confucian dialogue. In fact, he even suggests that Confucianism itself is a form of dialogue. He defends the thesis that East Asian civilization can be seen as the product of a dialogue process between the various intellectual forces that have shaped the region. He sees this happening in a number of stages, beginning with the classical legacy itself, which for the Confucian includes the contributions of the Sung Confucian revival, commonly called Neo-Confucianism. He traces the fortunes of all of these traditions through China's contact with the expansionist West in the modern period. He calls the contemporary intellectual horizon of East Asia "post-Confucian East Asia" because of the institutional disestablishment of the Confucian tradition (1988, 108). He notes the various factors, including political, economic and intellectual forces, that have led to this present condition.

De Bary observes that Confucianism had three main institutional strongholds in Chinese culture in the pre-modern period. These were the schools, the state and the family. It is clear that Confucianism no longer functions in any of these three areas as it did in imperial times. De Bary points out that at least for the present it is highly unlikely that Confucianism will regain any measure of direct influence in the state or the educational system (except for some success in places such as Singapore and Taiwan). He holds out more relevant chances for impact on the family, the social institution that is the bedrock of the Confucian world. In the realm of familial values it is clear that Confucianism dies hard, if at all, and in fact there seems to be something of a comeback or at least a serious discussion of these values throughout East Asia.

De Bary believes that many key Confucian values can provide material for the modernization process in East Asia. Not the least of these is the capacity to ask fundamental questions about modernization as Westernization. De Bary firmly believes that Confucianism, especially as expressed by Chu Hsi and his educational program, has a great deal to contribute to the emerging post-Confucian culture of East Asia, and indeed to the West if we are finally willing to take seriously East Asia intellectual culture.

De Bary asserts that Chu Hsi's curriculum for humane education is relevant for our present impasse. What North Atlantic civilization now needs is an educational curriculum starting from a personal reading and creative confrontation with the classics, followed by a study of the major histories of the civilized world, concluding with a lifelong commitment to the discussion of the values and problems of modern life—all mixed with an appreciation for the technical specialization needed for each of these disciplines. Chu Hsi recognized that this pattern of study and action rests on a "compelling need for spiritual and moral training alongside the reading and discussion of books" (1988, 137). Our understanding of history and the globalization of "classics" needs to be greatly expanded from Chu Hsi's day, although nothing in Chu Hsi's vision militates against just such an expansion of humane education within civilized society. The West needs to ponder afresh the East Asian challenge to look within, to control the self in order to find a new ecological balance before the entire environment is unfit for human habitation.

CONCLUSION

As we have seen, Mou, Tu and de Bary nicely complement each other. Mou and Tu demonstrate conclusively the religious spirit and flavor of the Confucian tradition, displaying the profound spiritual significance of the Confucian Way for modern Confucian scholarship. De Bary shows us the immense range of the liberal and dialogical traditions within the Confucian Way. He explores the humane learning requisite for any person to claim repossession of the Confucian way. Together the work of these three scholars shows what one can call the vertical and horizontal dimensions of the Confucian tradition— and indicate the direction for renewal needed within the tradition as it confronts contemporary global social, intellectual, ideological and religious pluralism.

This trend in the reinterpretation of the spiritual and religious nature of the Confucian tradition can also be found in the other two genres discussed above. In fact, the burden of a great deal of contemporary scholarship about the Confucian tradition is designed to indicate our failure to fully understand the complexity of the tradition. One of the paramount concerns of all three genres is to demonstrate that our inherited stereotype of the Confucian tradition as a narrow and provincial orthodoxy is unfounded. The attempt to show that the tradition is much more complicated, diverse and creative than we might have thought initially. In short, all of these studies demonstrate the extensive transformations and changes that have gone on within the Confucian tradition, whether understood in terms of institutional organization or in the spiritual quest of the Confucian scholar.

All three genres help us to have a more comprehensive understanding of the Confucian tradition. We can now see the tradition in some of its living vibrancy as it has unfolded over the ages. Further, I believe that through the medium of these new studies we can begin to understand why so many people dedicated themselves to living as Confucians. The Confucian Way lives on and continues to makes its contribution to the emergence of a new and hopefully expanded and enriched global consciousness and civilization.

Notes

INTRODUCTION

1. Richard J. Bernstein (Reynolds and Tracy 1992, 310–11) has neatly outlined the problem and promise of reflection on the otherness of different religious traditions from the perspective of contemporary North Atlantic philosophy. His outline of the six points of the spirit of the age of pluralism are an apt summary of the issues involved in the analysis of pluralism.

2. Tu Wei-ming has noted (1986, 1991, 1992), from the Confucian perspective, that people now often find direction for their lives in two rather contradictory ways. First, there is the new sense of global interconnection. We have become self-consciously aware of the unity of humankind in an unprecedented way. Second, we seek release from the tension of diversity in seeking the roots of our ethnic and cultural traditions. According to Tu, we seek the seemingly contradictory manifestations of a new ecumenical awareness running side by side with a renewed search for the fundamentals of each ethnic, cultural and religious community. Tu believes that it is too early to say which form of consciousness will dominate the postmodern age.

3. Richard Rorty (1989) is a happy exception to this rejection of relativism. In some highly influential essays he defends relativism as the way the world is; we ignore this relativity at our own peril.

4. The main focus of this essay is on the Chinese case. If we expanded the conversation to include Koreans and especially the Japanese, such generalizations about the modernization of the Confucian tradition would have to be modified. As Rodney Talyor's study (1988) of Okada Takehiko has shown, the Japanese Confucians have been busy reforming their tradition in terms of the Japanese response to the Western intellectual and spiritual challenge. Actually, as Harootunian (1970) has shown, the Japanese Neo-Confucian elite began the modernization process even before the Meiji Restoration.

5. In a recent study of Chu Hsi (Berthrong, 1993), I have applied the method of archic analysis developed by Walter Watson (1985) and David Dilworth (1989) to specific Chinese texts. While archic analysis is only one of many new methodological tools designed to promote comparative philosophy and theology, it is one that self-consciously takes Asian texts seriously.

6. Robert Neville, Roger Ames, David Hall, John Cobb and Steve Odin come to mind as scholars interested in comparative work based on various versions of process thought. Charles Hartshorne is also interested in comparative thought, though in a less focused fashion than the

younger generation of scholars indicated above. It is also doubtful that Neville still thinks of himself as a member of the movement even though he acknowledges its contribution to his own philosophic and theological project.

7. It should be noted that reflection on *ch'i*-theory does have a long and distinguished life in later Chinese, Korean and Japanese Confucian philosophy. In fact, a number of later Confucian scholars take Chu Hsi and his disciples to task for not paying much more attention to *ch'i* than they did. One of the strains of arguments is that Confucian pluralism and realism basically depends on appreciation of *ch'i* and not on speculation about principle or the Supreme Ultimate.

8. The terms form, dynamics and unification were first suggested to me by the Whiteheadian sociology of W. Widick Schroeder in "Religious Institutions and Human Society: A Normative Inquiry into the Appropriate Contribution of Religious Institutions to Human Life and to the Divine Live" (1976, 190–91). Whereas Schroeder limits the triad to an analysis of Western Christian institutions, there is no reason why the usage cannot be expand for the purposes of comparative theology.

CHAPTER ONE

1. Some of the New Confucians are interested in the Christian theological tradition and are more than willing to enter into dialogue. For instance, in his 1989 essay, Liu Shu-hsien offers a Confucian critique of Paul Tillich's doctrine of God and Christology. Clearly these are two issues at the heart of the modern interfaith debate between Confucianism and Christianity. It is interesting to note that Liu cites some of Charles Hartshorne's analysis of Tillich's position in his paper. Tu Wei-ming has signaled his interest in this topic by adding a chapter concerning the religious nature of the Confucian tradition to his essay on the *Chung-yung*. And Cheng Chung-ying (1991) has also written about the religious dimension of the tradition is his recent philosophic essays. A number of other Confucian responses have been collected in Peter Lee's (1991) volume from the first International Confucian-Christian Dialogue.

2. The term 'North Atlantic world' needs some explanation. Most of the drive for dialogue outside of Asia and Africa has come from the churches that find their origins in the countries surrounding the North Atlantic. I realize that this is not an entirely happy phrase, but it does point to the area of old Christendom which is now most concerned with the questions of interfaith dialogue and religious pluralism.

3. An example of the growing interest in pluralism in the interreligious dialogue movement is David J. Krieger's *The New Universalism: Foundations for a Global Theology* (1991). He devotes a subsection of chapter 1 (17–37) to the analysis of the emergence of radical pluralism in the agenda of ecumenical Christianity. The process movement philosophers have also been fascinated by this question. For instance, David L. Hall (1973, 1982a, 1982b) has addressed the issue of radical pluralism from the perspective of a Whiteheadian theory of culture. Given Whitehead's own commitment to a cosmological pluralism, most of his students and disciples have followed suit. Hall focuses his attention on the Taoist rather than the Confucian tradition that Robert Neville finds so stimulating.

4. Neville (1990, 46) has a very useful definition of "modernity" as a cultural force for theological reflection: "For purposes of theological discussion, modernity can be defined

precisely. It is that culture whose basic senses of the world have closure. Closure is a mathematical notion that defines a set of things as limited to certain specifiable properties and distinguished from things that might have contradictory properties."

5. Feminist and womanist theology will also have an impact on the way dialogue is carried out in the North Atlantic Christian community as feminist and womanist theologians add their voices to the literature. An example of this kind of critique is Maura O'Neill's *Women Speaking Women Listening* (1990).

6. Mark Edward Lewis (1990) has demonstrated in great detail the important role that sanctioned violence played in the formation of the early Han imperial state. This Warring State and Han interpretation of the role of violence, especially in its Confucian formulation, proved to be an extremely stable ideology. Only the impact of the West finally caused its collapse.

7. A considerable literature has been developed in the last decade dealing with the theological implications of the ecological crisis. For a sample of Christian opinion, see Charles Birch, William Eakin, Jay McDaniel (1990). Probably the most profound and sustained systematic attempt to frame an ecological ethic is Charles Birch and John B. Cobb, Jr. (1981).

8. The time frame I refer to here is from the great missionary meeting in Edinburgh in 1910 till Vatican II in 1964. What began in the mission field came to fruition with the ecumenical opening of John XXIII.

9. Hans Küng (1988) has devoted considerable attention to the application of Kuhn's paradigm hypothesis to the history of theology. Küng (1988, 123) argues that "the analysis of paradigms . . . helped me to see the contemporary crisis in a larger historical context: as conflict and controversy not just involving various theologians and theologies but large-scale paradigms." Slightly later in the same chapter (1988, 128) he outlines eleven major paradigms in the history of the development of the Christian church. While paradigms, according to Küng, do change throughout Christian history, most paradigms continue to survive somewhere in the ecumenical present. In some cases, individual Christians can maintain various paradigms at the cost of severe cognitive dissonance. And for all Christians, Küng (1988, 153) notes the continuity of received tradition which helps to distinguish the method of theology from that of the natural sciences.

10. This is a particularly pressing question for those three great historic missionary religions, Buddhism, Christianity and Islam. It will also become a question for the New Confucians as they argue for the universal validity of the Confucian message. As Mou Tsung-san has pointed out, the Confucian tradition was not historically a "universal" religion like Buddhism or Christianity, but it may become so as the great cultures of East Asia take their places in the modern world. Hence the question of truth and uniqueness might well become questions for thoughtful Confucians now even if they were not in the past. There are some traditions, such as Judaism, which have decided not to be missionary religions in the modern world even though they have a clear sense of universal mission. I should note that this is still an open question for modern Judaism, a tradition forced out of the missionary business by the early Christian church in the Greco-Roman world.

11. Both Livia Kohn (1991b) and Michael Saso (1990) are careful to point out that classical religious Taoism is not the same as what they call the popular religions of China. The religious scene in China is much more complicated and rich than the old typology of Confucianism, Taoism and Buddhist, would suggest.

12. The question of multiple religious participation also has a long history in India. In many ways this has been a most pressing issue for Christians and Hindus in the nineteenth and early twentieth centuries. The question was often asked, from the Hindu side it seems, whether or not one could be a Hindu-Christian. For a review of the theological implications of this question, see Jacques Dupuis (1991).

13. Ch'en (1986), in Wing-tsit Chan's excellent annotated English translation, devotes a whole section to a refutation of key Buddhist and Taoist notions such as "nonbeing" and "emptiness." For instance, Ch'en (1986, 169) states: "Take the doctrine of transmigration; it is definitely absurd." While Ch'en does not go on to call for a crusade against the Buddhists, he does not hide his conviction that Buddhism is a false doctrine.

14. We must recognize that this is the particular problem of the North Atlantic world and not for all sections of the Christian world. As Barrett (1982), the great demographer of religions, has pointed out, this is one of the great ages of the growth of the Christian church in Africa and Asia. But in all regions, even those of growth, there is a new demand for articulating the gospel in terms of that culture and time. Each area will have its special task, either for growth, renewal or simple survival with some kind of integrity.

15. Or as Smith put it on in an article on Christianity and religious pluralism (Oxtoby 1976, 9), "philosophy and science have impinged so far on theological thought more effectively than has comparative religion, but this will not last." Smith also points out in this article that Harvard undergraduates, in their student papers, were able to demonstrate that Paul Tillich really knew very little of other traditions. As we know from Tillich's last published work while teaching at the University of Chicage, it was unkind of the undergraduates to point out how little Tillich knew in detail of other religions as if this were something Tillich also did not keenly regret. It appears that Tillich was well aware of this fact and was on the road to rethinking his theological position on the basis of the encounter of Christianity and the world religions.

16. If Lucien Price (1954) is to be believed, Whitehead was less than enthusiastic about organized religion at least during his Harvard University period. But Whitehead would not be the first philosopher or theologian who was less than impressed with the churches around him while still remaining moved by the gospel account of the life, teachings and death of Jesus. One can be impressed with the Christian movement without finding a church for a home.

17. Parenthetically, I should note that I have not found the work being done in the discipline of comparative philosophy of much use for a theology of dialogue or religious pluralism. The obvious reason for this is that modern professional philosophers have very little serious interest in the classical religious issues of even the West; and to compound this problem, those seeking professional employment in departments of philosophy also show very little interest in mastering enough of the traditions of South and East Asia to be more than puzzled about why Eastern philosophy does not seem much like Western philosophy at all when judged by what it would take to get tenure in any serious department or publish in a prestigious philosophical journal.

Further, there is a rather bookish air to much of what comes out under the philosophic label. There are some notable exceptions, such as Halbfass (1988) in Indian philosophy, and the recent work of Walter Watson (1985) and David Dilworth (1989). I believe that much of this pervasive sense of unreality comes from the fact that philosophers are little involved in the day-to-day activities of the modern interfaith movement. In dialogue one learns rather quickly that people are not books and are prone to say things that do not, on the surface, seem possible given the tradition out of which they come.

We often talk these days of paradigm shifts, and the people involved in interfaith dialogue not only believe in such shifts, they have seen them happen in front of their own eyes and ears. Much of this disinterest can be analyzed in terms of power within a profession. The North Atlantic world has had a great success in imposing its conceptual patterns and its primary academic language, English, upon the rest of the world for the last three centuries. This phase of global history seems to be drawing to a close in interesting ways. It is obvious that East and South Asian thinkers have been enriched and transformed by their contact with the West; it is less clear that many Western thinkers have been transformed by their contacts. It is hoped that this is now changing, fuelled not only by intellectual curiosity but by a growing trade imbalance that even impacts the economic well-being of North American academics. More and more people are trying to figure out why East Asia is such a successful economic region. Part of this present success surely has to do with the intellectual heritage of the region and hence, a concomitant renewed interest in Confucianism, Buddhism, Taoism, Shinto and the I-Ching. Perhaps, for the first time in a long time, Western intellectuals are prone to consider that not all truth and light comes from the shores of the North Atlantic world.

18. The whole question of a common discourse is a difficult one indeed. Can anyone escape the fundamental perspectives and prejudices of his or her primary tradition? There is a growing literature related to comparative theology which tries to deal with this question. See Kreiger (1991), Nakamura (1975) and Halbfass (1988) for three different accounts as to how comparative theology *may* be possible.

19. Some modern students of religion, such as George A. Lindbeck (1984) in his influential *The Nature of Doctrine: Religion and Theology in a Postliberal Age*, argue that even beginning with "experience" prejudges the theological method involved in theological analysis. I have some sympathy with this argument, but continue to believe that without the modern experience of religiously pluralistic communities in the North Atlantic world, Western theologians would have never seriously considered this issue. Only the experience of a pluralistic world awoke them from their Barthian (from which, interestingly enough, the older Barth did not suffer) slumbers and orthodox dreams of a unified religious world. At least in systematic or biblical theology there were no movements which were overly concerned with religious pluralism or the other faith communities.

20. David McMullen (1988) notes that this is a very Neo-Confucian way to read the tradition, and in fact only dates from the Sung revival. The T'ang Confucians had a different way of viewing the history; they gave pride of place to the great commentators and not independent teachers such as Mencius or Hsün Tzu.

21. I have always found Mou's work to be the most philosophically brilliant of the New Confucians, and I say this even though I do not agree with his position. I am much more partial to Chu Hsi and the Chu Hsi tradition than he is; yet reading Mou has demonstrated to me the truth of the cliché that we can learn more from our critics than from our friends.

22. I will also make reference, especially in Chapter 4, to a more recent work (Mou 1983) in this regard. In his *Nineteen Lectures on Chinese Philosophy* he covers much of the same ground but is interested in the whole sweep of the Chinese philosophic tradition and not just the development of Confucianism. There is considerable continuity between the two summary

statements of Mou's interpretation of the three main Chinese intellectual traditions—Confucianism, Taoism and Buddhism.

CHAPTER TWO

1. I am well aware that this is not considered an authentic text of Aristotle. But then, there are some things which, as Ken Kesey once said, if not true, ought to be.

2. As we will note below, another counterexample is the conflict between the Japanese government and their Christian subjects in early Tokugawa Japan.

3. Another possible historical counterexample of the lack of hostility between Confucians and Christians is the conflict between the Tokugawa Bakufu and the Japanese Christians. This was certainly a clear case of suppression, and a bloody one at that. But as Herman Ooms (1985) has argued in his study of the formation of early Tokugawa ideology, it is unclear whether or not we can even call this a Confucian ideology. Confucianism was just one aspect of the mixture of Tokugawa politics, so this is not simply a religious conflict.

4. Institutionally this meant that the WCC Sub-Unit on Dialogue agreed to help convene the First International Confucian-Christian Dialogue in Hong Kong, June 1988. At the conclusion of the Second International Confucian-Christian Dialogue, July 1991, held at the Graduate Theological Union, Berkeley, California, there was an agreement that such consultations should continue to be held every four years. An international steering committee, coordinated by Dr. Peter Lee of the Christian Centre for the Study of Chinese Religion and Culture, Hong Kong, was charged to prepare the papers from several conference publications and to begin planning for a third conference in the mid-1990s.

5. In my 1993 analysis of Chu Hsi's concept of *ch'eng*, I have made use of the method of archic analysis for just this purpose. While based in a reformed Aristotelian reading of texts, archic analysis claims to be a hermeneutic tool capable of showing the affinities and dissimilarities between texts from all the great philosophic and religious traditions of humankind. One of the strong points of the Watson-Dilworth methodology is that they have attempted to apply it to the great Confucian tradition from the beginning. I have used archic analysis in order to see if we can discover the deep structures of the Confucian tradition. The results have been encouraging as far as showing some unexpected correlations with Western philosophers such as Whitehead.

As Mary Evelyn Tucker (conference presentation, 18–19 November 1992, Boston University) has suggested, the main problem with all such methodologies is that they work well for European and West Asian traditions and for the theistic aspects of the Hindu complex of schools and teachings. They begin to falter when confronted with the nontheistic teachings of South Asia, and become almost useless when we reach East Asia. One proof for this is the fact that Western scholars have had a difficult time deciding whether Confucianism is a religion.

6. Peter N. Gregory (1991) has shown just how difficult and transforming the process actually was through his study of the justly famous T'ang scholar-monk Tsung-mi (780–841). Anyone who thinks that interreligious borrowing is easy and quick needs to read this monograph to be persuaded by the evidence of Chinese Buddhist history.

7. As noted in the introduction, I owe the formulation of these traits as form, dynamics and unification to W. Widick Schroeder's Whiteheadian sociology of religion. In his 1976 study of religious institutions, Schroeder suggests that every aspect of human life can be analyzed

in terms of form, dynamics and unification. I have found this triad an effective and relatively neutral way to describe the metasystemic insights of the Chu Hsi school and process thought as two representatives of relational, processive and organic modes of discourse.

8. As the bibliography of this study will attest, the field of comparative theology or religion has already produced a prodigious amount in its most modern phase. For practical purposes, at least for the Christian churches, this new phase, often called "interfaith dialogue," began with the promulgation of the Vatican II teachings on ecumenical and interreligious relations. The World Council of Churches was not long delayed in joining the interfaith movement. One of the marks of any new or diverse movement in theology is the lack of consensus in terminology. There is no one term which has become the norm for talking about what I am attempting to do in this essay. Warren, in the late 1800s, called his early teaching comparative religion. This is a perfectly serviceable phrase and is actually more inclusive than comparative theology for, as Warren himself thought, it would include Buddhism as a religion though not a theistic tradition.

9. Even in North America the Christian community has been vaguely aware of religious pluralism—there have always been the Native Peoples and the Jews. But given the teachings of contempt which characterized so much early Christian thought about both traditions, the question of religious pluralism as we now find it never arose. The faith of the Jews was something, following St. Paul in *Romans*, which would be decided at the end of time, and Native Peoples would be dealt with by the missionaries, the residential schools and European diseases. In either case, Christian theology was not deflected from its dream of the conversion of the whole ecumenical world.

10. These charges, one must remember, are made from within the hermeneutic circle of process theology or postmodern philosophy. They are often highly polemical and may even violate some of the ethical dialogical norms which the dialogue movement proclaims as some of its most important virtues. For instance, would such self-description make much sense to a modern Thomistic theologian? If this not the case, it demonstrates yet another area where dialogue is necessary. A fine example of such a dialogue is to be found in David Lochhead's (1988) *The Dialogical Imperative* where in he shows how Barth's theology is much more open to interfaith dialogue than the master himself would have ever expected.

11. For instance, the great Ch'ing philosopher Tai Chen (1724–77) made a very cogent argument for such borrowing from the Taoists and Buddhists for Chu Hsi and Wang Yang-ming. See Ann-ping Chin and Mansfield Freeman (1990), *Tai Chen on Mencius* for an account of Tai's reservations.

CHAPTER THREE

1. While the main focus of the following introduction to Confucian thought focuses on the Chinese case, it is important to remember that Confucianism is an international movement. Historically it has served to define major aspects of the cultures of China, Korean, Japan and Vietnam. In the present religious scene, the Confucian tradition is having a global impact through its spread by the various East Asian diasporas. Confucianism gives every indication of spreading beyond East Asia and becoming another great inter-culturally defined Axial Age religion in terms of Jasper's definition of the Axial Age. I believe that Confucianism is now becoming a truly global religion (as well as philosophy, political science, poetics, etc.).

There is currently a lively debate about the question of what name we are to give this movement in its many forms deriving from the Northern Sung Confucian renaissance. As Hoyt Tillman (1992a) demonstrates, this is not just a pedantic quarrel among scholars. The name of a tradition is important in defining the self-identity of any group. The real problem is that none of the current English neologisms are a precise fit with the various Chinese terms used to define the great schools of the Sung, Yüan, Ming and Ch'ing dynasties. For instance, Tillman points out that the common English term 'Neo-Confucianism' does not even correspond exactly with the Chinese term *tao-hsüeh* or Learning of the Way. The problem, of course, is compounded by the fact that the Chinese thinkers themselves did not have just one term to describe their movement as a whole or even always their own particular school. But what they were sure of, as Peter Bol (1992) has shown, is that as Confucians they understood themselves as defending a shared notion of a common cultural heritage.

2. Of course this is a rhetorical overstatement. However, the point still stands that all of commentary, exegesis, religious practice and philosophic articulation are deployed in a historical framework. The sages are within history because they serve to define what is of worth remembering in that history.

Furthermore, we also need to remember that Judaism is another religion with a strong sense of history. It is as impossible to think of Judaism without a historical narration as to conceive of the Confucian Way without a historical past as canonized in the classics.

3. It is just this problem of the complex interaction of the imperial state and the Confucian tradition that de Bary (1991) has addressed in *The Trouble with Confucianism*. It is also an important topic in the emerging Confucian-Christian dialogue in that both parties are trying to find ways to reclaim the prophetic dimension of their traditions.

4. This is an interesting claim given that neither Mou or Tu, at least in their published works, would make this assertion. While it is obvious that both are definitely not partisans of the Chu Hsi school, it is much less clear about just how they see themselves in terms of the traditional debates between Chu Hsi and Wang Yang-ming. For instance, Mou is clear that his favorite Ming thinker is Liu Tsung-chou. My reading of the situation is that Mou and Tu are representative of a new generation of Confucians who are seeking to escape the confines of the old "school" quarrels and want to make use of the entire range of the Confucian tradition in order to commend this reformed Confucianism not only to their fellow East Asians but also to a globally educated public.

5. Benjamin Schwartz (1985) has probably written the best and most judicious rejoinder to Hall and Ames. Schwartz describes and analyzes the religious dimensions of the early Chinese tradition in contradiction to those who would refuse to see that aspect of classical Chinese thought.

6. Much the same point about the necessity for a tripartite formulation of "reality" is made by Charles Hartshorne (1965, x–xi) in terms of essence, existence and actuality. For Hartshorne this is a necessity if we are to make sense of Anselm's crucial ontological argument for God's existence. My reformulation of this insight attempts to be closer to the way Chu Hsi and Ch'en Ch'un stated the issue—if they had been writing in English and if they were interested in process theology, which is certainly an audacious leap of faith on my part. It is also interesting to note, and this is not lost of Hartshorne, that C. S. Peirce was intrigued by the role of triads in the formulation of anything altogether.

7. Giving an elegant, suitable and reliable English translation has been the despair of master sinologists from the beginning of the study of the Chinese philosophic tradition. I have come to believe that no one has yet to propose a single adequate English translation because *ch'i* plays such an enormously protean and important role in all Chinese thought. There is probably no way for a single English word or even phrase to capture all the shades of meaning of *ch'i* even in Chu Hsi's thought, much less in the works of other Neo-Confucians. The difficulties of translating *ch'i* expand even farther when we consider Taoist and Buddhist texts. Whatever else *ch'i* is, it is certainly vital, energetic, dynamic and capable of being configured in whatever modality it is as the very substrata of the spiritual, emotional, intellectual, transcendent world—or whatever other ways we may find to describe what is, is not, or might be.

8. Along with copious and meticulous notes for the exemplary and fluent translation, Chan has added an evaluation of the life and thought of Ch'en Ch'un. I have chosen to retain my own early renditions of Ch'en's philosophical glossary, based on the Chinese text of 1840, in order to highlight the specific philosophic issues I want to discuss. I commend Chan's translation and exposition of the entire text for anyone interested in Ch'en's interpretation of Chu Hsi.

9. Whitehead (1978, 4) speculated that true metaphysical concepts, if they could be discovered, would be very hard to identify because we cannot comprehend them in our normal fashion of noting differences by means of comparisons. "The metaphysical first principles can never fail of exemplification. We can never catch the actual world taking a holiday from their sway." I think that the notion of *ch'i* functions as such a metaphysical category in Chinese thought—it certainly never takes a holiday. It deserves much more careful study for just this reason. We can certainly make such an argument for Chang Tsai and Tai Chen (1724–77) in terms of *ch'i*'s role as a metaphysical notion in their philosophies.

10. I realize that this is a very truncated discussion of Whitehead's theory of the concrescence of mundane entities. For instance, I have chosen not to engage in an exegesis of the role of the divine reality in providing an initial aim for each emerging creature. I am aware of the complexity of the issue but am more interested here in Chu Hsi than in Whitehead.

CHAPTER FOUR

1. The very term "New Confucian" is ambiguous. Some of this ambiguity comes from the fact that the movement includes a number of different persons who have divergent agendas even though some of the most prominent of the group signed a common manifesto in 1957 (Chang 1962, vol. 2). For a discussion of this movement and its role in modern Chinese intellectual history, see Chang Hao (Furth 1976), "New Confucianism and the Intellectual Crisis of Contemporary China." In some cases, as is certainly the case for Mou, these agendas reflect what de Bary (1991b) has called the prophetic dimension of the tradition, the appeal to an original rereading of the classical Confucian texts which will renew the Confucian world in light of modern problems and challenges. There is nothing surprising about such an thematization; it is an appeal which almost all religious reformers have made as they attempt to convince their audiences that all they are doing is going back to the original fonts of wisdom to be found in the canonical texts of their tradition. However, it is quite clear that what Mou is actually doing is forging a modern "New" Neo-Confucianism and not a revived version of the classical texts of Confucius, Mencius, Hsün Tzu or their later Chou and Han followers. Mou is highly

selective in his sense of canon. He hardly ever deals with the *Ta-hsüeh*, which is certainly a key text for those he believes represent the Confucian mainline tradition. Perhaps one reason for this omission is the fact that Mou is not much concerned with the traditional Confucian interest in concrete political culture. There is nothing in his extensive corpus which could be called an engaged political vision in the same sense as Chu Hsi or Wang Yang-ming outlined for the Southern Sung or the mid-Ming. Although this could have been done on the basis of his texts, he has chosen not to do so. His particular interest has been to explain and expand what he takes to be Confucian moral metaphysics, the intellectual formulation of the tradition in terms which can be understood in the modern world. This is a kind of grand systematic philosophic metaphysics which is not much in favor these days, at least in Western-oriented philosophy departments.

Nonetheless, as we shall see, Mou is an important figure within the New Confucian movement as its chief philosophic systematician. This does not mean that all the other members of that movement or their students agree with his moral metaphysics. Nonetheless, it does mean that there is a general recognition of the importance of his attempt to reformulate the classical and Neo-Confucian heritage in terms of modern ecumenical philosophic concerns.

2. It is interesting to note that Tu Wei-ming, when he writes about the religious dimensions of the Confucian way, often calls this aspect of the tradition "religiosity." In some of his more recent writings, Tu shows more interest in explicating the religious dimension of the Confucian tradition than Mou. The reasons for Tu's usage are both sociological and theological. First, the Confucian tradition has no formal institutional religious structure as one finds for the great West Asian—Jewish, Christian and Muslim—family of faiths. Second, the Confucian tradition is not overtly theistic in that it locates the core of its religious dimension in self-transformation and human relatedness. Hence Tu discusses the issue in terms of "religiosity" and not religion as a formally organized historical tradition. See Tu's article (1985, 131–48), "Neo-Confucian Religiosity and Human-Relatedness."

3. As I have noted in the text, Mou Tsung-san has not been preoccupied with defending the religious dimension of the Confucian tradition, although he clearly recognizes a form of Confucian religiosity. One probable reason for this is Mou's continued defense of what can only be called the depth dimension of the Confucian Way. No one has done more to recast our understanding of the rise of Neo-Confucianism than Mou, and this exploration has lead him into not only an examination of Neo-Confucianism, but also the post-Enlightenment modern Western intellectual tradition, philosophic Taoism and Buddhism in its various Chinese manifestations.

The quest for the roots of the Sung-Ming Neo-Confucian revival began with the three volumes of *Hsin-t'i yü Hsing-t'i* in 1968–69. Reacting to discussion of his study of Northern and Southern Sung Neo-Confucianism down to Chu Hsi, he produced a number of other works. In 1971 he published *Chih te chih-chüeh yü Chung-kuo che-hsüeh*, an elaborate defense of the role of intellectual intuition in Chinese philosophy. This book was partially an attempt to show how the Chinese tradition differed from Kant and the later Continental traditions of Husserl and Heidegger. This was followed in 1975 by *Hsien-hsiang yü wu-tzu-shen*, yet another volume of comparative philosophy focused on the modern Continental German phenomenological and existential tradition. His students and critics also suggested that he had not paid sufficient attention to the high T'ang Buddhist synthesis. Mou attempted to correct this oversight in the two volumes of *Fo-hsing yü Pan-ro* in 1977. After having made these responses to perceived oversights in his history of the rise of Sung Neo-Confucianism, he returned to the Neo-Confucian tradition in his 1979 *Tsung Lu Hsiang-shan tao Liu Chi-shan*. This volume completed his study of the Neo-Confucian tradition down to the end of the Ming and the death of Liu Tsung-chou, the last great, creative figure in the Sung-Ming Neo-Confucian movement according to Mou. The two summary collections of lectures published in 1974 and 1983 outline, in some detail, his understanding of the whole of the Chinese tradition, including philosophical Taoism and Buddhism. Everywhere Mou seeks to describe the living reality of the Chinese intellectual experience and to commend it to the modern world as an important aspect of global culture.

See also Berthrong 1980a, 1980b, 1982 and 1987a for a further discussion of Mou's vision of the Confucian Way. Liu Shu-hsien (1989b) has an outline on Mou's scholarly career which also sheds light of Mou's concern for the depth of the dimensions of the Confucian tradition.

4. W. Halbfass (1988) surveys the history of similar debates in the Indian traditions and their encounter with Western modernity. It is fascinating to see how many of the great nineteenth and twentieth century Hindu reformers struggled with the same problem that bothers Mou Tsung-san. Clearly there is no easy way to identify precise Indian equivalents to the Western notions of religion and philosophy. Nonetheless the Neo-Hindu reformers are certain that the Indian tradition has such phenomena and Halbfass analyzes the linked conceptual pair of *darśana* and *dharma* in the debate about the nature and scope of Indian religious and philosophic discourse.

5. The term 'intersubjectivity' needs some comment in light of his English glosses (1974, 4) as subjectivity and inner morality. He argues that 'subjectivity' and 'inner morality' are keys for understanding the Confucian tradition. I have modified the usage by translating *chu t'i hsing* as 'intersubjectivity' because of the relational nature of Mou's thought. Mou certainly does not want to suggest that Chinese philosophy is a kind of individualistic subjectivism. By adding 'inter' to 'subjectivity' I hope to indicate the relational and pluralistic understanding which infuses all of Mou's moral metaphysics. According to Mou, we can only become human through interaction with other human beings. One can also note that the term intersubjectivity is important in some strains of modern Continental hermeneutic philosophy.

6. Much the same kind of criticism has been made of Fung by Wm. Theodore de Bary. De Bary (1989), it should be noted, pays generous tribute to Fung as a great, if flawed, historian of Chinese philosophy.

7. Liu Shu-hsien (1989b) reviews the intellectual contributions of four key New Confucians, including Mou Tsung-san, to the modern Confucian revival. It is clear from Liu's summary discussion of the work of these representatives of the New Confucianism that many of their interests in the "spirit" of the Chinese tradition would be part of the theological or religious dimension of Western European thought. The constant New Confucian emphasis on creativity and the balance between the transcendent and immanent dimensions of the cosmos constitute the background for the New Confucian development of Confucian religiosity.

8. There is quite a debate raging these days about who defines the "mainline" of the Sung Confucian renaissance. We must remember that Mou reads the tradition as a highly creative philosopher. While Mou is also often a fine textual critic, he does consistently read the texts with his own philosophy in mind. However, to paraphrase Whitehead, it is better for a philosopher to be interesting rather than correct in every detail. Mou is surprisingly good with details; and he is always interesting.

For two fine, and less polemical, studies of the rise of Sung though in general and Chu Hsi's dominance in particular, see Bol (1992) and Tillman (1992b). Bol described the development of the Confucian tradition from the late T'ang to Ch'eng I in the Northern Sung. Tillman's focus is on Chu Hsi's rise to intellectual prominence per se.

Both Bol and Tillman have challenged Mou's outline of Sung intellectual history as too simplistic to do justice to the complexity of the movement itself and the social situation that engendered it. Bol and Tillman agree that Mou has not expanded his list far enough. Mou has basically only dealt with the philosophic side of the movement and has failed to do justice to all those other Neo-Confucians who saw themselves as historians and poets. For instance, Tillman argues that if we are going to pay attention to Hu Hung, then we also need to pay much more attention to Chang Shih and Lü Tsu-ch'ien if we are to frame an accurate picture of what was really going on in the Southern Sung intellectual world. Tillman makes the interesting case that if Lü had lived a longer life he might have become the dominant Confucian of his age.

9. Mou is one of those students of the Confucian tradition who believes that the two major periods of creativity for the Confucian Way are to be found in the Chou and the Sung-Ming periods. These are the first and the fourth phases of the Confucian tradition as outlined in chapter 3. In a series of works devoted to the history of Chinese philosophy he demonstrates an active interest in the whole range of the Chinese tradition, including Buddhism and Taoism. But his style is to focus on what he takes to be the most philosophically creative and interesting eras of each tradition. Hence the jump from Mencius and Hsün Tzu to the Northern Sung for the Confucian tradition.

10. In his recent study of Hsün Tzu's ethical thought, Philip J. Ivanhoe (1991) notes that Hsün Tzu did indeed hold that reason was a very important part of the sage's ability to create civilizing norms, the Confucian rituals. According to Ivanhoe, Hsün Tzu believed that these proper norms of human behavior were developed through a struggle to understand the role of humanity in nature and their creation demanded a clarity of insight, a rationality of the highest order. In the sense that we must take the pluralism of the world seriously in our ethical reflection, Chu Hsi agrees with Hsün Tzu.

11. In the 1983 *Nineteen Lectures*, Mou sharpens his critique of Chu Hsi and his school and argues for its basic philosophic links to Hsün Tzu's pre-Han theories of mind and principle. He begins by noting (394) that Ch'eng I disagrees with his elder brother about the unity of perception and humanity (*jen*); the implication is that this separation of epistemological concerns from moral concerns, or at least an inclination to distinguish the analysis of the two, is typical of Ch'eng I and Chu Hsi in that Chu follows Ch'eng I and not Ch'eng Hao. Mou (394) notes that Ch'eng Hao sees a mutual implication of perception and humanity. This is the proper path of Confucian moral metaphysics and axiology. According to Mou (396), Chu Hsi, who follows Ch'eng I and not Ch'eng Hao, believes that intellectual achievement is crucial for the process of human self-transformation and therefore inverts the proper Confucian understanding that the moral must interpret the intellectual rather than the other way around. For Chu Hsi, Mou continues, creative reason is "mere reason." Hence for Chu (400–01), "humanity is mere reason and not mind," which Mou takes to be a form of active reason/mind. The real philosophic roots for Chu Hsi are to be found in the *Ta-hsüeh* and Hsün Tzu. "His (Chu's) raison-d'être is Hsün Tzu's raison-d'être." Mou (401–03) briefly outlines how Chu Hsi, from the age of 37 on, began this momentous and fatal deviation from proper Mencian Confucianism. Mou argues (403–05) that Chu Hsi is very much entranced by "ontological perfection" as found in his

intellectual understanding of principle, and is therefore more like Plato or St. Thomas in the West than Confucius, Mencius, Ch'eng Hao or Hu Wu-feng. Mou concludes (405) that this intellectual essentialism is the philosophic key for understanding both Hsün Tzu and Chu Hsi. While not filled with the details one finds in his major study of the rise of the Neo-Confucian tradition, this section is a lucid exposition of his philosophic critique of Chu Hsi and all who would follow him.

12. Of course, as Guy S. Alitto (1979) has demonstrated in his study of Liang Shu-ming, there were members of Mou's generation who took Confucian social reform most seriously.

13. David Tracy (1978) provides an excellent typology of the present theological situation. In this early work Tracy even adumbrates his own version of the process model which informs my own theological critique.

CHAPTER FIVE

1. Alasdair MacIntyre (1990) has made the same point in his Gifford Lectures. He argues that St. Thomas Aquinas faced the same problem in his attempt to reconcile the older Augustinian theology with the new Aristotelian sciences. One of the results of Aquinas' new integration of the various divine and secular sciences was a recognition of diversity as interpreted from within a new paradigm of knowledge, namely St. Thomas' new theology.

2. There is a growing body of literature that discusses the development of the process tradition, some of which is included in the bibliography. James R. Gray (1982) reminds us that Whitehead was not the only modern philosopher of process, although few would doubt that Whitehead's position has become the most influential. From within the Whiteheadian tradition, the most useful and basic exposition of process theology is John B. Cobb, Jr. and David Ray Griffin, *Process Theology: An Introductory Exposition* (1976).

3. At least three other names also come to mind in a description of the history of process thought, namely Peirce, James and Bergson. These thinkers all had an impact on the work of both Whitehead and Hartshorne. These three, no doubt, helped to create the intellectual environment in which process thought as a philosophic school could arise and flourish.

4. Not all of these thinkers see themselves as part of a Whiteheadian movement. For instance, David Tracy, although influenced in certain aspects of his work by Whitehead, is not identified as a process theologian. Yet the notions of process and relationality, key to the modern process tradition in all its forms, are still central to Tracy's thought.

5. Of the key group of process or process-influenced philosophers and theologians, Neville took an active role in both the 1988 and 1991 international Confucian-Christian dialogue conferences. His works since 1982 have reflected a growing fascination with the Confucian tradition. On the other hand, David Hall has also written about Confucianism but has not taken part in the formal dialogue programs. It is also fair to say that Hall is now much more interested in philosophic Taoism than Confucianism per se.

6. In 1975 Mou Tsung-san, during an interview with the author in Hong Kong, recounted the fact that he had been very interested in Whitehead's organic philosophy. Mou was particularly interested in the possible comparison of the primordial nature of God and Chu Hsi's concept of the Supreme Ultimate. Mou also went on to express an equal appreciation of Leibniz as an organic thinker interested in Asian thought.

7. As is well known, Hartshorne does not accept Whitehead's notion of God as an actual entity. For Hartshorne, God is more properly speaking a personally ordered society rather than an actual entity simpliciter.

8. The verbal formulation of these three notions, form, dynamics and unification, owe as much or more to Chu Hsi than they do to Whitehead. Reflection on the notion of principle, *ch'i* or matter-energy and the mind-heart, for instance, suggest the formal, dynamic and unifying traits of each person. While it is the case that most Neo-Confucian metasystematic thought is carried on in terms of the inherited dyads of the tradition, there is almost always a triadic method of relating the various balanced or correlative terms that suggests a tripartite ordering of Confucian cosmology.

9. While Whiteheadian scholars will, no doubt, have their lists of axioms, I take comfort that my set has been identified by two of the most careful of exegetes, Lewis Ford (1984) and Jorge Luis Nobo (1986). For instance, Nobo devotes three chapters to a discussion of the principles of relativity, ontology and creativity. As Ford notes in appendix 5 of his study of the emergence of Whitehead's metaphysics, Whitehead attempted to frame some of his principles as axioms in just this fashion.

10. Lewis Ford (1987) has made just this point that in terms of process biblical exegesis. He argues that a process reading of the biblical narrative makes a great deal more sense out of those parts of the tradition that speak of God's passionate concern and engagement with the world.

11. This is the way of stating the issue arising out of the Confucian-Christian dialogues in 1989 and 1991. It would not be an appropriate way to discuss the matter if the other tradition in dialogue were Buddhism. There is always a personal or agential voice in Christian theology and Confucian discourse that is alien to the Buddhist tradition.

12. One finds a similar need to explain the soul rather than explain it away in Whitehead's later reflections on the soul's nature in *Adventures of Ideas*, where he gives back to the soul what he has taken away in *Process and Reality*. Whitehead came to believe that the notion of an enduring soul or person needs an explanation within his system because it cannot be so easily dismissed as bad or muddled thinking when so many giants of the Western tradition have devoted so much time and energy to its defense.

13. Many later scholars of the Neo-Confucian movement will point out that Chang Tsai's thematization of the primordial *ch'i* is just such a cosmological principle of relativity even if Chang did not work out as complicated a cosmology as did Whitehead in *Process and Reality*.

14. The Church of the East, often called the Nestorian Church, faced these issues with a great deal of sensitivity centuries before all of Western Europe had even become Christian. It is a shame that we know so little about the theological dialogues that went on between the first Nestorian missionaries and their T'ang Buddhist, Taoist and Confucian colleagues. For a summary of the scant information about what we do know of this encounter, see Moffett (1992).

CHAPTER SIX

1. A crucial aspect of the success of the June 1988 international Hong Kong dialogue was the patient and effective leadership of Dr. Peter Lee of the Christian Centre for the Study

of Chinese Religion and Culture, Hong Kong. A similar constructive role was played by Dean Judith Berling for the July 1991 conference at Berkeley. It has been the hope of the WCC Sub-Unit on Dialogue that the various international Christian study centers will play a pivotal role in exploring the parameters of dialogue in their parts of the world. The Sub-Unit on Dialogue usually sponsors only projects under the direct supervision of the Geneva staff but in the case of the Hong Kong conference the Sub-Unit made an exception. The sponsorship and support of the Sub-Unit was key to the successful solicitations for grants and resources necessary for the realization of the Hong Kong conference. I should also not overlook the most important role played by the Departments of Theology and Philosophy of the Chinese University of Hong Kong. They were the co-hosts for the meetings under the able leadership of Prof. Liu Shu-hsien and Dean Philip Shen. Prof. Liu and Dean Shen helped to identity and invite the Confucian and Christian participants from Asia, hence the very planning process represented Confucian-Christian dialogue as a cooperative venture in search of the truth in encounter.

2. A number of the papers from the first conference have been edited by Peter K. H. Lee. See Peter K. H. Lee, ed., *Confucian-Christian Encounters in Historical and Contemporary Perspective* (Lewiston, N.Y.: The Edwin Mellen Press, 1991).

3. This does not mean that Confucians and Christians stopped talking in the late nineteenth and early twentieth century. Clearly this was not the case; nonetheless, the Hong Kong conference did mark a potential watershed in formal Confucian-Christian relations. The 1988 meeting acknowledged the recognition by both communities that Confucians and Christians need their own bilateral dialogue as part of the larger interfaith dialogue movement which began in the 1960s.

4. For an example of this kind of analysis with a special focus on the social sciences, see Tu Wei-ming, Milan Hejtmanek and Alan Wachman, eds., *The Confucian World Observed: A Contemporary Discussion of Confucian Humanism in East Asia* (Honolulu: University of Hawaii Press, 1992).

5. Wm. Theodore de Bary (1991) has addressed this problem in his *The Trouble with Confucianism*. The problem is that, along with the reformist element of the tradition, there is an equally strong conservative element. This politically conservative element can always be appealed to by the Chinese state. It evokes the ancient and pre-Confucian veneration of the elders that is so much part of the Chinese political scene. De Bary argues that one of the things that the New Confucians are going to have to learn is how to be a loyal opposition to the Chinese state. This is a difficult task for a tradition that rejected this notion for most of its career.

6. It was recognized that this was a very sophisticated question. It was hardly the kind of conversation that we would expect in nonscholarly dialogues. The discussion demanded a scholarly understanding of both traditions and a willingness to experiment with a highly novel comprehension of what we mean by tradition. Hence this is a proper conversation for scholars but may not be appropriate or even feasible outside that kind of dialogical setting.

7. Mou makes this point abundantly clear in his later work, *Yüan shan chiang* (On *Summum Bonum*). In this work published in 1985, he goes over, in great length, his reflections on the notion of autonomous morality. This is achieved through a long dialogue with Kant, his favorite Western interlocutor. He also goes over much the same ground in his 1983 lectures published as *Chung-kuo che-hsüeh shih-chiu chiang* (Nineteen Lectures on Chinese Philosophy), but with a great deal more commentary on the role of Chinese Buddhist philosophy.

8. While Mou argues for ritual action as key to the Confucian religious tradition, he is curiously silent about just what he takes to be ritual. This is a point of serious debate about Mou's place within the Confucian tradition because ritual means so much more than just specific personal actions. Ritual is also the key to the Confucian understanding of decent government. Therefore, if a Confucian thinker does not provide us with a social and political agenda guided by proper ritual, she or he has a very truncated Confucian vision. While I suspect that Mou would understand this criticism, I believe that he would restate his position as someone who has devoted himself to a different aspect of the Confucian tradition. Mou, stung by the persistent Western criticism of Chinese philosophy as lacking in critical analysis and sophistication, has sought to remedy this technical lack through the formulation of his moral metaphysics. While he has written about the philosophy of history, he has not sought an active role as a political reformer. This kind of response is not often considered normative from within the Neo-Confucian tradition. But then, Mou might well counter that the modern world is not the place for classical or Neo-Confucian responses, of more of the same.

9. Interestingly enough, Hans Küng (1991, 237–49) has argued recently that steadfastness is a virtue necessary for interfaith dialogue. If you are not steadfast in your own tradition, yet respectful of the dialogical partner, why would you bother to be in dialogue? Küng submits that there is enough indifferent relativism in secular society to keep us all happy.

10. Wm. Theodore de Bary (1991a) has devoted a whole volume of his ongoing study of the Neo-Confucian tradition to just this topic. In *Learning for One's Self* de Bary continues his exposition of the philosophic and religious dimensions of the Chu Hsi tradition and its critics down to the early Ch'ing period. De Bary argues that the persistent demand in the Chu Hsi school for "learning for one's self" was one driving force in the creation of the Neo-Confucian personality.

11. The New York City community of Roosevelt Island is another such example. However, in both cases a great deal of money has to be spent to maintain these mixed racial communities. Perhaps the answer is the allocation of resources to provide such opportunities for diversity if we are serious about learning to live together.

12. There is a great deal of discussion of the issue of syncretism in the modern ecumenical movement. One of the great founders of the movement, Visser 't Hooft (1963), devotes a volume to dangers posed to the ecumenical movement by syncretism in the form of Christian universalism. The *Guidelines on Dialogue with People of Living Faiths and Ideologies* rejects any positive appropriation of dialogue as contrary to its ecumenical understanding of interfaith encounter and relations. Probably the most balanced ecumenical Christian account of syncretism is found in Jerald Gort et al. (1989), *Dialogue and Syncretism: An Interdisciplinary Approach*. By interdisciplinary the authors mean an assessment of the phenomenon of syncretism in terms of the disciplines of biblical studies, the history of religions, philosophy and the sociology of knowledge. The volume manages to avoid much of the polemic so often found in discussions of syncretism.

13. Archic variables refer to the variables used by Watson (1985) and Dilworth (1989) in their comparative methodology. One of the interesting features of archic analysis, applied by Dilworth in particular to Asian texts, is the fact that it can demonstrate continuity or discontinuity within traditions using the same basic philosophic or theological vocabulary. Archic analysis is useful to show how similar terminology can mask profound differences in content.

14. Some argue that East Asian Manichaeism was absorbed into Buddhism; certainly it was tolerated and judged noncontradictory to the existing faiths.

15. Shils (1981, 275) notes that there are two possible outcomes for traditions in contact. "At one extreme, there is a possibility of a synthesis into a totally new tradition bearing none of the features of the parents. Another extreme would occur when one tradition extends its adherence so that it absorbs the other entirely without itself changing in any way; the other tradition disappears entirely." Shils argues that these are "ideal" types and are basically impossible outcomes of the process unless physical extermination occurs in the second case. One wonders if this may not be the case with many North American Native traditions when their populations have been reduced below a certain level by disease, war, intermarriage and quasi-forced conversions to various Christian sects.

16. The impact of Buddhist meditation in North America upon Christian laity may generate just such new themes. At least in the Protestant traditions, there is remarkably little sophisticated meditation practice. As lay people are trained in such spiritual disciplines, they are sure to bring these new techniques and ways of looking at the world back to their home religious base.

17. The late Joseph Levenson, in his brilliant conclusion to his trilogy on the modern fate of the Confucian tradition, pointed out (1968, 3:124), "Preserving the past by recounting it, or displaying its bequests, is not perpetuating it. But it does preserve." At best, Levenson, despairing for a tradition which he loved, felt that Confucianism would only live on in China as an artifact in the museum of culture. This was certainly not an unbelievable thought in the midst of Mao's Great Cultural Revolution. But as I have stressed in other parts of this essay, the Confucian tradition seems to be quite persistent in East Asia these days.

APPENDIX

1. In this Appendix I will confine my remarks to materials in English. I fully realize that this is a terribly parochial move, but I believe that the English material will demonstrate the full range of scholarly engagement in the study of the Confucian tradition. Of course, we must always remember that Western scholarship rides on the shoulders of the East Asian scholarly community.

2. For instance, many critics have noticed how often a modern New Confucian scholar such as Mou Tsung-san tends to gloss his Chinese text with English terms. Some have denounced this as the loss of the distinctive features of the Chinese tradition. On the contrary, Mou himself argues that it merely demonstrates the global nature of all modern intellectual discourse. No contemporary tradition can carry on its activities without noticing the modern global transformation of the 19th and 20th centuries.

3. Tu Wei-ming notes that the term "New Confucian" has also caught on in the PRC. The PRC scholars identify two distinct generations of New Confucians, the May Fourth and the post–World War II generations. The first generation includes Liang Shu-ming, Chang Chun-mai, Feng Yu-lan, Ho Lin and Hsiung Shih-li. The second generation includes Mou Tsung-san, T'ang Chün-i, Hsü Fu-kuan, Ch'ien Mu and Fang Tung-mei. Tu notes that separate consultations in Taiwan and Singapore arrived at almost the same list (Tu 1992, 103).

4. Charles Hartman (1986), Jo-Shui Chen (1992), David McMullen (1988) and Peter Bol (1992), in their respective studies of Han Yü, Liu Tsung-yüan and T'ang scholarly society, have demonstrated that we neglect the T'ang needlessly in terms of the Confucian tradition.

However, I still believe it true to say, at least in the English literature, that my generalization about the neglect of the T'ang Confucian tradition is true.

5. Neo-Confucianism is the most problematic of Western neologisms and is under sustained attack from Bol (1992) and Tillman (1992a, 1992b) as a term that covers a multitude of errors. In short, the problem Bol and Tillman identify is that Neo-Confucianism labels so many diverse T'ang, Sung, Yüan and Ch'ing movements—without even considering the fate of Confucianism in Korea and Japan during the period—that it must be abandoned for more precise terms derived from the history of Confucianism in China. One of Bol and Tillman's main criticisms is that the term Neo-Confucianism has served to highlight the supremacy of the Chu Hsi school to the detriment of other Sung options. According to Bol and Tillman, the bland term Neo-Confucianism hides the exuberance of the philosophic life of this great period of Confucian speculation. I believe that Bol and Tillman have a good point. We do need to define more accurately and precisely the various schools and movements that make up the Confucian Way during the post-T'ang and pre-modern period. But until a consensus arises about new terms, Neo-Confucianism is still the term most commonly used to define the whole period.

6. One has the hunch that Levenson, if he had lived, would be delighted with the signs of renewal now so evident in the Confucian tradition in East Asia. He was one who mourned the loss of vitality in the Confucian tradition, a tradition he loved so much and studied with such respect.

7. Another candidate for this list is Tu's revised edition of *Centrality and Commonality*. In this key study of the *Chung-yung* Tu added a fifth chapter devoted to the religious dimension of the Confucian tradition. The substance of Tu's argument is the same as in the works I will be citing from the other two studies. The interesting feature of this new chapter is that it is keyed to Tu's commentary on the *Chung-yung*.

8. There has been considerable debate over the last few years about the notion of Confucian transcendence. Hall and Ames (1987), in their influential study of Confucius, have argued that there is no such thing as a classical Confucian sense of transcendence on the analogy of the historic Western religious traditions. Hall and Ames contend that what we find in the Chinese case is a profound sense of immanence. Whatever marks of religious transcendence we find in the Neo-Confucian masters can be attributed to Buddhist and other non-Confucian influences. Tu Wei-ming and Mou Tsung-san counter this claim by pointing to a particular form of Confucian transcendence in the classical period. Tu calls this the "ethico-religious" aspect of the Confucian tradition; Mou calls it the vertical (transcendent) element of classical thought. While much of this debate may hinge on the semantics of the transcendent-immanent split, I do believe that Hall and Ames continue to illustrate the problem that even sophisticated Western scholars have with recognizing the distinctive marks of Confucian religiosity.

Chinese Glossary

There is no uniform system of romanization today used by the sinological community. Most scholars resort to a mixture of Wade-Giles and pinyin, and I will follow this practice here.

Analects (Lun-yü; Lun yu) 論語

Beijing 北京

Carsun Chang (Zhang Junmai) 張君勱

Chan Wing-tsit (Chen Rongjie) 陳榮捷

Ch'an (Chan) 禪

Chang Hsüeh-ch'eng (Zhang Xuecheng) 章學誠

Chang Li-wen (Zhang Liwen) 張立文

Chang Shih (Zhang Shi) 張栻

Chang Tsai (Zhang Zai) 張載

Chang-tzu Cheng-meng chu (Zhangzi Zhengmeng Zhu) 張子正
蒙注

Chao Shun-sun (Zhao Shunsun) 趙順孫

Chen Li Fu 陳立夫

Ch'en Ch'un (Chen Chun) 陳淳

Ch'en Liang (Chen Liang) 陳良

Cheng Chung-ying (Cheng Zhongying) 成中英

ch'eng (cheng) 誠

Ch'eng I, Yi-ch'uan (Cheng Yi; Yichuan) 程頤; 伊川

Ch'eng Ming-tao (Cheng Mingdao) 程明道

ch'i (qi) 氣

chia-ting (Jiating) 家庭

Chiang-hsi (Jiangxi) 江西

Chiao Hung (Jiao Hong) 焦竑

Ch'ien Mu (Qian Mu) 錢穆

chih (zhi) 智

Chih te chih-chüeh yü Chung-kuo che-hsüeh (Zhi de Zhijue yu Zhongguo Zhexue) 智的直覺與中國哲學

Chih-yen (Zhiyan) 知言

Chin-hsin shuo (Jin Xin Shuo) 盡心說

Ch'in (Qin) 秦

ching (jing) 經

ching (jing) 敬

Ching Feng (Jing Feng) 景風

ching-te (jingde) 敬德

Ch'ing (Qing) 清

ch'ing (qing) 情

Chou (Zhou) 周

Chou-i ts'an-t'ung-ch'i (Zhouyi cantongqi) 周易參同契

Chou Tun-i (Zhou Dunyi) 周敦頤

Chu Hsi (Zhu Xi) 朱熹

Chu Hsi ssu-hsiang yen-chiu (Zhuxi sixiang yanjiu) 朱熹思想研究

Chu-hung (Zhu Hong) 诛宏

chu-t'i hsing (zhu ti xing) 主體性

Chu-tzu che-hsüeh ssu-hsiang te fan-chan yü yuang ch'eng (Zhuzi zhexue sixiang de fazhan yu wancheng) 朱子哲學思想的發展與完成

Chu-tzu hsin hsüeh-an (Zhuzi xin xuean) 朱子新學案

Chu-tzu yü-lei ta-ch'üan (Zhuzi yulei daquan) 朱子語類大全

Chuang Tzu (Zhuangzi) 莊子

Chün-tzu (Junzi) 君子

Chung-kuo che-hsüeh shih-chiu chiang (Zhongguo zhexue shijiu jiang) 中國哲學十九講

Chung-kuo che-hsüeh te t'e-chih (Zhongguo zhexue de tezhi) 中國哲學的特質

Chung-kuo che-hsüeh yüan-lun: Tao-lun p'ien (Zhongguo zhexue yuanglun: Daolun pian) 中國哲學原論：道論篇

Chung-yung (Zhongyong) 中庸

Confucius (Kong Qiu, Kong Zhongni) 孔丘, 孔仲尼

Fan-shen (Fanxing) 反省

Fang I-chih (Fan Yizhi) 方以智

Fang Keli 方克立

Fang Tung-mei (Fang Dongmei) 方東美

Fo-hsing yü Pan-ro (Foxing yu Bore) 佛性與般若

Fu-chou (Fuzhou) 福州

Fung Yu-lan (Feng Youlan) 馮友蘭

Han (Han) 漢

Han Fei Tzu (Han Fei Zi) 韓非子

han-hsüeh (hanxue) 漢學

Han Yü (Han Yu) 韓愈

Ho Hsin-yin (He Xinyin) 何心隱

Ho Lin (He Lin) 賀麟

Ho Shang-kung (He Shanggong) 河上公

Hsi-tz'u (Xici) 繫辭

Hsien-hsiang yü wu-tzu-shen (Xianxiang yu wuzishen) 現象與物自身

hsin (xin) 心

hsin (xin) 信

hsin-hsüeh (xin-xue) 心學

Hsin Ju-chia te ching-shen fang-hsiang (Xinrujia de jingshen fang-xiang) 新儒家的精神方嚮

Hsin-t'i yü hsing-t'i (Xinti yu xingti) 心體與性體

hsing (xing) 性

Hsiung shih-li (Xiong Shili) 熊十力

Hsü Dau-lin (Xu Daling) 許大齡

Hsü Fu-kuan (Xu Fuguan) 徐復觀

hsüeh (xue) 學

Hsun Yuen (Xun Yue) 荀悅

Hsün Tzu (Xunzi) 荀子

Hu Hung (Hu Hong) 胡宏

Hu Shih (Hu Shi) 胡適

Hu Wu-feng (Hu Wufeng) 胡五峰

Hu Yüan (Hu Yuan) 胡瑗

Hua-yen (Hua-yan) 華嚴

Huang Chun-chieh (Huang Junjie) 黃俊傑

Huang-lao pao-shu (Huanglao Baoshu) 黃老寶書

Huang Siu-chi (Huang Xiuji) 黃秀璣

Huang Tsung-hsi (Huang Zongxi) 黃宗羲

Hui-tung yü chuan-hua (Huitong yu zhuanhua) 會通與轉化

hun-tun (hundun) 混沌

hou-wen 或問

i (yi) 義

I-Ching (Yijing) 易經

jen (ren) 仁

Jen-shuo (Renshuo) 仁說

Jen Wu Chih (Ren Wu Ji) 人物集

ju-chia (rujia) 儒家

ju-chiao (rujiao) 儒教

Ju-hsüeh ch'uan-t'ung yü wen-hua ch'uang-hsin (Ru xue chuan tong yu wenhua chuangxin) 儒學傳統與文化創新

ju-tao (rudao) 儒道

Kao P'an-lung (Gao Panlong) 高攀龍

Kuo Hsiang (Guo Xiang) 郭象

Lao Tzu (Laozi) 老子

li 理

li 禮

Li Ao 李翱

Li Chi (Li Ji) 李季

Li Ching-te (Li Jingde) 黎靖德

Li Jingquan 李錦全

li-i fen-shu (li yi fen shu) 理一分殊

Li-hsüeh (Lixue) 理學

Li Kou (Li Gou) 李覯

Li Chih (Li Zhi) 李贄

Liang Ch'i-chao (Liang Qichao) 梁启超

liang-chih (liangzhi) 良知

Liang Shu-ming 梁漱溟

Liang Yen-ch'ing (Liang Yancheng) 梁燕誠

Lin chao-en (Lin Zhaoen) 林兆恩

Liu Shao 劉邵

Liu Shu-hsien (Liu Shuxian) 劉述先

Liu Tsung-chou (Liu Zongzhou) 劉宗周

Liu Tsung-yüan (Liu Zongyuan) 柳宗元

Lo Chin-hsi (Luo Jinxi) 羅近溪

Lu 魯

Lu Chiu-yuan (Lu Jiuyuan) 陸九淵

Lü Liu-liang (Lu Liuliang) 呂留良

Lü K'un (Lu Kun) 呂坤

Lü Tsu-ch'ien (Lu Zuqian) 呂祖謙

Lun-yü (Analects; Lun-yu) 論語

Mao Tse-tung (Mao Zedong) 毛澤東

Master K'ung (Kongfuzi) 孔夫子

Mencius (Meng Ke) 孟軻

Meng Tzu (Mengzi) 孟子

Ming 明

ming-te (mingde) 明德

Mou Tsung-san (Mou Zongsan) 牟宗三

Ou-yang Hsiu (Ouyang Xiu) 歐陽修

p'an-chiao (panjiao) 判教

pao (bao) 報

Pei-hsi tzu-i (Beixi ziyi) 北溪字義

pen-hsin (benxin) 本心

Qian Wen-yuan 錢文源

san chiao ho-i (san jiao he yi) 三教合一

Shang 商

Shao Yung (Shao Yong) 邵雍

Shen Pu-hai (Shen Buhai) 申不害

sheng-sheng 生生

Shih-ching (Shijing) 詩經

Shih-hsuo hsin-yü (Shishuo Xinyu) 世說新語

shu 數

Ssu-shu (Sishu) 四書

Ssu-shu tsuan-shu (Sishu zuanshu) 四書纂疏

Sui-T'ang (Sui-Tang) 隨唐

Sung (Song) 宋

Sung Ming Li-hsüeh: Nan-Sung p'ien (Song Ming Lixue: NanSong pian) 宋明理學：南宋篇

Sung Ming Li-hsüeh: Pei-Sung p'ien (Song Ming Lixue: BeiSong pian) 宋明理學：北宋篇

Ta-hsüeh (Daxue) 大學

ta-tao (dadao) 大道

ta-te (dade) 大德

Tai Chen (Dai Zhen) 戴震

Taipei (Taibei) 臺北

t'ai-chi (taiji) 太極

T'ang (Tang) 唐

T'ang Chün-i (Tang Junyi) 唐君毅

tao-hsüeh (daoxue) 道學

Tao Te ching (Dao De Jing) 道德經

t'i (ti) 體

T'ien-chu Shi-i (Tianzhu shiyi) 天主實義

t'ien-ming (tianming) 天命

T'ien-t'ai (Tiantai) 天臺

t'ien-tao (Tiandao) 天道

Ts'ai Jen-hou (Cai Renhou) 蔡仁厚

Tso Chuan (Zuo Zhuan) 左傳

Tsing Hua (Qing Hua) 清華

Tsung Lu Hsiang-shan tao Liu Chi-shan (Cong Lu Xiangshan dao Liu Jishan) 從陸象山到劉蕺山

Tsung-mi (Zong Mi) 宗密

Tu Wei-ming (Du Weiming) 杜維明

Tung Chung-shu (Dong Zhongshu) 董仲舒

Tung-lin (Donglin) 東林

tzu-yüan (ziyuan) 自圓

Wang An-shih (Wang Anshi) 王安石

Wang Fu-chih (Wang Fuzhi) 王夫之

Wang Pi (Wang Bi) 王弼

Wang Yang-ming (Wang Yangming) 王陽明

Wei-Chin (Wei-Jin) 魏晋

Wei-hsin (weixin) 唯心

wei-hsüeh (weixue) 为學

Wen-kung (Wengong) 文公

wu 無

Wu Ch'eng (Wu Cheng) 吳澄

Xiandai Xinruxue Yanjiu Lunji 現代新儒家研究論集

yang 陽

Yang Hsiung (Yang Xiong) 楊雄

Yang Lien-sheng (Yang Liansheng) 楊聯陞

Yang Tingyun 楊廷筠

Yeh Shih (Ye Shi) 葉適

Yenching (Yanjing) 燕京

Yen Fu (Yan Fu) 嚴復

Yen Hui (Yan Hui) 顏回

Yi Ching (Yi Jing) 易經

yin 陰

Yü-chou Kuang (Yuzhou Guang) 宇宙光

Yü Ying-shih (Yu Yingshi) 余英时

Yüan (Yuan) 元

Yüan shan lun (Yuan shan lun) 圓善論

yung (yong) 用

Zen (Chan) 禪

Bibliography

Allen, E. L. 1960. *Christianity Among the Religions*. London: George Allen & Unwin, Ltd.

Allinson, Robert E., ed. 1989. *Understanding the Chinese Mind: The Philosophic Roots*. Oxford: Oxford University Press.

———. 1990. The Ethics of Confucianism and Christianity: The Delicate Balance. *Ching Feng* 33, no. 3 (September 1990): 158–175.

Alitto, Guy S. 1979. *The Last Confucian: Liang Shu-ming and the Chinese Dilemma of Modernity*. Berkeley: University of California Press.

Ames, Roger T. 1983. *The Art of Rulership: A Study in Ancient Chinese Political Thought*. Honolulu: University of Hawaii Press.

Anderson, Gerald H. and Thomas F. Stransky, eds. 1981a. *Christ's Lordship and Religious Pluralism*. Maryknoll, N. Y.: Orbis Books.

———. eds. 1981b. *Faith Meets Faith*. New York and Toronto: Paulist Press.

Anderson, Gerald H. 1988. American Protestants in Pursuit of Mission: 1886–1986. *International Bulletin of Missionary Research*, 12, no. 3 (June 1988): 98–118.

Ariarajah, S. Wesley. 1985. *The Bible and People of Other Faiths*. Geneva: World Council of Churches.

———. 1991. *Hindus and Christians: A Century of Protestant Ecumenical Thought*. Grand Rapids, Mich.: Wm. B. Eerdmans Publishing Co.

Arthur, C. J. 1986. *In the Hall of Mirrors: Problems of Commitment in a Religiously Plural World*. London: Mowbrary.

Balazs, Etienne. 1964. *Chinese Civilization and Bureaucracy: Variations on a Theme*. Trans. by H. M. Wright and edited by Arthur F. Wright. New Haven: Yale University Press.

Barnes, Johnathan, ed. 1984. *The Complete Works of Aristotle*. The revised Oxford ed. Bollingen Series 71. 2 vols. Princeton: Princeton University Press.

Barnes, Michael. 1989. *Christian Identity & Religious Pluralism: Religions in Conversations*. Nashville, Tenn.: Abingdon Press.

Barrett, David B. 1982. *World Christian Encyclopedia: A Comparative Study of Churches and Religions in the Modern World AD 1900–2000*. Oxford: Oxford University Press.

Barrett, T. H. 1992. *Li Ao: Buddhist, Taoist, or Neo-Confucian?* Oxford: Oxford University Press.

Bauer, Wolfgang. 1976. *China and the Search for Happiness*. Trans. by Michael Shaw. New York: Seabury Press.

Bellah, Robert N. 1970a. *Beyond Belief: Essays in Religion in a Post-traditional World*. New York: Harper & Row.

———. 1970b. *Tokugawa Religion: The Values of Pre-industrial Japan*. Boston: Beacon Press.

Benard, Henri. 1937. Chu Hsi's Philosophy and Its Interpretation by Leibniz. *T'ien Hsia Monthly* 5 (August 1937): 9–18.

Berger, Peter. 1977. *Facing Up to Modernity: Excursions in Society, Politics, and Religion.* New York: Basic Books.

————. 1980. *The Heretical Imperative: Contemporary Religious Affirmation.* Garden City and New York: Doubleday.

————. 1981. *The Other Side of God: A Polarity in World Religions.* Garden City and New York: Doubleday.

————. 1986. *The Capitalist Revolution: Fifty Propositions about Prosperity, Equality, & Liberty.* New York: Basic Books.

————. 1992. *A Far Glory: The Quest for Faith in an Age of Credulity.* New York: The Free Press.

Berling, Judith A. 1980. *The Syncretic Religion of Lin Chao-en.* New York: Columbia University Press.

Bernstein, Richard J. 1988. *Beyond Objectivism and Relativism: Science, Hermeneutics and Praxis.* Philadelphia: University of Pennsylvania Press.

————. 1992. *The New Constellation: The Ethical-Political Horizons of Modernity/Postmodernity.* Cambridge, Mass.: MIT Press.

Berry, Thomas. 1988. *The Dream of the Earth.* San Francisco: Sierra Club Books.

Berthrong, John H. 1980a. Suddenly Deluded Thoughts Arise. *Society for the Study of Chinese Religions Bulletin* 8 (1980): 32–55.

————. 1980b. The Thoughtlessness of Unexamined Things. *Journal of Chinese Philosophy* 7 (1980): 131–51.

————. 1982. The Problem of the Mind: Mou Tsung-san's Critique of Chu Hsi. *Journal of Chinese Religion* 10 (1982): 39–52.

————. 1987a. Chu Hsi's Ethics: *jen* and *ch'eng. Journal of Chinese Philosophy* 14 (1987).

————. 1987b. Tao and Logos: Confucian-Christian Dialogue. *China Notes* 15 (Winter 1986–87): 433–37.

————. 1989a. Human Nature Revisited: Prospects for Contemporary Confucian-Christian Dialogue. In *Pluralism, Tolerance and Dialogue: Six Studies,* M. Darrol Bryant, ed. Waterloo, Ontario: University of Waterloo Press.

————. 1989b. A Whiteheadian Interpretation of Interfaith Dialogue: Religious Pluralism as Scandal or Promise. *Journal of Ecumenical Studies* 26 (Winter 1989): 175–95.

————. 1989c. Wilfred Cantwell Smith: The Theological Necessity of Pluralism. *Toronto Journal of Theology* 5, no. 2 (Fall 1989): 188–204.

————. 1989d. Trends in the Interpretation of Confucian Religiosity. *Ching Feng: Quarterly Notes on Christianity and Chinese Religion and Culture.* 32, no. 4 (December 1989): 224–44.

————. 1991. Syncretism Revisted: Multiple Religious Participation. *China Notes.* 29, no. 4 (Autumn 1991): 654–55.

————. 1993. Master Chu's Self-Realization: The Role of *Ch'eng. Philosophy East and West* 43, no. 1 (January 1993): 39–64.

Bibby, Reginald W. 1990. *Mosaic Madness: The Poverty and Potential of Life in Canada.* Toronto: Stoddart Publishing Co.

Billeter, Jean-François. 1979. *Li Zhi, Philosophe Maudit (1527–1602).* Geneva: Librairie Droz.

Birch, Charles and John B. Cobb, Jr. 1981. *The Liberation of Life: From Cell to the Community.* Cambridge: Cambridge University Press.

Birch, Charles, William Eakin and Jay B. McDaniel, eds. 1990. *Liberating Life: Contemporary Approaches to Ecological Theology.* Maryknoll, N. Y.: Orbis Books.

Birdwhistell, Anne D. 1989. *Transition to Neo-Confucianism: Shao Yung and Symbols of Reality.* Stanford: Stanford University Press.

Bishop, Donald H., ed. 1985. *Chinese Thought: An Introduction.* New Delhi: Motilal Banarsidass.

Black, Alison Harley. 1989. *Man and Nature in the Philosophical Thought of Wang Fu-chih.* Seattle: University of Washington Press.

Bodde, Derk. 1981. *Essays in Chinese Civilization.* Edited by Charles Le Blanc and Dorthy Borei. Princeton: Princeton University Press.

————. 1991. *Chinese Thought, Society, and Science: The Intellectual and Social Background of Science and Technology in Pre-modern China.* Honolulu: University of Hawaii Press.

Bol, Peter K. 1992. *"This Culture of Ours": Intellectual Transitions in T'ang and Sung China.* Stanford: Stanford University Press.

Bosch, David J. 1988. The Church in Dialogue: From Self-delusion to Vulnerability. *Missology* 16, no. 2: 131–47.

————. 1991. *Transforming Paradigms: Paradigm Shifts in Theology of Mission.* Maryknoll, N.Y.: Orbis Books.

Braaten. Carl E. 1992 *No Other Gospel! Christianity among the World's Religions.* Minneapolis: Fortress Press.

Bruce, J. Percy. 1918. The Theistic Import of the Sung Philosophy. *Journal of the North-China Branch of the Royal Asiatic Society* 49 (1918): 111–17.

————. 1923. *Chu Hsi and His Masters.* London: Probsthain & Co.

Bryant, M. Darrol, ed. 1989. *Pluralism, Tolerance and Dialogue: Six Studies.* Waterloo, Ontario: University of Waterloo Press.

Buchler, Justus. 1966. *Metaphysics of Natural Complexes.* New York: Columbia University Press.

————. 1974. *The Main of Light: On the Concept of Poetry.* New York: Oxford University Press.

Callahan, Paul E. 1950. Chu Hsi and St. Thomas, a Comparison. *Papers on China* 4:1–23.

Chai, Ch'u and Winberg Chai. 1973. *Confucianism.* New York: Barron's Educational Series.

Chan, Alan K. L. 1991. *Two Visions of the Way: A Study of the Wang Pi and the Ho-shang Kung Commentaries on the Lao-tzu.* Albany, N.Y.: State University of New York Press.

Chan, Hok-lam. 1980. *Li Chih (1527–1602) in Contemporary Chinese Historiography: New Light on his Life and Works.* White Plains, N. Y.: M. E. Sharpe, Inc.

Chan, Hok-lam and Wm. Theodore de Bary, eds. 1982. *Yüan Thought: Chinese Thought and Religion under the Mongols.* New York: Columbia University Press.

Chan, Wing-Tsit. 1955. The Evolution of the Confucian Concept of Jen. *Philosophy East and West* 4 (January 1955): 229–319.

————. 1957. The Neo-Confucian Solution of the Problem of Evil. *The Bulletin of the Institute of History and Philology, Academia Sinica* 28 (1957): 773–91.

————. 1962. Syntheses in Chinese Metaphysics. In *The Chinese Mind: Essentials of Chinese Philosophy and Culture*, Charles E. Moore, Ed., Honolulu: East-West Press and University of Hawaii Press.

————. 1963. *A Source Book in Chinese Philosophy.* Princeton: Princeton Unviersity Press.

————. 1964. The Evolution of the Neo-Confucian Concept of Li as Principle. *Tsing Hua Jounral of Chinese Studies*, n.s., 4 (February 1964): 123–48.

————. 1967. Neo-Confucianism: New Ideas in Old Terminology. *Philosophy East and West* 17 (1967): 15–37.

————. 1969. *Religious Trends in Modern China*. New York: Octagon Books.

————. 1973. Chu Hsi's Completion of Neo-Confucianism. *Etudes Song* 2 (1973): 59–90.

————. 1986. *Chu Hsi and Neo-Confucianism*. Honolulu: University of Hawaii Press.

————. 1987. *Chu Hsi Life and Thought*. Hong Kong: Chinese University of Hong Kong Press.

————. 1989 *Chu Hsi: New Studies*. Honolulu: University of Hawaii Press.

Chang, Carsun. 1957–1962. *The Development of Neo-Confucian Thought*. 2 vols. New York: Bookman Associates.

Chang Hao. 1971. *Liang Ch'i-chao and Intellectual Transition in China (1890-1907)*. Cambridge, Mass.: Harvard University Press.

————. 1976. New Confucianism and the Intellectual Crisis of Contemporary China. In *The Limits of Change: Essays on Conservative Alternatives in Republican China*, Charlotte Furth, ed. Cambridge, Mass.: Harvard University Press.

Chang Li-wen. 1981. *Chu Hsi ssu-hsiang yen-chiu* [Investigations of Chu Hsi's Thought]. Beijing: Chinese Social Sciences Publishing Society.

Chao, Shun-sun (fl. 1243). 1973. *Ssu-shu tsuan-shu* [Collected Annotations on the Four Books]. Kao-hsiung, Taiwan: n.p. Cited as SSTS.

Chen, Charles K. H., comp. 1969. *Neo-Confucianism, Etc.: Essays by Wing-Tsit Chan*. Hanover, N. H.: Oriental Society.

Ch'en Ch'i-yn. 1980. *Hsün Yüeh and the Mind of Late Han China: A Translation of the Shen-chien with introductions and annotations*. Princeton: Princeton University Press.

Ch'en Ch'un (1159–1223). 1840. *Pei-hsi tzu-i* [Pei-hsi's Glossary]. Hsi Yin Hsüan Ts'ung-shu ed. Cited as PHTI.

————. 1986. *Neo-Confucian Terms Explained (The Pei-hsi tzu-i)*. Trans. and ed. by Wing-tsit Chan. Columbia: Columbia University Press.

Chen, Jo-Shui. 1992. *Liu Tsung-yüan and Intellectual Change in T'ang China, 773-918*. Cambridge University Press.

Chen Li Fu. 1948. *Philosophy of Life*. New York: The Philosophical Library.

Cheng Chung-ying. 1965. Inquiries into Classical Chinese Logic. *Philosophy East and West* 15 (July–October 1965): 195–216.

————. 1971. *Tai Chen's Inquiry into Goodness*. Honolulu: East-West Center Press.

————. 1991. *New Dimensions of Confucian and Neo-Confucian Philosophy*. Albany, N.Y.: State University of New York Press.

Ch'ien, Edward T. 1986. *Chiao Hung and the Restructuring of Neo-Confucianism in the Late Ming*. New York: Columbia University Press.

Ch'ien Mu. 1971. *Chu-tzu hsin hsüeh-an* [A New Study of Chu Hsi]. 5 vols. Taiwan: San Min shu-chü.

Chin Ann-ping, and Mansfield Freeman. 1990. *Tai Chen on Mencius: Explorations in Words and Meaning*. New Haven: Yale University Press.

Ching, Julia. 1972. *The Philosophical Letters of Wang Yang-ming*. Canberra: Australian National University Press.

————. 1972–73. Neo-Confucian Utopian Theories and Political Ethics. *Monumenta Serica* 30 (1972–73): 1–56.

————. 1974. The Goose Lake Monastery Debate (1175). *Journal of Chinese Philosophy* 1 (March 1974): 161–78.

————. 1976. *To Acquire Wisdom: The Way of Wang Yang-Ming*. New York: Columbia University Press.

————. 1977. *Confucianism and Christianity: A Comparative Study*. Tokyo: Kodansha International.

———. 1990. *Probing China's Soul: Religion, Politics, and Protest in the People's Republic.* San Francisco: Harper & Row.

Choo Hi. 1889. *La Siao Hio ou morale de la jeunesse.* Trans. by C. de Harlez. Paris: Annales de Musée Guimet.

Chow, Yih-ching. 1954. *La philosophie Morale dans le Neo-Confucianisme.* Paris: Presses Universitaires de France.

Chu Hsi. 1922. *The Philosophy of Human Nature.* Trans. by J. Percy Bruce. London: Probsthain & Co.

Chu Hsi and Lü Tsu-ch'ien. 1967. *Reflections on Things at Hand: The Neo-Confucian Anthology.* Trans. by Wing-Tsit Chan. New York: Columbia University Press.

Cobb, John B., Jr. 1965. *A Christian Natural Theology.* Philadelphia: The Westminster Press

Cobb, John B., Jr. and David Ray Griffith. 1976. *Process Theology: An Introductory Exposition.* Philadelphia: The Westminster Press.

Cobb, John B., Jr. 1975. *Christ in a Pluralistic Age.* Philadelphia: The Westminster Press.

———. 1979. *The Structure of Christian Existence.* New York: The Seabury Press.

———. 1982. *Beyond Dialogue: Toward a Mutual Transformation of Christianity and Buddhism.* Philadelphia: Fortress Press.

———. 1984. The Meaning of Pluralism for Christian Self-Understanding. In *Religious Pluralism,* L. S. Rouner, ed., Notre Dame, Ind.: University of Notre Dame Press.

———, and Christopher Ives, eds. 1990. *The Emptying God: A Buddhist-Jewish-Christian Conversation.* Maryknoll, N. Y.: Orbis Books.

Colvell, Ralph R. 1986. *Confucius, the Buddha, and Christ: A History of the Gospel in Chinese.* Maryknoll, N. Y.: Orbis Books.

A Concordance to Chuang Tzu. 1956. Cambridge, Mass., Harvard University Press.

A Concordance to Hsün Tzu. 1966. Taipei: Chinese Materials and Research Aids Service Center.

A Concordance to Meng Tzu. 1966. Taipei: Chinese Materials and Research Aids Service Center.

A Concordance to Yi Ching. 1966. Taipei: Chinese Materials and Research Aids Service Center.

Cook, Frank H. 1977. *Hua-yen Buddhism: The Jewel Net of Indra.* University Park: Pennsylvania State University Press.

Corless, Roger and Paul F. Knitter, eds. 1990. *Buddhist Emptiness and Christian Trinity: Essays & Explorations.* New York: Paulist Press.

Couvreur, Seraphin. 1949. *Les quatre livres.* Leiden: E. J. Brill.

Coward, Harold G. 1985. *Pluralism: Challenge to the World Religions.* Maryknoll, N. Y.: Orbis Books.

———. ed. 1987. *Modern Indian Responses to Religious Pluralism.* Albany, N. Y.: State University of New York Press.

———. 1988. *Sacred Word and Sacred Text: Scripture in World Religions.* Maryknoll, N. Y.: Orbis Books.

———. 1990. *Derrida and Indian Philosophy.* Albany, N. Y.: State University of New York Press.

Cox, Harvey. 1977. *Turning East.* New York: Simon and Schuster.

———. 1988a. Many Mansions or One Way? The Crisis in Interfaith Dialogue. *The Christian Century* 105, no. 24 (August 17–24, 1988): 731–35.

———. 1988b. *Many Mansions: A Christian's Encounter with Other Faiths.* Boston: Beacon Press.

Cracknell, Kenneth. 1986. *Toward a New Relationship: Christians and People of Other Faith.* London: Epworth Press.

Cragg, Kenneth. 1986. *The Christ and the Faiths: Theology in Cross-Reference*. London: SPCK.

Creel, Herrlee Glessner. 1929. *Sinism: A Study of the Evolution of the Chinese Worldview*. Chicago: The Open Court Publishing Co.

———. 1949. *Confucius and the Chinese Way*. New York: Harper & Row.

———. 1953. *Chinese Thought from Confucius to Mao Tse-tung*. Chicago: University of Chicago Press.

———. 1970a. *The Origins of Statecraft in China: The Western Chou Empire*, vol. 1. Chicago: University of Chicago Press.

———. 1970b. *What is Taoism? And Other Studies in Chinese Cultural History*. Chicago: University of Chicago Press.

———. 1974. *Shen Pu-hai: A Chinese Political Philosopher of the Fourth Century B.C.* Chicago: University of Chicago Press.

Cua, Antonio S. 1978. *Dimensions of Moral Creativity: Paradigms, Principles, and Ideals*. University Park and London: The Pennsylvania State University Press.

———. 1982. *The Unity of Knowledge and Action: A Study in Wang Yang-ming's Psychology*. Honolulu: University of Hawaii Press.

———. 1985. *Ethical Argumentation: A Study of Hsün Tzu's Epistemology*. Honolulu: University of Hawaii Press.

———. 1989. The Problem of Conceptual Unity in Hsün Tzu, and Li Kou's Solution. *Philosophy East & West* 39, no. 2 (April 1989): 115–34.

Cupitt, Don. 1984. *The Sea of Faith: Christianity in Change*. London: British Broadcasting Corporation.

Daedalus special issue. *The Living Tree: The Changing Meaning of Being Chinese Today*. 1991. *Journal of the American Academy of Arts and Sciences* 120, no. 2 (Spring 1991).

Daly, Herman E. and John B. Cobb, Jr. 1989. *For the Common Good: Redirecting the Economy toward Community, the Environment, and a Sustainable Future*. Boston: Beacon Press.

Dardess, John W. 1973. *Conquerors and Confucians: Aspects of Political Change in Late Yüan China*. New York: Columbia University Press.

———. 1983. *Confucianism and Autocracy: Professional Elites in the Founding of the Ming Dynasty*. Berkeley: University of California Press.

Davis, Charles. 1971. *Christ and the World Religions*. New York: Herder and Herder.

Davis, Winston. 1992. *Japanese Religion and Society: Paradigms of Structure and Change*. Albany, N.Y.: State University of New York Press.

Dawe, Donald G. and John B. Carman, eds. 1978. *Christian Faith in a Religiously Plural World*. Maryknoll, N. Y.: Orbis Books.

Dawson, Raymond, ed. 1964. *The Legacy of China*. Oxford: Clarendon Press.

———. 1981. *Confucius*. Oxford: Oxford University Press.

D'Costa, Gavin. 1986. *Theology and Religious Pluralism: The Challenge of Other Religions*. Oxford: Basil Blackwell.

———, ed. 1990. *Christian Uniqueness Reconsidered: The Myth of a Pluralistic Theology of Religions*. Maryknoll, N.Y.: Orbis Books.

de Bary, Wm. Theodore. 1953. A Reappraisal of Neo-Confucianism. In *Studies in Chinese Thought*, A. F. Wright, ed. Chicago: University of Chicago Press.

———. 1959. Some Common Tendencies in Neo-Confucianism. In *Confucianism in Action*, D. S. Nivison and A. F. Wright, eds. Stanford: Stanford University Press.

———. 1967a. Chinese Despotism and the Confucian Ideal: A Seventeenth-Century View. In *Chinese Thought and Institutions*, J. K. Fairbank, ed. Chicago; University of Chicago Press.

———. Wing-tsit Chan, and Burton Watson, eds. 1967b. *Sources of Chinese Tradition*. 2 vols. New York: Columbia University Press.

———. 1970. *Self and Society in Ming Thought*. New York: Columbia University Press.

———. 1975. *The Unfolding of Neo-Confucianism*. New York: Columbia University Press.

———, and Irene Bloom, eds. 1979. *Principle and Practicality: Essay in Neo-Confucianism and Practical Learning*. New York: Columbia University Press.

———. 1981. *Neo-Confucian Orthodoxy and the Learning of the Mind-and-heart*. New York: Columbia University Press.

———. 1983. *The Liberal Tradition in China*. Hong Kong and New York: The Chinese University Press and Columbia University Press.

———. and JaHyun Kim Haboush, eds. 1985. *The Rise of Neo-Confucianism in Korea*. New York: Columbia University Press.

———. 1988. *East Asian Civilizations: A Dialogue in Five Stages*. Cambridge, Mass.: Harvard University Press.

———. 1989a. *The Message of the Mind in Neo-Confucianism*. New York: Columbia University Press.

———. and John W. Chafee, eds. 1989b. *Neo-Confucian Education: The Formative Stage*. Berkeley: versity of California Press.

———. 1990. "The Prophetic Voice in the Confucian Nobleman." *Ching Feng*, 33, nos. 1 & 2 (April 1990): 3–19.

———. 1991a. *Learning For One's Self: Essays on the Individual in Neo-Confucian Thought*. New York: Columbia University Press.

———. 1991b. *The Trouble with Confucianism*. Cambridge, Mass.: Harvard University Press.

de Cusa, Nicholas. 1962. *Unity & Reform: Selected Writings of Nicholas de Cusa*. Edited by J. P. Dolan. Notre Dame, Ind.: Notre Dame University Press.

de Harlez, C. J. 1890. *L'Ecole philosophique moderne de la China ou système de la nature*. Brussels: Hayes.

———. 1896. *Tschu Hsi, his doctrine and his influence*. Louvain: Istas.

Deuchler, Martina. 1992. *The Confucian Transformation of Korea: A Study of Society and Ideology*. Cambridge, Mass.: Harvard University Press.

Dewey, John. 1934. *A Common Faith*. New Haven: Yale University Press.

Dennerline, Jerry. 1981. *The Chia-ting Loyalists: Confucian Leadership and Social Change in Seventeenth-Century China*. New Haven: Yale University Press.

———. 1988. *Qian Mu and the World of Seven Mansions*. New Haven: Yale University Press.

Dilworth, David, A. 1989. *Philosophy in World Perspective: A Comparative Hermeneutic of the Major Theories*. New Haven: Yale University Press.

Dimberg, Ronald G. 1974. *The Sage and Society: The Life and Thought of Ho Hsin-yin*. Honolulu: University Press of Hawaii.

Driver, Tom F. 1981. *Christ in a Changing World: Toward an Ethical Christology*. New York: The Crossroad Publishing Company.

———. 1991. *The Magic of Ritual: Our Need for Liberating Rites and Transform Our Lives & Our Communities*. San Francisco: Harper & Row.

Drummond, Richard Henry. 1985. *Toward a New Age in Christian Theology*. Maryknoll, N.Y.: Orbis Books.

Dschu Hsi. 1953. *Djin-si Lu: Dei songkonfuzianische summa*. Trans. by Olaf Graf. 3 vols. Tokyo: Sophia University Press.

Dubs, Homer H. 1966a. *Hsüntze: The Moulder of Ancient Confucianism*. Taipei: Ch'eng-Wen Publishing Company.

———. trans. 1966b. *The Works of Hsüntze*. Taipei: Ch'eng-Wen Publishing Company.

Dumoulin, Heinrich, S. J. 1974. *Christianity Meets Buddhism*. Trans. by J. C. Maraldo. LaSalle, Ill.: Open Court Publishing Company.

Dunne, George H., S. J. 1962. *Generations of Giants*. Notre Dame, Ind.: University of Notre Dame Press.

Dupuis, Jacques, S. J. 1991. *Jesus Christ at the Encounter of World Religions*. Trans. by Robert R. Barr. Maryknoll, N.Y.: Orbis Books.

Eber, Irene, ed. 1986. *Confucianism: The Dynamics of Tradition*. New York: Macmillian.

Ebrey, Patricia Buckley, trans. 1991a. *Chu Hsi's Family Rituals: A Twelth-Century Chinese Manual for the Performance of Cappings, Weddings, Funerals, and Ancestral Rites*. Princeton: Princeton University Press.

———. 1991b. *Confucianism and Family Ritual in Imperial China: A Social History of Writing about Rites*. Princeton: Princeton University Press.

Eliade, Mircea and Joseph M. Kitagawa, eds. 1959. *The History of Religions: Essays in Methodology*. Chicago: The University of Chicago Press.

Elison, George. 1973. *Deus Destroyed: The Image of Christianity in Early Modern Japan*. Cambrigde, Mass.: Harvard University Press.

Elman, Benjamin A. 1984. *From Philosophy to Philology: Intellectual and Social Aspects of Change in Late Imperial China*. Cambridge, Mass.: Council on East Asian Studies, Harvard University.

———. 1990. *Classicism, Politics, and Kinship: The Ch'ang-chou School of New Text Confucianism in Late Imperial China*. Berkeley: University of California Press.

Eno, Robert. 1990. *The Confucian Creation of Heaven: Philosophy and the Defense of Ritual Mastery*. Albany, N.Y.: State University of New York Press.

Fairbank, John King, ed. 1967. *Chinese Thought and Institutions*. Chicago: University of Chicago Press.

Fang Keli and Li Jinquan, eds. 1989. *Xiandai Xinruxue Yanjiu Lunji* [Disscussions of Research on Modern New Confucanism]. Beijing: Chinese Academy of Social Sciences.

Fang, Thomé H. n.d. *The Chinese View of Life: The Philosophy of Comprehensive Harmony*. Hong Kong: Union Press.

Fehl, Noah E. 1971. *Rites and Propriety in Literature and Life: A Perspective for a Cultural History of Ancient China*. Hong Kong: The Chinese University of Hong Kong.

Feyerabend, Paul. 1988. *Against Method*. Revised Edition. New York: Verso.

Fingarette, Herbert. 1972. *Confucius—the Secular as Sacred*. New York: Harper & Row.

Ford, Lewis S. 1978. *The Lure of God: A Biblical Background for Process Theism*. Philadelphia: Fortress Press.

———, and George L. Kline, eds. 1983. *Explorations in Whitehead's Philosophy*. New York: Fordham University Press.

———. 1984. *The Emergence of Whitehead's Metaphysics 1925–1929*. Albany, N.Y.: State University of New York Press.

Forke, Alfred. 1925. *The World Concept of the Chinese*. London: Arthur Probsthain.

———. 1964a. *Geschichte der alten chinesische philosophie*. Hamburg: Cram, de Gruyter & Co.

———. 1964b. *Geschichte der mittelalterichen chinesischen philosophe.* Hamburg: Cram, de Gruyter & Co.

———. 1964c. *Geschichte der neuren chinesischen philosophe.* Hamburg: Cram, de Gruyter & Co.

Franke, Herbert. 1976. *Sung Biographies.* 4 vols. Wiesbaden: Franz Steiner Verlag.

Freeman, Maurice. 1928. The Ch'ing Dynasty Criticism of Sung Politico-Philosophy. *Journal of the North China Branch Royal Asiatic Society* 59 (1929)

Fu, Charles Wei-hsun. 1973. Morality and Beyond: The Neo-Confucian Confrontation with Mahayana Buddhism. *Philosophy East and West* 23 (1973): 375–96.

Fuki, Kojun. 1974. A Study of *Chou-i Ts-an-t'ung-ch'i. Acta Asiatica* 27 (September 1974): 19–32.

Fung, Yu-lan. 1953. *A History of Chinese Philosophy.* Trans. by D. Bodde. 2 vols. Princeton: Princeton University Press.

———. 1964. *A Short History of Chinese Philosophy.* Edited by D. Bodde. New York: Macmillan C.

———. 1967. *The Spirit of Chinese Philosophy.* Edited by E. R. Hughes. Boston: Beacon Press.

Furth, Charlotte, ed. 1976. *The Limits of Change: Essays on Conservative Alternatives in Republican China.* Cambridge, Mass.: Harvard University Press.

Gadamer, Hans-Georg. 1975. *Truth and Method.* New York: The Seabury Press.

Gardner, Daniel K. 1986. *Chu Hsi and the Ta-hsüeh: Neo-confucian Reflection on the Confucian Canon.* Cambridge, Mass.: Council on East Asian Studies, Harvard University.

———. trans. and ed. 1990. *Learning to Be a Sage: Selections from the Conversations of Master Chu, Arranged Topically.* Berkeley: University of California Press.

Gedalecia, David. 1971. Wu Ch'eng: A Neo-Confucian of the Yüan. Ph.D. dissertation, Harvard University.

———. 1974. Excursion into Substance and Function: The Development of the *T'i-yung* Paradigm in Chu Hsi. *Philosophy East and West* 24 (October 1974): 443–51.

Gernet, Jacques. 1962. *Daily Life in China on the Eve of the Mongol Invasion: 1250–1276.* Trans. by H. M. Wright. Stanford: Stanford University Press.

———. 1985. *China and the Christian Impact.* Trans. by Janet Lloyd. Cambridge and Paris: Cambridge University Press and Editions de la Maison de Sciences de l'Homme.

Gimello, Robert M. 1976. Apophatic and Kataphatic Discourse in Mahayana: A Chinese view. *Philosophy East and West* 26 (April 1976): 117–36.

Girardot, N. J. 1983. *Myth and Meaning in Early Taoism: The Theme of Chaos (Hun-tun).* Berkeley: University of California Press.

Gort, Jerald D. et al. eds., 1989. *Dialogue and Syncretism: An Interdisciplinary Approach.* Grand Rapids, Mich.: William B. Eerdmans Publishing Company.

Goto, Toshimiduz. 1960. The Ontology of *Li* Philosophy of the Sung Dynasty of China. *Philosophical Studies of Japan.* 2 (1960): 119–43.

Graf, Olaf. 1970. *Tao und jen: Sein und sollen in sungchinesischen monismus.* Wiesbaden: Otto Harrassowitz.

Graham, A. C. 1958. *Two Chinese Philosophers: Ch'eng Ming-tao and Ch'eng Yi-ch'uan.* London: Lund Humphries.

———. 1961. *The Problem of Value.* London: Hutchinson University Library.

———. 1978. *Later Mohist Logic, Ethics and Science.* Hong Kong: The Chinese University Press.

———. 1985. *Reason and Spontaneity: A New Solution to the Problem of Fact and Value.* London: Curzon Press.

———. 1986a. *Studies in Chinese Philosophy and Philosophical Literature.* Singapore: The Institute for East Asian Philosophies.

————. 1986b. *Yin-yang and the Nature of Correlative Thinking*. Singapore: The Institute of East Asian Philosophies.

————. 1989. *Disputers of the Tao: Philosophical Argument in Ancient China*. La Salle, Ill.: Open Court Publishing Company.

Granet, Marcel. 1968. *La pensée Chinoise*. Paris: Editions Albin Michel.

————. 1975. *The Religion of the Chinese People*. Translated by Maurice Freedman. New York: Harper & Row.

Gray, James R. 1982. *Modern Process Thought: A Brief Ideological History*. Lanham, Md.: University Press of America.

Gregory, Peter N. 1991. *Tsung-mi and the Sinification of Buddhism*. Princeton: Princeton Univesity Press.

Grieder, Jerome B. 1970. *Hu Shih and the Chinese Renaissance: Liberalism in the Chinese Revolution, 1917–1937*. Cambridge, Mass.: Harvard University Press.

Griffin, David Ray. 1973. *A Process Christology*. Philadelphia: The Westminster Press.

————. and Huston Smith. 1989. *Primordial Truth and Postmodern Theology*. Albany, N.Y.: State University of New York Press.

————. 1991. *Evil Revisited: Responses and Reconsiderations*. Albany, N.Y.: State University of New York Press.

Griffiths, Paul L. 1991. *An Apology for Apologetics: A Study in the Logic of Interreligious Dialogue*. Maryknoll, N.Y.: Orbis Books.

Guidelines on Dialogue with People of Living Faiths and Ideologies. 1973. Geneva: World Council of Churches, Sub-Unit on Dialogue.

Haboush, JaHyun Kim. 1988. *A Heritage of Kings: One Man's Monarchy in the Confucian World*. New York: Columbia University Press.

Haeger, John Winthrop. 1972. The Intellectual Context of Neo-Confucian Syncretism. *The Journal of Asian Studies* 31 (May 1972): 499–513.

————. ed. 1975. *Crisis and Prosperity in Sung China*. Tucson, Ariz.: The University of Arizona Press.

Hahn, Lewis Edwin, ed. 1991. *The Philosophy of Charles Hartshorne*. La Salle, Ill.: Open Court Publishing Company.

Halbfass, Wilhelm. 1988. *India and Europe: An Essay in Understanding*. Albany, N.Y.: State University of New York Press.

Hall, David L. 1973. *The Civilization of Experience: A Whiteheadian Theory of Culture*. New York: Fordham University Press.

————. 1982a. *Eros and Irony: A Prelude to Philosophical Anarchism*. Albany, N.Y.: State University of New York Press.

————. 1982b. *The Uncertain Phoenix: Adventures Toward a Post-cultural Sensibility*. New York: Fordham University Press.

————. and Roger T. Ames. 1987. *Thinking through Confucius*. Albany, N.Y.: State University of New York Press.

Handlin, Joanna F. 1983. *Action in late Ming Thought: The Reorientation of Lü K'un and Other Scholar-Officials*. Berkeley: University of California Press.

Hansen, Chad. 1983. *Language and Logic in Ancient China*. Ann Arbor: The University of Michigan Press.

Harootunian, H. D. 1970. *Toward Restoration: The Growth of Political Consciouness in Tokugawa Japan.* Berkeley: University of California Press.

———. 1988. *Things Seen and Unseen: Discourse and Ideology in Tokugawa Japan.* Chicago: University of Chicago Press.

Hartman, Charles. 1986. *Han Yü and the T'ang Search for Unity.* Princeton: Princeton University Press.

Hartshorne, Charles, and William L. Reese, eds. 1953. *Philosophers Speak of God.* Chicago: University of Chicago Press.

Hartshorne, Charles. 1962. *The Logic of Perfection and Other Essays in Neoclassical Metaphysics.* Lasalle, Ill.: Open Court Publishing Company.

———. 1964. *The Divine Relativity: A Social Conception of God.* New Haven: Yale University Press.

———. 1965. *Anselm's Discovery: A Re-Examination of the Ontological Proof for God's Existence.* La Salle, Ill.: Open Court Publishing Company.

———. 1967. *A Natural Theology for Our Time.* Lasalle, Ill.: Open Court Publishing Company.

———. 1970. *Creative Synthesis & Philosophic Method.* La Salle, Ill.: The Open Court Publishing Co.

———. 1972. *Whitehead's Philosophy: Selected Essays, 1935–1970.* Lincoln: University of Nebraska Press.

———. 1973. Ideas and Theses of Process Philosophers. In *Two Process philosophers: Hartshorne's Encounter with Whitehead,* L. S. Ford, ed. Tallahasse, Fla.: American Academy of Religion.

———. 1976. *Aquinas to Whitehead: Seven Centuries of Metaphysics of Religion.* Milwaukee, WI: Marquette University Publications.

———. 1983. *Insights & Oversights of Great Thinkers: An Evaluation of Western Philosophy.* Albany, N.Y.: State University of New York Press.

———. 1984a. *Creativity in American Philosophy.* Albany, N.Y.: State University of New York Press.

———. 1984b. *Omnipotence and Other Theological Mistakes.* Albany, N.Y.: State University of New York Press.

———. 1987. *Wisdom as Moderation: A Philosophy of the Middle Way.* Albany, N.Y.: State University of New York Press.

Henderson, John B. 1984. *The Development and Decline of Chinese Cosmology.* New York: Columbia University Press.

———. 1991. *Scripture, Canon, and Commentary: A Comparison of Confucian and Western Exegesis.* Princeton: Princeton University Press.

Henke, Frederick Goodrich. 1964. *The Philosophy of Wang Yang-ming.* 2nd ed. New York: Paragon Book Reprint Corp.

History of Religions 1978. Current Perspectives in the Study of Chinese Religions. *History of Religions* 17, nos.3 & 4 (February–May 1978).

Hick, John. 1985. *Problems of Religious Pluralism.* London: Macmillan Press.

———. and Paul F. Knitter, eds. 1987. *The Myth of Christian Uniques: Toward a Pluralistic Theology of Religions.* Maryknoll, N.Y.: Orbis Books.

———. 1989. *An Interpretation of Religion: Human Responses to the Transcendent.* New Haven: Yale University Press.

Hickley, Dennis. 1980. *The First Christians in China.* London: China Study Project.

Hillman, Eugene. 1989. _Many Paths: A Catholic Approach to Religious Pluralism._ Maryknoll, N.Y.: Orbis Books.

Ho Peng Yoke. 1985. _Li, Qi and Shu: An Introduction to Science and Civilization in China._ Hong Kong: Hong Kong University Press.

Hoang, Pierre. 1902. De l'origine et du développement du systèmede Tchou Hi et son influence sur l'esprit de lettres. _Varietés Sinologiques_ 21 (1902): 147–64.

Hocking, William Ernest. 1936. Chu Hsi's Theory of Knowledge. _Harvard Journal of Asiatic Studies_ 1 (1936): 109–27.

Hong, Choi Min. 1980. _A Modern History of Korean Philosophy._ Seoul: Seong Moon Sa.

Hood, Robert E. 1990. _Must God Remain Greek? Afro Culture and God-Talk._ Minneapolis: Fortress Press.

Hospital, Cifford G. 1985. _Breakthrough: Insights of the Great Religious Discoverers._ Maryknoll, N.Y.: Orbis Books.

Houston, G. W., ed. 1985. _The Cross and the Lotus: Christianity and Buddhism in Dialogue._ Delhi: Motillal Banarsidass.

Hsiao, Kung-chuan. 1979. _A History of Chinese Political Thought: From the Beginnings to the Sixth Century A.D._ vol. 1. Trans. by F. W. Mote. Princeton: Princeton University Press.

Hsieh, Shan-yuan. 1972. The Life and Thought of Li Kou (1009–1059). Ph.D. dissertation, University of Chicago.

Hsü Dau-lin. 1971. The Myth of the 'Five Human Relationships' of Confucius. _Monumenta Serica_ 29 (1970–71): 27–37.

Hsü, P. C. 1933. _Ethical Realism in Neo-Confucian Thought._ Yenching: n.p.

Hu, Shih. 1928. _The Development of the Logical Method in Ancient China._ Shanghai: Oriental Book Company.

———. 1962. The Scientific Spirit and Method in Chinese Philosophy. In _Philosophy and Culture East and West_, Charles A. Moore, ed. Honolulu: University of Hawaii Press.

Huang Chun-chieh. 1986. _Ju-hsüeh ch'uan-t'ung yü wen-hua ch'uang-hsin_ [Confucian Tradition and Cultural Renewal]. Taipei: Tung Ta Library Publishing Company.

Huang, Ray. 1981. _1587, A Year of No Significance: The Ming Dynasty in Decline._ New Haven: Yale University Press.

———. 1988. _China: A Macro History._ Armonk, N.Y.: M. E. Sharpe.

Huang, Siu-chi. 1968. Chang Tsai's Concept of Ch'i. _Philosophy East and West_ 18 (October 1968): 247–60.

———. 1971. The Moral Point of View of Chang Tsai. _Philosophy East and West_ 21 (April 1971): 141–56.

———. 1974. The Concept of T'ai-chi (Supreme Ultimate) in Sung Neo-Confucian Philosophy. _Journal of Chinese Philosophy_ 1 (June and September 1974): 275–94.

———. 1977. _Lu Hsiang-shan: A Twelth Century Chinese Idealist Philosopher._ Westport, Conn.: Hyperion Press.

Hughes, Edward J. 1986. _Wilfred Cantwell Smith: A Theology for the World._ London: SCM Press Ltd.

Hughes, E. R. 1943. _The Great Learning and the Mean-in-Action._ New York: Button & Co.

———. 1967. Epistemological Methods in Chinese Philosophy. In _The Chinese Mind_, C. A. Moore, ed. Honolulu: East-West Center Press.

Hummel, Arthur W., ed. 1943. *Eminent Chinese of the Ch'ing Period (1644–1912).* 2 vols. Washington, D.C.: United States Government Printing Office.

Hutchinson, William. R. 1987. *Errand to the World: American Protestant Thought and Foreign Mission.* Chicago: University of Chicago Press.

Hymes, Robert P. 1986. *Statesmen and Gentlemen: The Elite of Fu-Chou, Chiang-Hsi, in Northern and Southern Sung.* Cambridge: Cambridge University Press.

I-ching: Book of Changes. 1964. Trans. by James Legge. New York: University Books.

Ivanhoe, Philip J. 1990. *Ethics in the Confucian Tradition: The Thought of Mencius and Wang Yang-ming.* Atlanta: Scholars Press.

———. 1991. A Happy Symmetry: Xunzi's Ethical Thought. *Journal of the American Academy of Religion.* 59, no. 2 (Summer 1991): 309–22.

Jeanrond, Werner G. and Jennifer L. Rike, eds. 1991. *Radical Pluralism & Truth: David Tracy and the Hermeneutics of Religion.* New York: Crossroad.

Johnson, A. H. 1983. *Whitehead and His Philosophy.* Lanham, Md.: University Press of America.

Kallgren, Gerty. 1958. Studies in Sung Time Colloquial Chinese as Revealed in Chu Hsi's *Ts'üanshu. Bulletin of the Museum of Far Eastern Antiquities* 30 (1958): 1–165.

Kalton, Michael C., trans. and ed. 1988. *To Become a Sage: The Ten Diagrams on Sage Learning by Yi T'oegye.* New York: Columbia University Press.

Kane, Robert and Stephen H. Phillips, eds. 1989. *Hartshorne, Process Philosophy and Theology.* Albany, N.Y.: State University of New York Press.

Katz, Steven T., ed. 1978. *Mysticism and Philosophical Analysis.* Oxford: Oxford University Press.

———. ed. 1983. *Mysticism and Religions Tradition.* Oxford: Oxford University Press.

Keenan, John P. 1989. *The Meaning of Christ: A Mahayana Theology.* Maryknoll, N.Y.: Orbis Books.

Kilgore, Kathleen. 1991. *Transformations: A History of Boston University.* Boston: Boston University.

Kim, Sung-Hae. 1985. *The Righteous and the Sage: A Comparative Study on the Ideal Images of Man in Biblical Israel and Classical China.* Seoul: Sogang University Press.

———. 1990. Liberation through Humanization: With a Focus on Korean Confucianism. *Ching Feng* 33, nos. 1 & 2 (April 1990): 20–46.

Kitagawa, Joseph M., ed. 1967. *The History of Religions: Essays on the Problem of Understanding.* Chicago: University of Chicago Press.

Kitagawa, Joseph Mitsuo. 1990. *The Quest for Human Unity: A Religious History.* Minneapolis: Fortress Press.

Knoblock, John. 1988–1990. *Xunzi: A Translation and Study of the Complete Works.* Vol. I, books 1–6; vol. II, books 7–16. Stanford: Stanford University Press.

Knitter, Paul F. 1985. *No Other Name? A Critical Survey of Christian Attitudes Toward the World Religions.* Maryknoll, N.Y.: Orbis Books.

Kohn, Livia. 1987. *Seven Steps to the Tao: Sima Chengzhen's Zuowanglun.* Nettetal: Steyler Verlag.

———, ed. 1989. *Taoist Meditation and Longevity Techniques.* Ann Arbor: The University of Michigan Center for Chinese Studies.

———. 1991a. *Taoist Mystical Philosophy: The Scripture of Western Ascension.* Albany, N.Y.: State University of New York Press.

———. 1991b. *Early Chineses Mysticism: Philosophy and Soteriology in the Taoist Tradition.* Princeton: Princeton University Press.

Kracke, E. A. 1953. *Civil Service in Early Sung China: 960–1067*. Cambridge. Mass.: Harvard University Press.

Kraus, Elizabeth M. 1979. *The Metaphysics of Experience: A Companion to Whitehead's Process and Reality*. New York: Fordham University Press.

Krieger, David J. 1991. *The New Universalism: Foundations for a Global Theology*. Maryknoll, N.Y.: Orbis Books.

Kuhn, Philip A. 1990. *Soulstealers: The Chinese Sorcery Scare of 1768*. Cambridge, Mass.: Harvard University Press.

Küng, Hans et al. 1986. *Christianity and the World Religions: Paths to Dialogue with Islam, Hinduism, and Buddhism*. Garden City, N.Y.: Doubleday.

———. 1988. *Theology for the Third Millennium: An Ecumenical View*. New York: Doubleday.

———. and Julia Ching. 1989. *Christianity and Chinese Religions*. New York: Doubleday.

Lach, Donald F. 1957. *The Preface of Leiniz's Novissima Sinica*. Honolulu: University of Hawaii Press.

Lai, Whalen. 1977. The Meaning of "mind-only" *(wei-hsin)*: An Analysis of a Sinitic Mahayana Phenomenon. *Philosophy East and West* 27 (January 1977): 65–83.

Lampe, G. W. H. 1977. *God As Spirit*. Oxford: Clarendon Press.

Lamont, H. G. 1973–1974. An Early Ninth Century Debate on Heaven: Liu Tsung-yüan's *T'ien-Shou* and Liu Yü-hsi's *T'ien Lun*. *Asia Major* 18 (1973): 181–209; 19 (1974): 37–85.

Lango, John W. 1972. *Whitehead's Ontology*. Albany, N.Y.: State University of New York Press.

Larson, Gerald J. and Eliot Deutsch, eds. 1988. *Interpreting Across Boundaries: New Essays in Comparative Philosophy*. Princeton: Princeton University Press.

Lau, D. C. 1967. A Note on *Ke Wu*. *Bulletin of the School of Oriental and African Studies* 30 (1967): 353–57.

Leclerc, Ivor. 1958. *Whitehead's Metaphysics: An Introductory Exposition*. London: George Allen and Unwin Ltd.

Lee, Jung Young. 1979. *The Theology of Change: A Christian Concept of God in an Eastern Perspective*. Maryknoll, N.Y.: Orbis Books.

Lee, Thomas H. C., ed. 1991. Christianity and Chinese Intellectuals: From the Chinese Point of View. In *China and Europe: Images and Influences in Sixteenth to Eighteenth Centuries*. Hong Kong: The Chinese University Press.

Lee, Peter K. H., ed. 1991. *Confucian-Christian Encounters in Historical and Contemporary Perspective*. Lewiston/Queenstown: The Edwin Mellen Press.

Le Gall, Stanislas., S. J. 1923. Le philosophe Tchou Hi, sa doctrine, son influence. *Varietés Sinologiques* 3 (1923): 1–132.

Legge, James, trans. 1960. *The Chinese Classics*. 5 vols. Hong Kong: Hong Kong University Press.

———. 1966. *The Nestorian Monument of Hsian Fu in Shen-hsi, China*. New York: Paragon Book Reprint Corp.

———. trans. 1968. *The Li Ki*. 2 vols. Delhi: Motilal Barnarsidass.

Leibniz, Gottfried Wilhelm. 1977. *Discourse on the Natural Theology of the Chinese*. Trans. by Henry Rosemont, Jr. and Daniel J. Cooks. Honolulu: University of Hawaii Press.

Levenson, Joseph P. 1968. *Confucian China and its Modern Fate: A Trilogy*. Berkeley: University of California Press.

Lewis, Mark Edward. 1990. *Sanctioned Violence in Early China*. Albany, N.Y.: State University of New York Press.

Li, Chi. 1972. Chu Hsi the Poet. *T'oung Pao* 58 (1972): 55–119.

Li Ching-te (fl. 1263), ed. 1973. *Chu-tdu yü-lei ta-ch'üan* [The Dialogues of Chu Hsi]. 8 vols. Tokyo: n.p.

Liang Ch'i-ch'ao. 1959. *Intellectual Trends in the Ch'ing Period*. Trans. by Immanuel C. Y. Hsü. Cambridge, Mass.: Harvard University Press.

Lindbeck, George A. 1984. *The Nature of Doctrine: Religion and Theology in a Postliberal Age*. Philadelphia: The Westminster Press.

Liu, I-ch'ing. 1976. *Shih-shuo Hsin-yü: A New Account of Tales of the World*. Trans. by Richard B. Mather. Minneapolis: University of Minnesota Press.

Liu, James J. Y. 1975. *Chinese Theories of Literature*. Chicago: University of Chicago Press.

Liu, James T. C. 1959. *Reform in Sung China: Wang An-shih (1021–1086) and His New Policies*. Cambridge, Mass.: Harvard University Press.

————. 1967. *Ou-yang Hsiu: An Eleventh-Century Neo-Confucianist*. Stanford: Stanford University Press.

————. and Peter J. Golas, eds. 1969. *Change in Sung China: Innovation or Renovation*. Lexington, Mass.: D. C. Heath & Co.

Liu, Shu-hsien. 1971. The Religious Import of Confucian Philosophy: Its Traditional Outlook and Contemporary Significance. *Philosophy East and West* 21 (April 1971): 157–75.

————. 1972a. The Confucian Approach to the Problem of Transcendence and Immanence. *Philosophy East and West* 22 (January 1972): 45–52.

————. 1972b. The Contemporary Development of a Neo-Confucian Epistemology. In *Invitation to Chinese Philosophy*, A. Naess and A. Hanny, eds. Oslo: Scandinavian University Books.

————. 1972c. A Philosophical Analysis of the Confucian Approach to Ethics. *Philosophy East and West* 22 (October 1972): 417–25.

————. 1978. The Functions of the Mind in Chu Hsi's Philosophy. *Jounral of Chinese Philosophy* 5 (1978): 204.

————. 1982. *Chu-tzu che-hsüeh ssu-hsiang te fa-chan yü yuan-ch'eng* [The Development and Completion of Chu Hsi's Philosophic Thought]. Taipei: Student Book Company.

————. and Robert Allinson, eds. 1988. *Harmony and Strife: Contemporaru Perspectives East & West*. Hong Kong: The Chinese University Press.

————. 1989a. A Critique of Paul Tillich's Doctrine of God and Christology from an Oriental Perspective. In *Religious Issues and Interreligious Dialogues*, Charles Wei-hsun Fu and Gerhard E. Spiegler, eds. New York: Greenwood Press.

————. 1989b. Postwar Neo-confucian Philosophy: Its Development and Issues. In *Religious Issues and Interreligious Dialogues*. Charles Wei-hsun Fu and Gerhard E. Spiegler, eds. New York: Greenwood Press.

————. 1989c. Some Reflections on What Contemporary Neo-Confucian Philosophy May Learn from Christianity. *Ching Feng* 32, no. 3 (September 1989): 145–58.

————. 1990a. Some Reflections on the Sung-Ming Understanding of Mind, Nature, and Reason. *The Journal of the Institute of Chinese Studies of The Chinese University of Hong Kong* 21, (1990): 331–43.

————. and Peter K. H. Lee. 1990b. A Confucian-Christian Dialogue: Liberating Life as a Commitment to Truth. *Ching Feng* 33, no. 3 (September 1990): 113–35.

Liu Wu-chi. 1965. *A Short History of Confucian Philosophy.* New York: Dell Publishing Company.

Lo, Winston Wan. 1974. *The Life and Thought of Yeh Shih.* Gainesville, Fla. and Hong Kong: University of Florida Press & The Chinese University of Hong Kong.

Lochhead, David M. 1988. *The Dialogical Imperative: A Christian Reflection on Interfaith Encounter.* Maryknoll, N. Y.: Orbis Books.

Loewe, Michael. 1968. *Everyday Life in Early Imperial China.* New York: Harper & Row.

————. 1979. *Ways to Paradise: The Chinese Quest for Immortality.* London: George Allen & Unwin.

————. 1982. *Chinese Ideas of Life and Death: Faith, Myth and Reason in the Han Period (202 B.C.–A.D. 220).* London: George Allen & Unwin, Ltd.

Lowe, Victor. 1962. *Understanding Whitehead.* Baltimore: The Johns Hopkins Press.

Magliola, Robert. 1984. *Derrida on the Mend.* West Lafayette, Ind.: Purdue University Press.

Malenbranche, Nicole. 1980. *Dialogue Between a Christian Philosopher and a Chinese Philosopher on the Existence of God.* Trans. by D. A. Iorio. Washington, D.C.: University Press of America.

Margolis, Joseph. 1986. *Pragmatism Without Foundations: Reconciling Realism and Relativism.* Oxford: Basil Blackwell.

Martinson, Paul Varo. 1987. *A Theology of World Religions: Interpreting God, Self, and World in Semitic, Indian, and Chinese Thought.* Minneapolis: Agusburg Publishing House.

Maruyama, Masao. 1974. *Studies in the Intellectual History of Tokugawa Japan.* Trans. by Mikiso Hane. Princeton and Tokyo: Princeton University Press and University of Tokyo Press.

Mays, Wolf. 1959. *The Philosophy of Whitehead.* London: George Allen and Unwin Ltd.

McDaniel, Jay B. 1989. *Of God and Pelicans: A Theology for Reverence for Life.* Louisville: Westminister/John Knox Press.

McFague, Sallie. 1987. *Models for God: Theology for an Ecological, Nuclear Age.* Philadelphia: Fortress Press.

MacIntyre, Alasdair. 1984. *After Virtue: A Study in Moral Theory.* 2d ed. Notre Dame, Ind.: Notre Dame University Press.

————. 1988. *Whose Justice? Which Rationality?* Notre Dame, Ind.: Notre Dame University Press.

————. 1990. *Three Rivial Versions of Moral Enquiry: Encyclopaedia, Genealogy, and Tradition.* Notre Dame, Indiana: Notre Dame University Press.

McMullen, David. 1988. *State and Scholars in T'ang China.* Cambridge: Cambridge University Press.

Mencius. 1963. Trans. by W. A. C. H. Dobson. Toronto: University of Toronto Press.

Mencius. 1970. Trans. by D. C. Lau. Baltimore: Penguin Books.

Metzger, Thomas A. 1977. *Escape from Predicament: Neo-Confucianism and China's Evolving Political Culture.* New York: Columbia University Press.

Moffett, Samuel Hugh. 1992. *A History of Christianity in Asia: Beginnings to 1500.* vol. 1. San Francisco, Harper & Row.

Moore, Charles A., ed. 1962. *Philosophy and Culture East and West.* Honolulu: University of Hawaii Press.

————. ed. 1967. *The Chinese Mind.* Honolulu: University of Hawaii Press.

Moran, Gabriel. 1992. *Uniqueness: Problem or Paradox in Jewish and Christian Traditions.* Maryknoll, N.Y.: Orbis Books.

Mote, Frederick W. 1989. *Intellectual Foundations of China.* 2nd ed. New York: McGraw-Hill.

Mou, Tsung-san. 1968–69. *Hsin-t'i yü hsing-t'i* [Mind and Nature]. 3 vols. Taiwan: Cheng-chu shu-chu.

———. 1971. *Chih te chih-chüeh yü Chung-kuo che-hsüeh* [Intellectual Intuition and Chinese Philosophy]. Taipei: Student Book Company.

———. 1974. *Chung-kuo che-hsüeh te t'e-chih* [The Uniqueness of Chinese Philosophy]. Taipei: Student Book Company.

———. 1975. *Hsien-hsiang yü wu-tzu-shen* [Phenomenon and Thing-in-itself]. Taipei: Student Book Company.

———. 1977. *Fo-hsing yü Pan-ro* [Buddha Nature and *Prajna*]. 2 vols. Taipei: Student Book Company.

———. 1979. *Tsung Lu Hsiang-shan tao Liu Chi-shan* [From Lu Hsiang-shan to Liu Chi-shan]. Taipei: Student Book Company.

———. 1983. *Chung-kuo che-hsüeh shih-chiu chiang* [Nineteen Lectures on Chinese Philosophy]. Taipei: Student Book Company.

———. 1985. *Yüan shan lun* [On the *Summum Bonum*]. Taipei: Student Book Company.

Mungello, David E. 1971. Leibniz's Interpretation of Neo-Confucianism. *Philosophy East and West* 21 (January 1971): 3–22.

———. 1976. The Reconciliation of Neo-Confucianism with Christianity in the Writings of Joseph de Premare, S. J. *Philosophy East and West* 26 (October 1976): 389–410.

———. 1977. *Leibniz and Confucianism: The Search for Accord*. Honolulu: The University Press of Hawaii.

———. 1985. *Curious Land: Jesuit Accommodation and the Origins of Sinology*. Stuttgart: Franz Steiner Verlag Wiesbaden GMBH.

Munro, Donald J. 1969. *The Concept of Man in Early China*. Stanford: Stanford University Press.

———. 1977. *The Concept of Man in Contemporary China*. Ann Arbor: University of Michigan Press.

———. 1988. *Images of Human Nature: A Sung Portrait*. Princeton: Princeton University Press.

Haas, William S. 1956. *The Destiny of the Mind: East and West*. New York: Macmillan.

Naess, Arne and Alastir Hanny, eds. 1972. *Invitation to Chinese Philosophy*. Oslo: Scandinavian University Books.

Nakamura, Hajime. 1965. *Ways of Thinking of Eastern Peoples: India, China, Tibet and Japan*. Honolulu: East-West Center Press.

———. 1975. *Parallel Developments: A Comparative History of Ideas*. Tokyo: Kodansha.

Nakayama, Shigeru. 1984. *Academic and Scientific Traditions in China, Japan, and the West*. Trans. by J. Dusenbury. Tokyo: University of Tokyo Press.

Najita, Tetsuo and Irwin Scheiner, eds. 1978. *Japanese Thought in the Tokugawa Period: Methods and Metaphors*. Chicago: University of Chicago Press.

Najita, Tstsuo. 1987. *Visions of Virtue in Tokugawa Japan: The Kaitokudo—Merchant Academy of Osaka*. Chicago: University of Chicago Press.

Nasr, Seyyed Hossein. 1981. *Knowledge and the Sacred: The Gifford Lectures*. New York: Crossroad.

Needham, Joseph. 1943. *Time the Refreshing River: Essay and Addresses, 1932–1942*. London: George Allen & Unwin.

———. 1954–. *Science and Civilization in China*. 8 vols. Cambridge: Cambridge University Press.

———. 1969a. *The Grand Titration: Science and Society in East and West*. London: George Allen & Unwin.

————. 1969b. *Within the Four Seas: The Dialogue of East and West.* Toronto: University of Toronto Press.

————. 1970. *Clerks and Craftsmen in China and the West.* Cambridge: Cambridge Unviersity Press.

————. 1981. *Science in Traditional China: A Comparative Perspective.* Cambridge, Mass., and Hong Kong: Harvard University Press and the Chinese University Press.

Neville, Robert C. 1968. *God the Creator: On the Transcendence and Presence of God.* Chicago: University of Chicago Press.

————. 1974. *The Cosmology of Freedom.* New Haven: Yale University Press.

————. 1978. *Soldier Sage Saint.* New York: Fordham University Press.

————. 1980. *Creativity and God: A Challenge to Process Theology.* New York: The Seabury Press.

————. 1981. *Reconstruction of Thinking.* Albany, N.Y.: State University of New York Press.

————. 1982. *The Tao and the Daimon: Segments of a Religious Inquiry.* Albany, N.Y.: State University of New York Press.

————. 1987. *The Puritan Smile: A Look Toward Moral Reflection.* Albany, N.Y.: State University of New York Press.

————. 1989. *Recovering the Measure: Interpretation and Nature.* Albany, N.Y.: State University of New York Press.

————. 1991a. *Behind the Masks of God: An Essay Toward Comparative Theology.* Albany, N.Y.: State University of New York Press.

————. 1991b. *A Theology Primer.* Albany, N.Y.: State University of New York Press.

————. 1992. *The Highroad Around Modernism.* Albany, N.Y.: State University of New York Press.

Newman, Paul W. 1987. *A Spirit Christology: Recovering the Biblical Paradigm of Christian Faith.* Lanham, Md. University Press of America.

Nivison, David S. 1966. *The Life and Thought of Chang Hsüeh-ch'eng (1738–1801).* Stanford: Stanford University Press.

————. and Arthur F. Wright, eds. 1959. *Confucianism in Action.* Stanford: Stanford University Press.

Nobo, Jorge Luis. 1986. *Whitehead's Metaphysics of Extension and Solidarity.* Albany, N.Y.: State University of New York Press.

Nosco, Paul, ed. 1984. *Confucianism and Tokugawa Culture.* Princeton: Princeton University Press.

Northrop, F. S. C. 1947. *The Meeting of East and West: An Inquiry Concerning World Understanding.* New York: Macmillan.

Odin, Steve. 1982. *Process Metaphysics and Hua-yen Buddhism: A Critical Study of Cumulative Penetration vs. Interpenetration.* Albany, N.Y.: State University of New York Press.

O'Neill, Maura. 1990. *Women Speaking Women Listening: Women in Interreligious Dialogue.* Maryknoll, N.Y.: Orbis Books.

Ooms, Herman. 1985. *Tokugawa Ideology: Early Constructs, 1570–1680.* Princeton: Princeton University Press.

Organ, Troy. 1975. *Western Approaches to Eastern Philosophy.* Athens, Ohio: Ohio University Press.

Overmyer, Daniel L. 1976. *Folk Religion: Dissenting Sects in Late Traditional China.* Cambridge, Mass.: Harvard University Press.

————. 1986. *Religions of China: The World as Living System.* San Francisco: Harper & Row.

Oxtoby, Willard G., ed. 1976. *Religious Diversity: Essays by Wildred Cantwell Smith.* New York: Harper & Row.
————. 1983. *The Meaning of Other Faiths.* Philadelphia: The Westminster Press.
Pang Ching-jen. 1942. *L'Idée de Dieu chez Malebranche et L'Idée de Li chez Tchou Hi.* Paris: Librairie Philosophique.
Panikkar, Raimundo. 1978. *The Intrareligious Dialogue.* New York: Paulist Press.
————. 1979. *Myth, Faith and Hermeneutics: Cross Cultural Studies.* New York: Paulist Press.
————. 1989. *The Silence of God: The Answer of the Buddha.* Maryknoll, N.Y.: Orbis Books.
Parrinder, Geoffrey. 1987. *Encountering World Religions: Questions of Religious Truth.* New York: The Crossroad Publishing Company.
Peerenboom, R. P. 1990. Natural Law in the *Huang-Lao Boshu. Philosophy East & West,* 40, no. 3 (July 1990): 309–29.
Pepper, Stephen C. 1942. *World Hypothesis: A Study in Evidence.* Berkeley: University of California Press.
————. 1967. *Concept and Quality: A World Hypothesis.* La Salle, Ill.: Open Court Publishing Company.
Peterson, Willard J. 1979. *Bitter Gourd: Fang I-chih and the Impetus for Intellectual Change.* New Haven: Yale University Press
Pieris, Aloysius, S. J. 1988a. *An Asian Theology of Liberation.* Maryknoll, N.Y.: Orbis Books.
————. 1988b. *Love Meets Wisdom: A Christian Experience of Buddhism.* Maryknoll, N.Y.: Orbis Books.
Pols, Edward. 1967. *Whitehead's Metaphysics: A Critical Examination of Process and Reality.* Carbondale, Ill.: Southern Illinois University Press.
Pontifical Council for Interreligious Dialogue and the Congregation for the Evangelization of Peoples. 1991. Dialogue and Proclamation: Reflections and Orientations on Interreligious Dialogue and the Proclamation of the Gospel of Jesus Christ. *Origins.* 21, no. 8 (4 July 1991): 121–35.
Price, Lucien. 1954. *Dialogues of Alfred North Whitehead.* Boston: Little, Brown and Company.
Proudfoot, Wayne. 1985. *Religious Experience.* Berkeley: University of California Press.
Pulleyblank, Edward C. 1960. Neo-Confucianism and Neo-Legalism in T'ang Intellectual Life. In *The Confucian Persuasion,* A. R. Wright, ed. Stanford: Stanford Unviersity Press.
Qian, Wen-yuan. 1985. *The Great Inertia: Scientific Stagnation in Traditional China.* London: Croom Helm.
Race, Alan. 1983. *Christians and Religious Pluralism: Patterns in the Christian Theology of Religions.* London: SCM Press.
Reynolds, Frank and David Tracy, eds. 1992. *Discourse and Practice.* Albany, N.Y.: State University of New York Press.
Ricci, Matteo, S. J. 1985. *The True Meaning of the Lord of Heaven (T'ien-chu Shi-i).* Trans. by Douglas Lancashire and Peter Hu Kuo-chen, S. J. Taipei, Paris, Hong Kong: Ricci Institute.
Richards, I. A. 1932. *Mencius on the Mind: Experiments in Multiple Definition.* London: Kegan Paul, Trench, Trubner & Co.
Ro Young-Chan. 1989. *The Korean Neo-Confucianism of Yi Yulgok.* Albany, N.Y.: State University of New York Press.

Ropp, Pauld S., ed. 1990. *Heritage of China: Contemporary Perspectives on Chinese Civlizations.* Berkeley: University of California Press.

Rorty, Richard. 1979. *Philosophy and the Mirror of Nature.* Princeton: Princeton University Press.

————. 1989. *Contingency, Irony, and Solidarity.* Cambridge: Cambridge University Press.

Rosemont, Henry, Jr., ed. 1984. *Explorations in Early Chinese Cosmology.* Chico, Calif.: Scholars Press.

————. ed. 1991. *Chinese Texts and Philosophical Contexts: Essays Dedicated to Angus C. Graham.* La Salle, Ill.: Open Court Publishing Company.

————. and Benjamin I. Schwartz, eds. 1979. *Studies in Classical Chinese Thought.* Ann Arbor, Michigan: American Academy of Religion. *Journal of the American Academy of Religion,* Thematic Issue 47, no. 3 (September 1979).

Ross, Stephen David. 1983. *Perspective in Whitehead's Metaphysics.* Albany, N.Y.: State University of New York Press.

Rubin, Vitaly A. 1976. *Individual and State in Ancient China: Essays on Four Chinese Philosophers.* Trans. Steven I. Levine. New York: Columbia University Press.

Rusch, Walter G. 1988. *Reception: An Ecumenical Opportunity.* Philadelphia: Fortress Press.

Said, Edward W. 1978. *Orientalism.* New York: Vintage Books.

Samartha, Stanley J. 1981. *Courage for Dialogue: Ecumenical Issues in Inter-religious Relationships.* Geneva: World Council of Churches.

————. 1991. *One Christ-Many Religions: Toward a Revised Christology.* Maryknoll, N.Y.: Orbis Books.

Sargent, Galen Eugène. 1955. *Les debats personnels de Tchou Hi en matière de methodolgie. Journal Asiatique* 243 (1955): 213–28.

————. 1957. Tchou Hi contre le Bouddhisme. *Paris Université Mélanges* (1957): 1–157.

Sariti, Anthony William. 1972. Monarch, Bureaucracy, and Absolutism in the Political Thought of Ssu-ma Kuang. *The Journal of Asian Studies* 32 (Novemember 1972): 53–76.

Saso, Michael. 1990. *Blue Dragon White Tiger: Taoist Rites of Passage.* Washington, D. C.: The Taoist Center.

Scharfstein, Ben-Ami. 1974. *The Mind of China.* New York: Dell.

————. 1978. *Philosophy East/Philosophy West: A Critical Comparison of Indian, Chinese, Islamic, and European Philosophy.* New York: Oxford University Press.

Schillp, Paul Arthur, ed. 1941. *The Philosophy of Alfred North Whitehead.* Lasalle, Ill.: Open Court Publishing Company.

Schirokauer, Conrad M. 1960. The Political Thought and Behavior of Chu Hsi. Ph.D. dissertation, University of Chicago.

————. 1962. Chu Hsi's Political Career: A Study in Ambivalence. In *Confucian Personalities,* A. F. Wright and D. Twichett, eds. Stanford: Stanford University Press.

————. 1975. Neo-Confucians Under Attack: The Condenmation of *Wei-hsüeb.* In *Crisis and Prosperity in Sung China,* J. W. Haeger, ed. Tucson: University of Arizona Press.

Schroeder, W. Widick. 1976. Religious Institutions and Human Society: A Normative Inquiry into the Appropriate Contribution of Religious Institutions to Human Life and to the Divine Life. In *Belonging and Alienation: Religious Foundations for the Human Future,* P. Heffner and W. W. Schroeder, eds. Chicago: Center for the Scientific Study of Religion.

————. 1981. Structure and Context in Process Political Theory: A Constructive Formulation. In *Process Philosophy and Social Thought,* J. B. Cobb, Jr. and W. W. Schroeder, eds. Chicago: Center for the Scientific Study of Religion.

Schwartz, Benjamin I. 1959. Some Polarities in Confucian Thought. In *Confucianism in Action*, David S. Nivison and Arthur F. Wright, eds. Stanford: Stanford University Press.

———. 1964. *In Search of Wealth and Power: Yen Fu and the West*. Cambridge, Mass.: The Belknap Press of Harvard University Press.

———. 1985. *The World of Thought in Ancient China*. Cambridge, Mass.: The Belknap Press of Harvard University.

Schwartz, Vera. 1986. *The Chinese Enlightenment: Intellectuals and the Legacy of the May Fourth Movement of 1919*. Berkeley: University of California Press.

Secreatariatus Pro Non Christian. 1984. *The Attitude of the Church Towards the Followers of Other Religions: Reflections and Orientations on Dialogue and Mission*. Ottawa: Canadian Conference of Catholic Bishops.

Shao Yong. 1986. *Dialogue between a Fisherman and a Wood-cutter*. Trans. by Knud Lundbaek. Hamburg: C. Bell Verlag.

Sharpe, Eric J. 1977. *Faith Meets Faith: Some Christian Attitudes to Hinduism in the Nineteenth and Twentieth centuries*. London: SCM Press.

———. 1983. *Understanding Religion*. London: Duckworth.

Sheard, Robert B. 1987. *Interreligious Dialogue in the Catholic Church since Vatican II: An Historical and Theological Study*. Lewiston/Queenstown, N.Y.: The Edwin Mellin Press.

Sherburne, Donald W. 1966. *A Key to Whitehead's Process and Reality*. Bloomington, Indiana University Press.

Shih, Vincent Y. C. 1963. Metaphysical Tendencies in Mencius. *Philosophy East and West* 12 (January 1963): 319–41.

Shils, Edward. 1981. *Tradition*. Chicago: The University of Chicago Press.

Shorter, Aylward. 1988. *Toward a Theology of Inculturation*. Maryknoll, N.Y.: Orbis Books.

Shryock, J. K. 1937. *The Study of Human Abilities: the Jen Wu Chih of Liu Shao*. New Haven: American Oriental Society.

Sivin, Nathan. 1968. *Chinese Alchemy: Preliminary Studies*. Cambridge, Mass.: Harvard University Press.

Smith, D. Howard. 1968. *Chinese Religions*. New York: Holt, Rinehart and Winston.

———. 1973. *Confucius*. New York: Charles Scribner's Sons.

Smith, Kidder, Jr., Peter K. Bol, Joseph A. Adler, and Don J. Wyatt. 1990. *Sung Dynasty Uses of the I Ching*. Princeton: Princeton University Press.

Smith, Jonathan Z. 1982. *Imagining Religion: From Babylon to Jonestown*. Chicago: University of Chicago Press.

Smith, Wilfred Cantwell. 1972. *The Faith of Other Men*. New York: Harper & Row.

———. 1976. *Questions of Religious Truth*. New York: Charles Scribner's Sons.

———. 1977. *Belief and History*. Charlottesville: University Press of Virginia.

———. 1978. *The Meaning and End of Religion*. San Francisco: Harper & Row.

———. 1979. *Faith and Belief*. Princeton: Princeton University Press.

———. 1981. *Towards a World Theology: Faith and the History of Religion*. Philadelphia: The Westminster Press.

Spae, J. J., C.I.C.M. 1980. *Buddhist-Christian Empathy*. Chicago and Tokyo: The Chicago Institute of Theology and Culture and Oriens Institute for Religious Research.

Spence, Jonathan D. 1984. *The Memory Palace of Matteo Ricci*. New York: Viking.

———. 1988. *The Question of Hu*. New York: Knopf.

————. 1990. *The Search for Modern China*. New York: W. W. Norton.

Stackhouse, Max L. 1988. *Apologia: Contextualization, Globalization, and Mission in Theological Education*. Grand Rapids, Mich.: William B. Eerdmans Publishing Company.

Standaert, N. 1988. *Yang Tingyuan, Confucian and Christian in Late Ming China*. Leiden: E. J. Brill.

————. 1991. Confucian-Christian Dual Citizenship: A Political Conflict? *Ching Feng* 34, no. 2 (June 1991): 109–14.

Stockwell, Eugene, ed. 1988. Tambaram Revised [Special issue]. *International Review of Mission* 78, (no. 307 (July 1988).

Struve, Lynn A. 1988. The Early Ch'ing Legacy of Huang Tsung-hsi: A Reexamination. *Asia Major*, third series, 1, part 1.

Suchocki, Marjorie H. 1982. *God Christ Church: A Practical Guide to Process Theology*. New York: Crossroad.

————. 1988. *The End of Evil: Process Eschatology in Historical Context*. Albany, N.Y.: State University of New York Press.

Sun, George Chih-hsin. 1971. Chinese Metaphysics and Whitehead. Ph.D. dissertation, Southern Illinois University.

Sun, Stanislaus, S. J. 1966. The Doctrine of *Li* in the Philosophy of Chu Hsi. *International Philosophic Quarterly* 6 (1966): 153–88.

Swidler, Leonard, ed. 1987. *Toward a Universal Theology of Religion*. Maryknoll, N. Y.: Orbis Books.

————. 1990. *After the Absolute: The Dialogical Future of Religious Reflection*. Minneapolis: Fortress Press.

T'ang, Chün-i. 1956. Chang Tsai's Theory of Mind and Its Metaphysical Basis. *Philosophy East and West* 6 (1956): 113–36.

————. 1962. The *T'ien Ming* (Heavenly Ordinance) in pre-Ch'in China. *Philosophy East and West* 11 (January 1962): 195–218.

————. 1972. The Spirit and Development of Neo-Confucianism. In *Invitation to Chinese Philosophy*, A. Naess and A. Hanny, eds. Oslo: Scandinavian University Press.

————. 1974. *Chung-kuo che-hsüeh yüan-lun: Tao-lun p'ien* [Fundamental Exposition of Chinese Philosophy: Introduction]. Kowloon, Hong Kong: New Asia Research Institute.

Taylor, Mark C. 1989. *Altarity*. Chicago: University of Chicago Press.

Taylor, Rodney L. 1975. Neo-Confucianism, Sagehood and the Religious Dimension. *Journal of Chinese Philosophy* 2 (September 1975): 386–415.

————. 1978. *The Cultivation of Sagehood as a Religious Goal in Neo-Confucianism: A Study of Selected Writings of Kao P'an-lung*. Missoula, Mont.: Scholars Press.

————. 1988. *The Confucian Way of Contemplation: Okada Takehiko and the Tradition of Quiet-sitting*. Columbia, S.C.: University of South Carolina Press.

————. 1990a. *The Religious Dimensions of Confucianism*. Albany, N.Y.: State University of New York Press.

————. 1990b. The Study of the Confucianism as a Religious Tradition: Notes on Some Recent Publications. *Journal of Chinese Religions* 18 (Fall 1990).

Thelle, Notto R. 1987. *Buddhism and Christianity in Japan: From Conflict to Dialogue, 1854–1899*. Honolulu: University of Hawaii Press.

Tillich, Paul. 1952. *The Courage to Be*. New Haven: Yale University Press.

————. 1963. *Christianity and the Encounter of the World Religions*. New York: Columbia University Press

Tillman, Hoyt Cleveland. 1982. *Utilitarian Confucianism: Ch'en Liang's Challenge to Chu Hsi*. Cambridge, Mass.: Council on East Asian Studies, Harvard University.

————. 1992a. A New Direction in Confucian Scholarship: Approaches to Examining the Differences between Neo-Confucianism and *Tao-hsüeh. Philosophy East and West* 42, no. 3 (July 1992): 455–74.

————. 1992b. *Confucian Discourse and Chu Hsi's Ascendancy*. Honolulu: University of Hawaii Press.

Tomoeda, Ryutaro. 1971. The Characteristics of Chu Hsi's Thought. *Acta Asiatica* 21 (1971): 52–72.

Tracy, David. 1975. *Blessed Rage for Order: The New Pluralism in Theology*. New York: The Seabury Press.

————. 1981. *The Analogical Imagination: Christian Theology and the Culture of Pluralism*. New York: Crossroad.

————. 1987. *Plurality and Ambiguity: Hermeneutics, Religion, Hope*. San Francisco: Harper & Row.

————. 1990. *Dialogue with the Other: The Inter-religious Dialogue*. Louvain and Grand Rapids, Mich.: Peeters Press and William B. Eerdmans Publishing Company.

Ts'ai Jen-hou. 1979. *Sung Ming li-hsüeh: Pei-Sung p'ien* [Sung-Ming Neo-Confucianism: The Northern Sung]. Taipei: Student Book Company.

————. 1980. *Sung Ming li-hsüeh: Nan-Sung p'ien* [Sung-Ming Neo-Confucianism: The Southern Sung]. Taipei: Student Book Company.

————. 1982. *Hsin Ju-chia te ching-shen fang-hsiang* [The Direction of the Neo-Confucian Spirit]. Taipei: Student Book Company.

————. Chou Tsung-hua and Liang Yen-ch'eng. 1985. *Hui-tung yü chuan-hua* [Comprehension and Transformation]. Taipei: Yu-Chou Kuang Publishers.

Ts'ai, Yung-ch'un. 1950. The Philosophy of Ch'eng I. Ph.D. dissertation, Columbia University.

Tu, Wei-meng. 1971. Review of *Hsin-t'i yü hsing-t'i* [Mind and Nature], by Mou Tsung-san. *Journal of Asian Studies* 30 (May 1971): 642–47.

————. 1974. Reconstituting the Confucian Tradition. *Journal of Asian Studies* 33 (May 1974): 441–54.

————. 1976a. Hsiung Shih-li's Quest for Authentic Existence. In *Limits of Change: Essays on Conservative Alternatives in Republican China*, C. Furth, ed. Cambridge, Mass.: Harvard University Press.

————. 1976b. *Neo-Confucian Thought in Action: Wang Yang-ming's Youth (1472–1509)*. Berkeley: University of California Press.

————. 1979. *Humanity and Self-Cultivation: Essays in Confucian Thought*. Berkeley: Asian Humanities Press.

————. 1985. *Confucian Thought: Selfhood as Creative Transformation*. Albany, N.Y.: State University of New York Press.

————. 1989a. *Centrality and Commonality: An Essay on Confucian Religiousness*. A revised and enlarged edition of *Centrality and Commonality: An Essay on Chung-yung*. Albany, N.Y.: State University of New York Press.

———. 1989b. *Way, Learning, and Politics: Essays on the Confucian Intellectual.* Singapore: The Institute of East Asian Philosophies.

———. Milan Hejtmanek, Alan Wachman. 1992. *The Confucian World Observed: A Contemporary Discussion of Confucian Humanism in East Asia.* Honolulu: University of Hawaii Press.

Tucker, Mary Evelyn. 1989. *Moral and Spiritual Cultivation in Japanese Neo-Confucianism: The Life and Thought of Kaibara Ekken (1630–1714).* Albany, N.Y.: State University of New York Press.

Van Zoeren, Steven. 1991. *Poetry and Personality: Reading, Exegesis and Hermeneutics in Traditional China.* Stanford: Stanford University Press.

Verdu, Alfonso. 1974. *Dialectical Aspects in Buddhist Thought: Studies in Sino-Japanese Mahayana Idealism.* Lawrence, Kan.: Center for East Asian Studies.

———. 1981. *The Philosophy of Buddhism: A "Totalistic" Synthesis.* The Hague: Martinus Nijhoff Publishers.

———. 1985. *Early Buddhist Philosophy: In the Light of the Four Noble Truths.* Delhi: Motilal Banarsidass.

Visser 't Hooft, W. A. 1963. *No Other Name: The Choice Between Syncretism and Christian Universalism.* London: SCM Press.

von Brück, Michael. 1991. *The Unity of Reality: God, God-Experience, and Meditation in the Hindu-Christian Dialogue.* Trans. by James T. Zeitz. New York: Paulist Press.

Vroom, Hendrik M. 1989. *Religions and the Truth: Philosophical Reflections and Perspectives.* Grand Rapids, Mich., and Amsterdam: William B. Eerdmans Publishing Company and Editions Rodopi.

Wakeman, Federic, Jr., ed. 1970. *Nothing Concealed: Eassy in Honor of Liu Yü-yün.* Taipei: Chinese Materials and Research Aids Service Center.

———. 1973. *History and Will: Philosophical Perspectives on Mao Tse-t'ung's Thought.* Berkeley: University of California Press.

Waley, Arthur. 1938. *The Analects of Confucius.* London: Allen & Unwin.

———. 1939. *Three Ways of Thought in Ancient China.* Garden City, N.Y.: Doubleday.

Wang Fu-chih (1619–92). 1974. *Chang-tzu Cheng-meng chu* [A Commenatry on Chang Tsai's *Cheng-meng*]. Taiwan: San-jen hsing ch'u-pan she.

Wang, Yang-ming. 1963. *Instructions for Practical Living and Other Neo-Confucian Writings.* Trans. by Wing-sit Chan. New York: Columbia University Press.

Ward, Keith. 1987. *Images of Eternity: Concepts of God in Five Religions.* London: Danton, Longman and Todd.

Warren, G. G. 1924. Was Chu Hsi a Materialist? *Journal of North-China Branch of the Royal Asiatic Society* 55 (1924): 28–44.

Watson, Burton, trans. 1967. *Basic Writings of Mo Tzu, Hsün Tzu, and Han Fei Tzu.* New York: Columbia University Press.

———. trans. 1989. *The Tso Chuan: Selections from China's Oldest Narrative History.* New York: Columbia University Press.

Watson, Rubie S. and Patricia Buckley Ebrey, eds. 1991. *Marriage and Inequality in Chinese Society.* Berkeley: University of California Press.

Watson, Walter. 1985. *The Architectonics of Meaning: Foundations of the New Pluralism.* Albany, N.Y.: State University of New York Press.

Weber, Max. 1951. *The Religion of China: Confucianism and Taoism.* Trans. by Hans H. Gerth. New York: Macmillan.

Werblowsky, R. J. Zwi. 1976. *Beyond Tradition and Modernity: Changing Religions in a Changing World.* London: The Athlone Press.

Whitehead, Alfred North. 1925. *Science and the Modern World.* New York: Macmillan.

―――. 1927. *Religion in the Making.* Cambridge: Cambridge University Press.

―――. 1928. *Symbolism: Its Meaning and Effect.* Cambridge: Cambridge University Press.

―――. 1929a. *The Aims of Education and other Essays.* New York: Macmillan.

―――. 1929b. *The Function of Reason.* Princeton: Princeton University Press.

―――. 1933. *Adventures of Ideas.* New York: Macmillan.

―――. 1938. *Modes of Thought.* New York: Macmillan.

―――. 1978. *Process and Reality: An Essay in Cosmology.* David Ray Griffin and Donald W. Sherburne, eds. Revised ed. New York: The Free Press.

Whitehead, James D., Yu-ming Shaw, and N. J. Giradot, eds. 1979. *China and Christianity: Historical and Future Encounters.* Notre Dame: Center for Pastoral and Social Ministry, University of Notre Dame.

Whyte, Bob. 1988. *Unfinished Encounter: China and Christianity.* London: Collins.

Wieger, P. Leon., S. J. 1930. *Textes Philosophiques: Confucianisme, Taoisme, Buddhisme.* Hien-hien: n.p.

Wilhelm, Hellmut. 1960. *Change: Eight Lectures on the I-Ching.* Trans. by Cary R. Baynes. New York: Harper & Row.

―――. 1971. On Ming Orthodoxy. *Monumenta Serica* 29 (1970–71): 1–26.

Wilhelm, Richard. 1931. *Confucius and Confucianism.* Trans. by George H. Danton and Annaina Periam Danton. New York: Harcourt Brace Jovanovich.

―――, trans. 1950. *The I-Ching or Book of Changes.* 3d ed. Trans. by Cary F. Baynes. Bollingen Series XIX. Princeton: Princeton University Press.

Williamson, H. R. 1973. *Wang An Shih: A Chinese Statesman and Educationalist of the Sung Dynasty.* 2 vols. Westport, Conn.: Hyperion Press.

Wilmot, Laurence F. 1979. *Whitehead and God: Prolegomena to Theological Reconstruction.* Waterloo, Ontario: Wilfred Laurier University Press.

Wittenborn, Allen, trans. and ed. 1991. *Further Reflections on Things at Hand: A Reader.* Lanham, Md.: University Press of American.

Wood, Thomas E. 1991. *Mind Only: A Philosophical and Doctrincal Analysis of the Vijnanavada.* Honolulu: University of Hawaii Press.

Wright, Arthur F. and Denis Twitchett, eds. 1962. *Confucian Personalities.* Stanford: Stanford University Press.

―――, ed. 1960. *The Confucian Persuasion.* Stanford: Stanford University Press.

Wu, Joseph S. 1971. Whitehead and the Philosophical Meeting of East and West. *Chinese Culture* 12 (December 1971): 84–91.

―――. 1973. Philosophy and Revolution: Confucianism and Pragmatism. *Philosophy East and West* 23 (July 1973): 323–32.

Wu, Pei-yi. 1990. *The Confucian's Progress: Autobiographical Writings in Traditional China.* Princeton, N.J.: Princeton University Press.

Yagi, Seiichi and Leonard Swidler. 1990. *A Bridge to Buddhist-Christian Dialogue.* New York: Paulist Press.

Yang, C. K. 1967. *Religion in Chinese Society*. Berkeley: University of California Press.

Yang, Lien-sheng. 1957. The Concept of *Pao* as a Basis for Social Relations in China. In *Chinese Thought and Institutions*, J. K. Fairbank, ed. Chicago: University of Chicago Press.

Yearly, Lee H. 1990. *Mencius and Aquinas: Theories of Virtue and Conceptions of Courage*. Albany, N.Y.: State University of New York Press.

Yeh, Theodore T. Y. 1969. *Confucianism, Christianity and China*. New York: Philosophical Library.

Yen, Yüan. 1972. *Preservation of Learning*. Trans. by Maurice Freeman. Los Angeles: Monumenta Serica.

Young, Henry James. 1990. *Hope in Process: A Theology of Social Pluralism*. Minneapolis: Fortress Press.

Young, John D. 1983. *Confucianism and Christianity: The first Encounter*. Hong Kong: Hong Kong University Press.

Yu, David. 1959. A Comparative Study of the Metaphysics of Chu Hsi and A. N. Whitehead. Ph.D. dissertation, University of Chicago.

————. 1969. Chu Hsi's Approach to Knowledge. *Chinese Culture* (December 1969): 1–14.

Zaehner, R. C. 1970. *Concordant Discord: The Interdependence of Faiths*. Oxford: Clarendon Press.

Index

261